LANGUAGE ETHICS

LANGUAGE
ETHICS

Edited by

Yael Peled

and

Daniel M. Weinstock

McGill-Queen's University Press

Montreal & Kingston • London • Chicago

ISBN 978-0-2280-0158-4 (cloth)
ISBN 978-0-2280-0159-1 (paper)
ISBN 978-0-2280-0292-5 (ePDF)
ISBN 978-0-2280-0293-2 (ePUB)

Legal deposit third quarter 2020
Bibliothèque nationale du Québec

Printed in Canada on acid-free paper that is 100% ancient forest free
(100% post-consumer recycled), processed chlorine free

This book has been published with the help of a grant from the Canadian
Federation for the Humanities and Social Sciences, through the Awards to
Scholarly Publications Program, using funds provided by the Social
Sciences and Humanities Research Council of Canada.

We acknowledge the support of the Canada Council for the Arts.

Nous remercions le Conseil des arts du Canada de son soutien.

Library and Archives Canada Cataloguing in Publication

Title: Language ethics / edited by Yael Peled and Daniel M. Weinstock.
Names: Peled, Yael (Language ethicist), editor. | Weinstock, Daniel M.,
    editor.
Description: Includes bibliographical references and index.
Identifiers: Canadiana (print) 20200198645 | Canadiana (ebook)
    20200198750 | ISBN 9780228001591 (softcover) | ISBN 9780228001584
    (hardcover) | ISBN 9780228002925 (PDF) | ISBN 9780228002932 (ePUB)
Subjects: LCSH: Language policy. | LCSH: Language and languages—Moral
    and ethical aspects. | LCSH: Language and languages—Political aspects.
Classification: LCC P119.3 .L36 2020 | DDC 306.44/9—dc23

CONTENTS

ACKNOWLEDGMENTS

This book has been in the making for a long time. It emerged from an international workshop that took place in Montreal in November 2011, entitled "Language Ethics as a Field of Inquiry." The workshop sought to bring together leading experts from philosophy, political science, and linguistics (broadly construed), to explore a shared interest in the complex interface between ethics, power, and language. It was guided by a hope that, through intensive interdisciplinary discussion, a common notion of a language ethics, on par with that of bioethics or environmental ethics, could be identified and articulated by the participants. That hope relied, among other things, on an attitude of intellectual and professional generosity on the part of presenters and attendees alike, and it has not only facilitated a productive workshop discussion, but also set the tone for the book more broadly, in terms of the individual contributions and even more so when taken as a whole.

We are grateful, in the first instance, to the contributors to this volume, and for their continuous faith in this project through an extended period of time, resulting in part from the necessity to navigate ongoing uncertainties – and sometimes anxieties and tensions – in contemporary academia, with regard to the knowledge institutionalization of highly interdisciplinary research endeavours. We thank the contributors for their endless patience and strong sense of commitment throughout the longer, more complex and uncertain process undertaken by this project's transformation from a workshop into a book, and for continuing to develop their chapters throughout that time, responding to the growing body of literature that can be said to come under the title of "language ethics," often by leading these cutting-edge developments themselves.

We also wish to express our deep gratitude to McGill-Queen's University Press, where this book has found a welcoming and committed home. In particular, we are grateful to our editor Mark Abley for his continuous support of this project from its earliest stages, and for his unwavering confidence in the broader vision that guides it. At McGill-Queen's University Press we are also thankful to our managing editor Kathleen Fraser, and to our copy-editor Grace Rosalie Seybold. We thank Jeremy Parker for designing the cover. And we thank the two anonymous reviewers for their constructive comments and encouragement, which contributed to better consolidating the book as a whole and in line with its broader intellectual aims. We also thank Alice Everly for the preparation of the index and the watchful proofreading.

Finally, we wish to acknowledge the financial and institutional support that has sustained this project to its successful conclusion. The 2011 workshop was generously funded by an Aid to Workshops and Conferences grant from the Social Sciences and Humanities Research Council of Canada, as well as the Department of Philosophy at the Université de Montréal. This book has been published with the help of a grant from the Federation for the Humanities and Social Sciences, through the Awards to Scholarly Publications Program, using funds provided by the Social Sciences and Humanities Research Council of Canada. And last but certainty not least, the final manuscript was prepared and completed at the Forschungskolleg Humanwissenschaften, and has benefited immeasurably from the Kolleg's generous intellectual and material support.

Yael Peled and Daniel M. Weinstock, Montreal, August 2019

LANGUAGE ETHICS

INTRODUCTION

The Idea of Language Ethics as a Field of Inquiry

YAEL PELED

1. THE COMMONALITY OF DIFFERENCE

In an insightful chapter reflecting on the place of animals in political philosophy, Kymlicka and Donaldson point out the longstanding centrality of linguistic agency in conceptions of social and political membership, going as far back as Aristotle's linking of "the power of speech" with the "sense of good and evil, of just and unjust" (Aristotle, in Kymlicka and Donaldson 2016, 696). The centrality of language to political relationships and membership, they conclude, means that "[t]he link between linguistic agency and political membership runs deep in Western political thought, found equally in the liberal and republican traditions, and in both Anglo-American and continental traditions. And it is reflected in our everyday understanding of 'politics', 'the public', 'citizenship' and 'the public sphere', all of which are seen as constituted by linguistic acts" (Kymlicka and Donaldson 2016, 696).

Kymlicka and Donaldson's insightful analysis goes on to consider the ways in which animals, as non-linguistic agents, may nonetheless be imagined as political actors and participants in political relationships. At the same time, it seems worthwhile to point out that, while political philosophy can certainly be said to have a long tradition of attributing great importance to language, its underlying conception of what language is, or how to understand it, may be neither as fully theorized nor as empirically informed as is sometimes assumed. For example, as Schmidt notes, "democratic theorists working in the tradition of participatory democracy have had little, if anything, substantive to say about reconciling linguistic diversity with democratic theory in practice" (Schmidt 2014, 396; see also Peled and Bonotti 2019). Similar critiques have also been directed towards liberal rights-based democratic theorists, and the linguistic assumptions – overt or covert – that underlie their conceptions of language (see Wee 2011; Ives 2015; May 2015; Wright 2015; Peled 2017; Oakes and Peled 2018; Ives 2018).

This long-enduring gap between the centrality of language to political philosophy, on the one hand, and the under-theorizing of language by political philosophers, on the other hand, highlights the importance of a common epistemic framework that is capable of constructive bridging across and between disciplines that share an interest in language, ethics, and power. The vision for that common epistemic framework, which underlies this book, aims to embrace the longstanding centrality of language to moral reasoning as a human commonality, and reinterpret it in a manner that draws on the social and political life of real-world language rather than being alienated from it. That common epistemic framework can be labelled "language ethics."

The notion of "language ethics" as a comprehensive and distinct domain in ethics (theoretical and applied) begins from the view that the capacities for moral reasoning and language are humanity's two most distinct features, and that they are interrelated. Where it differs from more traditional notions in the political philosophy of language, is, first, in the recognition that these two forms of human commonality are *dividing* commonality. That is, the shared capacity for moral reasoning manifests itself in a plurality of moral theories, principles, and values. The shared capacity for language, similarly, manifests itself as a diversity of languages (see Peled 2014; 2018a; 2018b). The two combined create a shared human experience of difference, along both moral and linguistic lines, whose commonality lies, paradoxically, not in the abstract shared capacities but rather in their divided (and dividing) manifestations.

The experience of moral difference in political life necessitates political ethics, in the sense that political ethics – like politics itself – arises from the reality of human difference and interdependence (Schmidt 2006, 98) as well as uncertainty (Peled 2018a). Similarly, the need for language ethics arises from the experience of an ineliminable linguistic difference (for example, in an interaction between two monolingual English and French speakers), and even linguistic alterity (for example, in an interaction between a monolingual and a multilingual, with their differing experience of linguistic agency [Peled 2019]).[1] The experience of a language barrier as (paradoxically) a common human experience is elemental for the notion of language ethics proposed here, putting language on par with morality at the centre of human moral and political agency.

The human commonality of the experience of a language barrier, rather than merely the universal capacity for language, has important implications for the political theory and philosophy of language. In other words, what is crucial about the linguistic nature of political actors and political memberships and relationships is not merely that they require *a* language, but the fact that, in real-world cases and contexts, they more often than not take place in an intertwined multiplicity of languages alongside a plurality of moral values, principles, and beliefs. Democratic theorists naturally tend to focus on the role of political institutions when considering the importance of a common language to sustain a *demos*, morally (providing political transparency and accountability) as well as practically (ensuring the efficient working of public institutions) (see De Schutter and Robichaud 2015a). But this focus on political institutions often overlooks other social institutions, such as hospitals, community centres, or the police, where the existence of a language barrier is an ineliminable reality in the everyday life of ordinary citizens. The same also holds for residents who are (partly or entirely) without political rights, such as temporary residents, refugees, and undocumented immigrants, who are nonetheless under the responsibility of these institutions and must navigate their linguistic environments and perceptions.

The upshot of the discussion above is that the notion of language ethics proposed here, originating from a common experience of linguistic difference, necessitates a rethink of some of the underlying assumptions – covert or overt – that are still commonplace among theorists and philosophers interested in the moral and political life of language. This is because this notion of language ethics is grounded in a lived rather than an abstracted (or generic) experience of linguistic agency. Because of that, this notion requires a much greater input from and engagement with empirically oriented researchers in the language disciplines, such as sociolinguistics and applied linguistics, social psychology and linguistic anthropology. At the same time, given the significance of the ethical inquiry to the notion of a language ethics, being party to that inquiry similarly requires empirically oriented researchers to rethink some of their underlying *normative* assumptions, with regard to the substance of normative key concepts such as power, justice, authority, and legitimacy. These epistemic conditions imply that the proposed notion of language ethics is intrinsically interdisciplinary. This interdisciplinary challenge will be considered more closely in the final section of this chapter.

It has become somewhat of a commonplace, in the political theory and philosophy of language, to comment on the scarcity of normative work dedicated to language, in comparison with the plenitude of offerings that make a periodic general nod to language as part of a more comprehensive discussion on culture, and/or bodies of work dedicated to other forms of human difference such as race, ethnicity, gender, or sexuality. This state of affairs, fortunately, is changing. It is motivated in part by a greater awareness of the political life of language – and the political life of ineliminable language barriers – on the part of a growing number of political theorists and philosophers, who seek a greater dialogue with research originating in the language disciplines, in order to inform and strengthen their normative inquiry. The last decade in particular has seen an impressive rise in the number of not only published articles but also book chapters (Shorten 2018; Peled 2019; Ives 2019; Petrovic 2019), edited volumes (Kymlicka and Patten 2003; Kraus and Grin 2018), handbook chapters (Réaume and Pinto 2012; De Schutter and Robichaud 2012; Peled 2018a; Ives 2018), special issues (Tonkin 2015; Léger and Lewis 2017; Ricento, Peled, and Ives 2014; De Schutter and Robichaud 2015b [the latter two also published as edited volumes]), and monographs (Van Parijs 2011; Petrovic 2014; Oakes and Peled 2018; Cetrà 2019) dedicated to an evolving normative inquiry on language.

Perhaps the most distinct component in that developing body of work concerns the question of linguistic justice, responding in part to Van Parijs's seminal *Linguistic Justice for Europe and for the World* (Van Parijs 2011) and to its predecessor *Language Rights and Political Theory* by Will Kymlicka and Alan Patten (Kymlicka and Patten 2003). As De Schutter and Robichaud identify in their comprehensive overview of this emerging debate, linguistic justice theories aim to "provide an answer to the question: what is the just political management of the presence of different language groups within a political community? This question comprises different sub-questions: Should we go for equality or inequality of recognition between the different languages? Should we go for sub-state territories with monolingual policies, or for states that instantiate statewide multilingualism or for some combination of both? Should linguistic minorities receive special linguistic benefits? Should we endeavour to save moribund languages? Should states have one common language that all speak and understand?" (De Schutter and Robichaud 2015a, 88).[2]

The contribution of the linguistic justice debate to the idea of language ethics as a distinct domain of ethics is elemental. At the same time, it is important to remain mindful of the fact that justice does not in itself encapsulate the entirety of ethics, or at least not necessarily. The promotion of justice as the "value of values" (Sandel 1988, 16, following on Bickel 1975, 5), an "'Archimedean point' from which to assess the basic structure of society" (Sandel 1988, 16), seems natural in the specific context of a Rawlsian-inspired (or Rawlsian-responsive) political theory and philosophy grounded in the idea that "justice is the first virtue of social institutions" (Rawls 1999, 3), which has been perhaps the most powerful impetus for liberal theory and theories of rights since the 1970s. Indeed, as Robichaud points out in his chapter in this volume, "[m]ost of these research results proposed institutional solutions, legal and/or political … The debates so far have mostly highlighted political problems and have suggested legal and political measures as possible solutions" (Robichaud, this volume, 90). But for all its normative utility in defining and defending the moral entitlements of individuals, the primacy of justice over all other social values, virtues, and goods nonetheless gives rise to a conception of selfhood and agency that may seem overly individualistic and procedural, and detached from a fuller and more relational account of human life (e.g. Sandel 1988; Taylor 1985a; 1985b; 1989).

For the purpose of a comprehensive notion of language ethics as proposed in this introduction, the conflation of linguistic justice with language ethics is as unhelpful as it is unnecessary. It is unhelpful because justice can be argued to comprise part of ethics rather than embody it, just as *liberal* justice comprises only part of the idea of justice and not its full embodiment. Indeed, liberal linguistic justice arguments can be challenged by competing understandings of what linguistic justice requires and entails from both within and outside the liberal tradition. Thus Robichaud, for example, highlights an important moral shortcoming in a language ethics that is grounded in a *laisser-faire* approach to language rights, in the form of linguistic free-riding

(Robichaud, this volume). In another type of critique of a liberal approach to linguistic justice, Edwards points to the limitations of its rights-based rhetoric, and argues that the widespread focus on language rights and their conflation with language claims (and language-related hopes) is not only analytically problematic, but also paradoxically unsuccessful in realizing well-intentioned ends, such as the protection of vulnerable linguistic minorities, by pushing for utopian policies supported more by the force of normative rhetoric than actual obligations grounded in existing forms of political legitimacy and authority (Edwards, this volume).

The conflation of language ethics and linguistic justice is not only unhelpful but also epistemically unnecessary, because linguistic justice can still play a central role in a more comprehensive notion of language ethics without being pressured into providing more impact, outcomes, or solutions than it can realistically deliver. To understand that, it is important to consider not just the scope of the linguistic justice debate, but also its limitations. The prioritization of justice over benevolence, of the right over the good, is a genuine challenge in the case of language, and even more so in the case of a language barrier. This is because linguistic interaction between institutions and citizens, and even more so between co-citizens, can only be procedurally regulated to a certain extent (Peled 2017).

For example, it can be justified for a political community to make sovereign decisions on the particular linguistic prioritization it wishes to promote and defend (for example, French in Quebec or Hebrew in Israel), provided it meets certain normative criteria that safeguard linguistic minorities from linguistic discrimination. But to what extent should that prioritization be rigidly upheld in complex interactive situations, such as equal access to health and social services for linguistic minorities, and especially emergency services? Or, for example, as Avnon explores in his chapter, in pedagogical contexts situated in active sites of ethnic and national conflict between linguistic communities? Is it just for a doctor or a police officer to refuse to serve a member of the public in a language other than the official one, even when they are capable of using it – at least to some degree – and can do so at no personal cost or professional liability? Is it just for citizens to purposefully interact only in the common language and refuse to communicate with co-citizens in any other language, even when they, too, are capable of it to a certain extent? If the primacy of the linguistically just (i.e. the promotion and protection of the common language) always overrides the competing moral claim of the linguistically good (i.e. a temporary accommodation in the face of a language barrier), for example as follows from Van Parijs's coercive approach to the linguistic territoriality principle (Van Parijs 2011), can it really still be said to result in overall moral betterment?

Of course, Van Parijs's main concern in proposing a coercive territorial approach is to counter the threat from the powerful global English to national languages and, more specifically, to the equal linguistic dignity of their speakers. This concern is entirely legitimate and understandable. Yet the coerciveness of that approach does seem to place an unequal linguistic burden not only on powerful Anglophones but also on all other linguistic minorities, notably immigrants, who may already be more disadvantaged than their linguistic majority co-citizens. In many parts of the world that are even less demolinguistically "tidied up" than Belgium, normative challenges regarding linguistic minorities in political life and in interaction with political institutions further extend to, in addition to immigrants, Indigenous people within and especially outside their communities. Another crucial challenge is the one facing Deaf communities, which are often overlooked not only in the growing normative linguistic justice debate, but also in more general frameworks and theories in the field of language policy.

The concern for equal linguistic dignity, or "parity of esteem" (Van Parijs 2011, 117–32), is a foundational concern in any theory of moral agency in language. Yet equal linguistic dignity is most tested – and needed – in circumstances where a language barrier cannot be simply eliminated by a general call for linguistic safeguarding through territory-grabbing. This is the reason why a more comprehensive notion of language ethics, which acknowledges the existence of a language barrier as a feature of political life rather than a bug, is needed to complement linguistic justice theories, when they reach the limits of their utility to instruct political actors how to react in complex linguistic environments that cannot be morally regulated in any clear-cut way. A more comprehensive notion of language ethics, one that extends beyond the specific boundaries of the linguistic justice debate, aims to recognize and address those grey zones of moral and practical uncertainty, where justice alone cannot serve as the single most important value that guides moral agency, overriding other weighty values such as care, friendship, or hope (see Peled 2017; 2018a).

Linguistic justice asks, "What is the right thing to do?" But the question of what is the right thing to do can yield only limited results in circumstances when knowing the right thing to do is not very clear-cut or straightforward (for example, in the case of the ethics of the linguistic integration of adult migrants). In cases such as these, where the degree of moral and practical uncertainty is high, it is less clear precisely how linguistic burdens should be distributed among members of a political community. Similarly, the question of "what is the right thing to do" in the face of ineliminable language barriers does not in itself provide a definitive answer to the question of "what is the good thing to do," nor does it offer much help in deciding how to weigh the respective strengths of the moral claims of these two questions against each other. Doing so requires a more comprehensive framework for theorizing language, power, and ethics, which is the substance of the notion of language ethics understood as a distinct field of inquiry.

2. THE SUBSTANCE OF LANGUAGE ETHICS

The previous section outlined a notion of language ethics that is centred on the common human experience of an ineliminable linguistic difference. What makes language a domain of ethical inquiry, on that account, as well as giving it its urgency, is the reality of a language barrier. It is true that linguistic difference is not fixed, and that it may be influenced and shaped by historical, social, and political forces. Indeed, it is precisely the acknowledgment that linguistic identities are adaptable which underlies language policy as a practice (e.g. state interventions in citizens' linguistic repertoires) as well as a field of study. But the very existence of that difference, and the reality of a language barrier that transpires from it, cannot be completely eliminated. Centring the linguistic human condition on linguistic difference challenges utopian conceptions of an aesthetically neat and clear-cut overlap between a language, a nation, and a territory. (In so doing, it provides, among other things, an important corrective to the populist notion of the people as a linguistically indivisible body.[3]) Similarly, it calls into question ontological approaches that perceive language as some kind of universal and generic capacity that can be fully detached from its particular manifestations in the form of different languages, including those that sometimes are not even recognized as such, such as non-standard varieties and sign languages.

What does all of this mean for the notion of language ethics? What is its substance? Where is it situated, and what are its limits? "Language ethics" is defined throughout the remainder of this introduction as the set of values, norms, and principles that govern our thinking on moral agency in language in the face of a reality of linguistic (as well as moral) difference. It can be understood as an ethical framework that "applies philosophical methods to analyse the moral issues that pertain to language, such as those related, for example, to questions of linguistic freedoms, equality, autonomy, legitimacy, and dignity in multilingual societies" (Peled 2018a, 144). Or, as formulated by Avnon in this volume, "[a]pplied to language, ethics pertains to considerations guiding our understanding of the purposes and benefits of language for individual and communal well-being, and the conduct that comes in the wake of such understanding" (Avnon, this volume, 32). Under such linguistic, moral, and political conditions, what is a good life and how is it to be led? What kind of duties do we owe each other? How may we judge what is good or bad, right or wrong? And (as the previous section inquires) how should we weigh competing moral claims on language between the right and the good?

The above serves as an entry point to a more concrete outlining of the notion of language ethics, and the important role that *normative* ethics play within it. This importance can be attributed to the prominence of a normative *approach* to the social and political life of language in contemporary political philosophy, for example the linguistic justice debate, and to the normative *interest* that is motivating contemporary language policy research, for example in pedagogy, especially on the part of more critical approaches in the field (see Ricento 2000; Oakes and Peled 2018). Indeed, one promising way of bridging the gap between political theory and philosophy of language and language policy is through the framework of "normative language policy" (Peled 2014; Oakes and Peled 2018). The moral and practical significance of normativity for language ethics stems from the argument, as mentioned above, that language ethics is particularly useful – and needed – in situations of moral un-certainty, which render the questions "what is the right thing to do" and "what is the good way to act" even more urgent.

Normative ethics is, of course, not the only type of ethics to have a legiti-mate claim under the umbrella term of language ethics. As Kymlicka and Donaldson point out, the language *of* political life, and especially democratic life, is heavily reliant on linguistic acts in constituting the respective (linguis-tic) notions of "the public," "citizenship," and "the public sphere" (Kymlicka and Donaldson 2016, 696). This suggests that the nexus between ethics, power, and language is far more complex than the limited set of normative questions that pertain to linguistic prioritization in multilingual societies. It also en-compasses, on that view, meta-ethics and descriptive ethics approaches to language ethics. The former may include, for example, the *meaning* of moral propositions as expressed through language, while the latter may investigate the linguistic encoding of value systems, for example, within and across dif-ferent languages.[4] The question of the inclusivity of meaning is an important one for the notion of language ethics, and it will be revisited in later sections of this chapter. For the purpose of this introductory discussion, and the broader thematic and (inter)disciplinary vision of this book as a whole, the primary type of ethics considered here, at this point in the development of this inquiry, is normative ethics.

Normative ethics in language are necessitated by real-world politics of lan-guage that emerge, as Schmidt proposes, from the reality of difference and in-terdependence (Schmidt 2006, 98) – more specifically, in this case, linguistic difference and social interdependence. The contributors to this volume offer an important insight into the complex nature of the topic, as well as the com-plex entities that comprise it. The idea of the "social," for example, invoked by the framing of language ethics as situated in the social experience of lin-guistic difference, is approached in this book in an expansive manner, and as an umbrella term for social, political, economic, and other domains of human activity and life as a social entity. This intrinsic plurality of the "social" is well-reflected in the chapters that explore the shared theme of language ethics from the perspectives of political philosophy and theory as well as public policy (Avnon, Robichaud, De Schutter, Weinstock), economics (Robichaud, Grin, Ricento), development studies (Ricento), and education (Avnon, De Schutter).

Furthermore, many of the chapters make the clear point that different dimensions of the "social" are not isolated but are rather strongly interconnected. Thus Grin, for example, argues for the interconnectedness of economic, social, and cultural factors, by making the point that "[c]ontrary to a widespread belief, non-material and symbolic dimensions are a legitimate, even necessary, part of the economic assessment of policy choices" (Grin, this volume, 123).

"Language," too, is approached in this volume as a multifaceted entity. Commenting on the gap between popular perceptions of language and more nuanced professional approaches, De Schutter makes the point that "when we talk about or learn a language, we refer to and learn the 'standard' version of the language. The standard version of the language is granted higher status than all other versions. It forms the basis for the (often official) grammar, dictionary, and spelling, and it is the version used for the codification of law, in public debate, and in the educational system" (De Schutter, this volume, 146). Similarly, Ricento's reflection on the epistemic distance between political theory and sociolinguistics concludes that "Western political theorists, generally non-experts in the language sciences, whose principal aim is often to advance normative theories on desirable states of affairs within liberal democratic states, tend to deal with language as a stable nominal category, as something that one 'has' or 'doesn't have,' that can be labelled as one thing (e.g. English) or another thing (e.g. French), that may be learned for defined purposes, that has instrumental and symbolic value, that is used principally as a modality for interpersonal communication, with 'speakers,' possibly with associated geographic territories, and with cultural affiliations and traditions 'attached' to named languages and varieties" (Ricento, this volume, 203).

The meaning of "language," therefore, is expanded in this volume so as to further take into account non-standardized varieties ("dialects"), or otherwise languages that have not undergone extensive standardization and codification processes. This extension, in turn, allows the expansion of normative theorizing to engage not only with *interlinguistic* ethics but also with *intralinguistic* ethics. De Schutter's chapter, dedicated to a normative exploration of justice *between* language varieties, indeed makes the point that *intralinguistic* justice comprises "another dimension of language policy, to which barely any normative attention has been paid so far: the political management of linguistic diversity occurring within one and the same language group" (De Schutter, this volume, 146). De Schutter's chapter demonstrates the relevance and utility of expanding the scope of normative language theorizing to the intralinguistic domain. Similarly, it demonstrates its usefulness in producing a more nuanced, or "layered," reflection on the complex interrelations between social interdependence and linguistic difference, shedding light on an important, yet largely under-theorized, area of normative language policy and politics.[5] This is also echoed in Ricento's analysis of the relative prestige of *particular* varieties of English (notably those that are linked to high educational qualifications), rather than of "English" in the general and abstract (Ricento, this volume).

The contributors to this volume, in addition to interrogating the substance of both "social" and "language" as applied to language ethics, also examine what, precisely, the "difference" in "linguistic difference" entails. The contributors note this element in the social and political life of language – and its normative challenges – within the complex overlap of political and linguistic borders. At the same time, they also examine its analytical utility and limitations. Grin, for example, in his critique of the language of language rights, points out that "difference" possesses a certain normative overtone of "otherness" which is often both essentialized and under-theorized. For this reason, he proposes, thinking constructively about linguistic difference is better pursued through the notion of diversity (Grin, this volume, 122–3).

There exist additional reasons that highlight the conceptual significance of "diversity" for a more comprehensive framework of language ethics. Besides the great popularity the concept already enjoys at present among political theorists and philosophers and language policy researchers alike, "diversity" enables the debate on the normative theorizing of linguistic difference to direct its attention not only towards linguistically diverse societies, but also linguistically diverse *individuals*, further taking into consideration, as Grin notes, not only actual linguistic skills but also their usage (Grin, this volume, 119; see also Avnon and Robichaud, this volume). In so doing, it makes the notion of language ethics more language-aware, by recognizing the *internal* linguistic plurality of individuals, and the set of normative beliefs, attitudes, anxieties, and hopes – sometimes in tension with one another (Peled 2019) – that emerge from moral agency in a multilingual repertoire. The significance of this subtle yet meaningful shift lies in making linguistic repertoires more prominent as objects of analysis, on the part of individual political actors, as well as of state actors and policy-makers, with regard to the permissibility of intervention in interlinguistic (Robichaud and Weinstock) and intralinguistic (De Schutter) contexts. The focus on diversity also raises the important point, hinted at in the previous section, that "linguistic difference" may also be interpreted as difference not only between distinct linguistic groups (for example, Anglophones and Francophones), but also between different types of linguistic alterity (monolinguals and multilinguals) (see also Avnon, this volume, 37).

Interpreting "difference" as "diversity" therefore re-centres the normative debate on the linguistic experience and agency of individuals, rather than taking as a starting point some general features of a desired language regime. In so doing, it better connects individual moral and political agency in language with the various normative orders proposed for advancing individual and social linguistic justice and well-being. The idea that normative orders in language should be meaningfully connected to individuals' lived experience of moral and political agency in language(s), rather than some generic formulation of that agency, should hopefully not be viewed as a strange proposition. All it does is extend into the normative realm the argument according to which language policy cannot be detached from the particularities of local linguistic cultures (Schiffman 1996) – or, in other words, the argument that *normative* considerations on language cannot be formulated, implemented, and evaluated without being meaningfully engaged with local linguistic and political cultures (see Oakes and Peled 2018). This raises a third interpretation, or type, of linguistic difference, that pertains not to a specific language or linguistic alterity, but rather to linguistic culture.

The notion of diversity, therefore, is clearly significant for the vision of language ethics proposed in this volume. At the same time, as Grin notes, it is important to remain mindful of the analytical limitations of some of the ways it is currently used. More specifically, Grin critiques more expansive interpretations of diversity that seek to challenge the distinctiveness of its constitutive elements. Taking diversity seriously, Grin argues, is at odds with perceptions according to which "the very notion that people use 'languages' ought to be replaced by the notion that people are 'languaging' … that is, they are using a linguistic repertoire in which languages such as 'English,' 'French,' 'Swahili,' and 'Kurdish,' far from being discrete entities, blend into each other; *ergo*, languages as they are used blend into each other to such an extent that it no longer makes sense to refer to 'named' languages" (Grin, this volume, 127). Such perceptions, Grin points out, are problematic on both moral and feasibility grounds: "[d]ismissing languages to celebrate diversity or claiming that diversity ought to be dissolved in a 'super-diversity' whose elements are made invisible does seem self-contradictory. After all, the very idea of diversity is meaningless if it is not made up of identifiably different elements – even if, obviously, the nature and extent of the differences between them do change over time" (Grin, this volume, 129). Grin's caution about the imperative of acknowledging linguistic difference, rather than seeking to eliminate it, mirrors this volume's underlying vision of language ethics as rooted in a human commonality of linguistic difference.

3. THE DISCORDANT PARITY OF REAL-WORLD LANGUAGE ETHICS

The sections above argued for the importance of grounding the idea of language ethics in an understanding of language that is more nuanced and socially embedded, rather than one that is abstracted, platonic, and/or generic. Rather than thinking about the normative ethics of Language (in the uppercase), in other words, the proposed notion of language ethics seeks to situate itself against a much more contextual backdrop, focusing instead on linguistic repertoires and identities, and what they entail for the normative ordering of the political life of language (in the lowercase). In so doing, the proposed notion of language ethics aims to examine moral and political agency in language in the context in which it develops and which provides it with its meaning and significance. This "lowercase conception" stems directly from the central role that the notion of language ethics designates for the experience of language barriers as a human commonality.

On the face of it, a lowercase conception of language ethics might seem less philosophically rigorous than competing approaches that aim to explore language, including moral agency in language, from a more universal standpoint. But taking as a starting point the particular rather than the universal nonetheless offers important advantages, by challenging prevailing assumptions and convictions, linguistic and political alike. For example, as Riera-Gil notes in her critique of certain varieties of liberal linguistic justice theories, the tendency to presuppose the instrumental superiority of majority languages "can be viewed as a deviation from the liberal principle of neutrality; the reason is that this assumption privileges particular options of good life, namely those that measure success according to the rules of knowledge economy as if they were the only worth for any individual" (Riera-Gil 2019, 3).

Furthermore, a serious philosophical consideration of a different form of linguistic alterity, and the type of moral and political agency born out of it, holds great promise for a normative debate on language, in terms of further developing and refining its analytical capacity and real-world applicability. This is because "the capacity to use different languages provides not only more opportunities, but also more choice options for conducting different and valuable kinds of good life. And the relative importance of mastering each of these languages for a particular individual will depend, to a great extent, on the kind of life she desires to live" (Riera-Gil 2019, 15).

The contributors to this volume clearly articulate the theoretical and practical value of approaching language ethics in the lowercase rather than the uppercase. Avnon's contribution, for example, which draws on an experience (and reflection) situated in a site of significant political and linguistic conflict, demonstrates the practical significance of a language ethics that extends beyond universal and abstracted constructs, and is considered for the purpose of practical action-guidance, especially when the social and political stakes involved are high. This significance makes language ethics particularly meaningful as *applied* ethics. Without at least some kind of an underlying systematic and principled ethical theory of language, as Avnon emphasizes, there exists the risk of relevant decisions and judgments being made on the base of unreflective language beliefs and attitudes. Especially in the realm of public policy-making, working primarily on the basis of moral and linguistic knowledge of that type may lead to highly adverse results.

To appreciate that, consider Avnon's reflection on a period spent as a director of a research centre at the Hebrew University of Jerusalem, one of whose main missions was the teaching of civics to Hebrew- and Arabic-speaking high school students. Regarding the language of instruction, Avnon notes that "[a]lthough we did have a clear sense of our overall purpose and of activities that we hoped would lead to attainment of the goal of creating a shared civic language across the entire Israeli secondary-school system, we did not have a language ethics to guide us through the issues and programs that we initiated" (Avnon, this volume, 41). Consequently, he goes on, "[s]ince we did not have a language ethics as an external referent for our discussions, debates, and arguments, we negotiated according to our beliefs and convictions" (Avnon, this volume, 43).

The strongly applied nature of language ethics, invoked by Avnon in his discussion of the philosophy and praxis of civic education in a deeply divided society, is similarly echoed in many of the chapters included in this volume. Edwards's critique of the language of language rights, and its prevalence in the ecolinguistics discourse, is motivated by his wariness of the potential adverse impact of this theoretical framework on the very real well-being of those communities this rhetoric aims to protect. De Schutter's discussion of intralinguistic justice, namely of justice *between* varieties of the same language, draws precisely on an aspect of the "linguistic real world" that is often neglected in comparison with its interlinguistic counterpart. Ricento's analysis of the power structures that connect English as a world language to neoliberal economics is likewise grounded in a detailed examination of empirical findings on the role of (certain varieties of) English in the global economy of high-income versus low-income countries, particularly with regard to the knowledge economy. Grin's chapter, exploring the challenges (and possibilities) of operationalizing the concept of diversity to address pressing ethical concerns, similarly highlights the nature of a lowercase language ethics as applied ethics. Robichaud's and Weinstock's engagement with language protection as a collective action problem and the challenge of free riders, with their respective connections to the Quebec case, clearly demonstrates the relevance and utility of language ethics to developed as well as developing nations. Offering a general reflection on the importance of a situated inquiry (in this case on the justification of linguistic coercion and its limits), Weinstock proposes that "considering language choice within a strategic context … allows us to identify with greater precision the moral dilemmas that attend speakers of smaller languages who find themselves in situations in which they must coerce fence-sitters and defectors in order to protect those languages" (Weinstock, this volume, 198).

The strong applied nature of language ethics is reflected in the complementarity of the normative and empirical work upon which the chapters draw. The finely tuned theorization of the normative chapters by Avnon, Robichaud, De Schutter, and Weinstock is complemented by the more empirically oriented chapters by Edwards, Grin, and Ricento. Furthermore, *within* individual chapters many of the authors call on both normative and empirical sources in constructing their understanding of the interface between language, power, and ethics, and the shape in which this interface is manifested in real-world contexts, issues, and challenges. In so doing, the authors make a particularly important contribution to the ongoing effort to bridge the existing gap between political theory and philosophy on the one side and language policy on the other.

Taken together, the chapters included in this volume outline the current boundaries of the notion of language ethics as a more comprehensive framework that examines the interrelations between ethics, power, and language. Each chapter can be seen as holding a distinct piece of the theoretical, conceptual, and methodological elements that comprise the broader puzzle of language ethics as a distinct field of inquiry. Each of the chapters addresses, from its own perspective, the moral challenge of a human commonality rooted in the experience of linguistic difference. At the same time, the individual chapters, and even more so the volume as a whole, nonetheless situate the discussion not only in different research and geographical contexts, but also as part of a broader general conversation on human agency in the face of the ineliminable reality of a language barrier. This may seem like an internal contradiction, given the significance of a lowercase conception of language ethics as reasoned above, and the effort to distinguish it from more abstracted and platonic conceptions. But it is in fact fully compatible with the broader vision that underlies the book as a whole, which envisages both contextual and universal dimensions of the notion of real-world language ethics as existing in a state of "discordant parity" (Benvenisti and Harel 2017).

The idea of discordant parity originates in human rights theory, where it was recently proposed as a manner of reconciling the irresolvable conflict between constitutional law on the one hand, and international law on the

other hand. What underlies this idea is the recognition of the equal importance of the two for securing human rights despite their inner tensions, which
makes the relationship between the two discordant. As the originators of the
idea propose, "[t]he parity between international and constitutional norms
does not rest on harmonious interdependence. Parity implies friction; but
friction is a positive, indeed, a necessary element for ensuring individual liberty. Hence the 'discordant parity': international norms and constitutional
norms compete with each other and seek to dominate the normative sphere"
(Benvenisti and Harel 2017, 39).

The notion of "discordant parity" serves a useful purpose in thinking about
how to understand the relationship between the contextual and the general
scopes of the notion of language ethics. More specifically, the principle of discordant parity helps to situate the respective roles of a context-sensitive
inquiry on the political life of language with a general discussion on moral
and political agency in language more broadly. In so doing, it avoids the clear
pitfalls that stem from fully embracing a highly particularistic inquiry over
a more generalized approach, especially with regard to the capacity to address
more general questions concerning the human linguistic experience, such as
those underlying this volume. What it aims at, rather, is highlighting the productive "unsettled" interdependence between a more general theoretical
inquiry on the one hand, and one that is more closely immersed in the particularities of specific cases and contexts, on the other hand. This is in the hope
that the two engage in a process of mutual shaping and re-shaping, rather than
seek to impose on different cases specific notions of moral and political
agency in language that may themselves be just as context-dependent (Oakes
and Peled 2018; Morales-Gálvez 2018; Riera-Gil 2019). The fact that there exists
an "uneasy interface between the universality of a general theory and the particularity of the various contexts in which it is grounded" (Oakes and Peled
2018, 157) should therefore be viewed as an important feature of the theory of
language ethics rather than a bug.

A more generalized discussion of what language ethics are and entail, when
informed by a more real-world and context-sensitive inquiry, has the important task of revisiting, re-examining, and redefining fundamental ethical
questions that stem from the human commonality of linguistic difference.
Under such starting conditions, what constitutes a linguistically good life?

What forms of moral and political self-direction exist in a multilingual world, and how may we assess their relative moral strengths and weaknesses? If the difference between how monolinguals and multilinguals experience the world can be said to constitute a form of substantive if not radical alterity, what does it mean for the way in which important notions such as linguistic dignity or linguistic equality are approached and utilized in linguistic justice theories, and/or invoked and then institutionalized through public policy interventions? What does it mean for the way in which civic life is imagined and reasoned? Or for more cosmopolitan forms of identity, affinity, and action? What does it entail for understanding moral and political agency in cases or situations in which that very essence of being a linguistic agent participating in political life comes under substantive pressure? For example, in mental illness, such as the experience of "indescribability" in depression (Ratcliffe 2015, 1–2), or "language nausea," the feeling of alienation from one's own words and utterances and the disturbance of their practical significance in relation to the world (Ratcliffe 2019)?

These and other similar such questions hint at the broader philosophical horizons of the notion of language ethics as a distinct field of ethical inquiry, and chart for it some possible thematic, conceptual, and methodological paths forward as it develops. In that process, there is much to be gained from closer interaction with other domains in ethics where language and linguistic interaction play a pivotal role. In political ethics this includes, for example, recent normative explorations on the nature of political listening that draw in part on important work in feminist ethics (Dobson 2014). Relatedly, feminist ethics also offers a more general consideration on the role of the senses in the shaping and cultivation of moral agency (e.g. Holler 2012), providing an insightful perspective on the often covert political dynamics of real-world linguistic interaction in multilingual democracies (Peled and Bonotti 2019). Another important venue for exploring language ethics lies in post-colonial political philosophy, and its inquiry on the difficulty of the enduring moral presence of the past, as Weinstock notes (Weinstock, this volume). Language ethics also plays a vital role in professional ethics, such as education (Avnon 2006) and healthcare (Peled 2018c). Another important source of a potentially productive joint theory-building effort is environmental ethics, which is ideally situated to bring together a language ethics perspective with the important (and timely) body of work on ecolinguistics (e.g. Romaine and Nettle 2001; Harrison 2007; Fill and Penz 2018). These collaborative horizons highlight the contours of the ethical inquiry embodied not only in the notion of language ethics, but also in its intrinsically interdisciplinary nature.

4. THE EPISTEMIC JURISDICTION

The topic and concept of language ethics have been discussed thus far in this introduction in terms of their experiential grounding (the common human experience of linguistic difference), as part of an attempt to identify their theoretical substance (especially vis-à-vis the more particular debate on linguistic justice), and in relation to their real-world orientation. In this final section of the introduction, my aim is to complete this "mapping" of the notion of language ethics by considering the complex (inter)disciplinary terrain in which it is situated.

At a first glance, "ethics" and "language" seem instantaneously associated with the respective disciplines of philosophy and linguistics. "Language ethics," this suggests, could be mapped as a bridging intellectual terrain, or an intellectual crossover, under an appropriately vague heading such as "philosophy of language." The semantic content of "philosophy of language," however, already refers not only to an entirely different established area of inquiry, but also to one in which both ethics and language (in the lowercase) are, at best, marginal. To make matters even more complicated, the positioning of language ethics as arising from the reality of politics introduces political science as a third discipline into the mix, by incorporating a strong component of normative political theorizing into the descriptive study of the social life of language. The neatness of this tripartite description, however, collapses fairly quickly when we consider the range of adjacent disciplines present in this volume: Grin, Robichaud, and Ricento all draw on economics in conceptualizing the "disciplinary repertoire" of language ethics, with Ricento further expanding it so as to include international development. Avnon highlights the crucial importance of education. An overarching perspective (or otherwise constructive input) from the sociology of language is already present in the majority of chapters (Avnon, De Schutter, Grin, Ricento). An even more fine-grained account of the *sub-disciplines* invoked and utilized throughout the book, such as political economy or the history of ideas, would have yielded an even more kaleidoscopic account (of course, both sociolinguistics and political philosophy/theory can be thought of in themselves as sub-disciplines or interdisciplines).

It might seem that what we end up with here is a disciplinarily disputed territory, in which it is not clear who, if anyone, holds a legitimate and authoritative claim for an overriding epistemic jurisdiction. This is because the entities on which this volume focuses, namely ethics and language, are multifaceted phenomena that extend over a variety of domains and practices of human life. Ethics might well be identified as part of the rightful intellectual territory of philosophy, but it is difficult to think about normative or applied ethics without considering at least some insights from disciplines such as political science, sociology, or economics. Language, similarly, is a field in which linguists are the most obvious candidates to be held as epistemic authorities, but it is hard to think about a meaningful account of human language, and, even more so, human agency in language, that does not require at least some input from disciplines such as history, psychology, or anthropology. In truth, these two "dividing commonalities" are irreducible to the self-contained domains of a single discipline. There ought to be nothing surprising about this statement: the real world, after all, does not occur in a particular discipline. Rather than being perceived as discrete vehicles of truth-discovery, disciplinary perspectives are better understood as particular lenses which we may use to observe phenomena in the world. Our understanding and thinking are therefore lens-dependent. This is why intrinsically interdisciplinary notions, such as language ethics, necessitate a discussion on thinking *about* thinking.

At the same time, to reiterate Grin's warning on the conceptualization of diversity, it is imperative not to lose the capacity for analytical discussion even in the face of what are, for all purposes, intrinsically multifaceted entities. The temptation to opt for "a view from everywhere" might be intellectually alluring, but should be resisted on grounds of, as it were, epistemic feasibility and/or fallibility. A "view from everywhere" runs the risk of being analogous to the crude characterization of a cosmopolitan as an individual who regards the entire world as their home, but never feels at home in any part of it. Paradoxically, perhaps, interdisciplinary work necessitates a robust disciplinary-conscious framework, which is sensitive to its advantages (theoretical, conceptual, methodological) as well as to its limitations. A more promising approach for interdisciplinary work in this complex area is to shift our outlook from the self-identifying labels of the disciplines to the scientific epistemologies that underlie them. Different disciplines, after all, are well-known to offer a significant variety in what they identify as important or relevant questions, in their discovery procedures, and in what they consider as admissible evidence.[6] The "disciplinary-disputed territory" of language ethics therefore seems to exhibit the very same tension between (disciplinary) difference and (epistemic) interdependence as does this notion itself.

Language ethics has been identified throughout this introduction as located primarily in normative and applied ethics. Such identification, subsequently, charts general – if not absolute – contours that situate this notion primarily in political philosophy, with "special relations" with the language disciplines. This identification is grounded in the primacy of political philosophy in theorizing normative and applied ethics, by offering a rigorous and nuanced analysis of how and why we ought to act in the context of language, in the same way that parallel topics in ethics consider how we ought to act in contexts such as healthcare (bioethics), gender (feminist ethics), or the environment (environmental ethics). Keeping in mind this thematic ecology in the process of developing a more systematic account of what language ethics is and entails can inform the debate on the possible trajectories, structures, argumentation, principles, and modes of reasoning that it may utilize as it develops. This is not meant, however, to imply the appropriation of epistemic jurisdiction by political philosophers to their exclusive use. Prioritizing the scientific epistemology of political philosophy above those of the language disciplines would be tantamount to the erroneous attempt to "solve away" the tension between disciplinary difference and epistemic interdependence. The main goal therefore should not be to conclusively settle this important tension, but rather to find suitable theoretical, conceptual, and methodological forms of transforming it into a creative tension. (See also De Schutter, this volume, 156–8, on the important tension between political theorists and sociolinguists on the normative ethics of intralinguistic prioritizing, and the constructive contribution this topic may inspire nonetheless.)

The dissatisfaction with the adequacy of the frameworks currently present in the (broadly construed) field of normative language theorizing and the politics of language is iterated in several of the chapters included in this volume. Grin comments that, as far as public policy is concerned, "interdisciplinary linkage often remains aspirational. Important tracts of sociolinguistic literature, while mentioning language policy and using the word 'policy' in their titles, turn out not to address policy questions" (Grin, this volume, 137). Edwards observes the unease often felt by social scientists faced with normative questions "because they believe it is outside their remit to venture into prescriptive or 'normative' territory" (Edwards, this volume, 56). Ricento argues that the "lack of clarity on key terms and concepts leads to disputes and contrary positions on important issues where there might otherwise be greater agreement, or at least a basis for identifying common ground, which could lead to a greater possibility of consilience" (Ricento, this volume, 204), referring in particular to language policy scholars whose "lack of sophistication in political economy impacts their ability to critically address the effects of neoliberal economic policies on the status and utility of global languages" (Ricento, this volume, 204). The debate on language ethics therefore clearly invites, if not necessitates, a conversation that goes beyond the question of which particular theories, concepts, or methods to import or adapt – namely, a discussion which engages directly with the process of "thinking about thinking." The substantive stakes of not doing so are highlighted, for example, by Avnon, pointing out that, in the absence of a systematic engagement with the ethical substratum of language politics, the normative theorizing of language tensions and conflicts, and the subsequent policy measures that transpire from them, are most likely to be shaped around intuitive beliefs and convictions, without any principled checks (Avnon, this volume, 43). This clearly is an unfortunate state of affairs, both in terms of the theoretical deficiencies it exhibits and in the subsequent problematic consequences such deficiencies risk when translated into public policy.

Nothing mandates, however, that this state of affairs cannot or should not be changed. The overarching tone of the chapters included in this volume is not one of defeatism but rather one of constructive and creative thinking on how our understanding of the common human experience of linguistic difference may be successfully advanced. This is an encouraging and hopeful message for academic researchers, policy-makers, activists, and citizens who are faced with moral questions pertaining to language in their everyday lives and the lives of their political communities. The importance of pragmatic and action-guiding reasoning is highlighted, for example, in Grin's critique of the limited utility of some of the conceptual vocabulary of critical sociolinguistics (Grin, this volume), and in Robichaud's important emphasis that coercive linguistic norms must not be regarded as arbitrary (Robichaud, this volume, 113).

A fine yet robust thematic line connects the seemingly disparate cases of language anxieties in Quebec, the language of civic education in Israel, and the power structures that determine the utility of English in a global market. What these cases – and many similar ones – have in common is an underlying multifaceted nexus between ethics and language, born out of real-world necessities rather than pure intellectual pursuit. Exploring how we ought to treat one other, as humans whose moral and linguistic commonality is only realizable in the particular, is the primarily goal of this volume, and of its conception of the field of language ethics as a distinct field of inquiry.

NOTES

1   For an insightful account of Levinasian radical alterity in the context of linguistic and cultural diversity, and its implications for an inclusive approach to care in liberal democracies, see Kirmayer 2015.

2   See also Alcalde 2018 for comprehensive interdisciplinary review of the linguistic justice literature.

3   Peled 2019. The linguistic challenge to the populist notion of an indivisible body exists on both interlinguistic and intralinguistic levels.

4   See, for example, Peled and Bonotti 2016; Patrão 2018.

5   See Oakes and Peled 2018 and Peled and Bonotti 2019 for an application of De Schutter's theory of intralinguistic justice to pluricentric contexts in the French-speaking world and the political life of accent.

6   See Peled 2014; Oakes and Peled 2018; Peled 2018a.

REFERENCES

Alcalde, Javier. 2018. "Linguistic Justice: An Interdisciplinary Overview of the Literature." In *Language Policy and Linguistic Justice: Economic, Philosophical and Sociolinguistic Approaches*, edited by Michele Gazzola, Torsten Templin, and Bengt-Arne Wickström, 65–149. Berlin: Springer.

Avnon, Dan. 2006. *Civic Language in Israel*. Jerusalem: Magnes Press.

Benvenisti, Eyal, and Alon Harel. 2017. "Embracing the Tension between National and International Human Rights Law: The Case for Discordant Parity." *International Journal of Constitutional Law* 15, no. 1: 36–59.

Cetrà, Daniel. 2019. *The Politics of Language and Nationalism*. London: Palgrave Macmillan.

De Schutter, Helder, and David Robichaud. 2012. "Language Is Just a Tool! On the Instrumentalist Approach to Language." In *The Cambridge Handbook of Language Policy*, edited by Bernard Spolsky, 124–46. Cambridge: Cambridge University Press.

– 2015a. "Van Parijsian Linguistic Justice – Context, Analysis and Critiques." *Critical Review of International Social and Political Philosophy* 18, no. 2: 87–112.

Dobson, Andrew. 2014. *Listening for Democracy: Recognition, Representation, Reconciliation*. Oxford, UK: Oxford University Press.

– eds. 2015b. "Linguistic Justice. Van Parijs and His Critics." *Critical Review of International Social and Political Philosophy* 18, no. 2 (special issue).

Fill, Alwin A., and Hermine Penz. 2017. *The Routledge Handbook of Ecolinguistics*. London: Routledge.

Harrison, David K. 2007. *When Languages Die: The Extinction of the World's Languages and the Erosion of Human Knowledge*. Oxford, UK: Oxford University Press.

Holler, Linda. 2012. *Erotic Morality: The Role of Touch in Moral Agency*. New Brunswick, NJ, and London: Rutgers University Press.

Ives, Peter. 2015. "Global English and the Limits of Liberalism: Confronting Global Capitalism and Challenges to the Nation-State." In *Language Policy and Political Economy: English in a Global Context*, edited by Tom Ricento, 48–71. Oxford, UK: Oxford University Press.

– 2018. "Language and the State in Western Political Theory: Implications for Language Policy and Planning." In *The Oxford Handbook of Language Policy and*

Planning, edited by James W. Tollefson and Miguel Pérez-Milans, 183–201. Oxford, UK: Oxford University Press.

– 2019. "Putting Canadian Language Politics in a Global Context." In *Language Politics and Policies: Perspectives from Canada and the United States*, edited by Thomas Ricento, 78–94. Cambridge: Cambridge University Press.

Jones, Rhys, and Huw Lewis. 2019. *New Geographies of Language: Language, Culture and Politics in Wales*. London: Palgrave Macmillan.

Kirmayer, Laurence. 2008. "Empathy and Alterity in Cultural Psychiatry." *Ethos* 36, no. 4: 457–74.

Kraus, Peter A., and François Grin, eds. 2018. *The Politics of Multilingualism: Europeanisation, Globalisation and Linguistic Governance*. Amsterdam and Philadelphia, PA: John Benjamins.

Kymlicka, Will, and Alan Patten. 2003. *Language Rights and Political Theory*. New York: Oxford University Press.

Kymlicka, Will, and Sue Donaldson. 2016. "Locating Animals in Political Philosophy." *Philosophy Compass* 11, no. 11: 692–701.

Léger, Rémi, and Huw Lewis, eds. 2017. "Normative Approaches to Language Policy and Planning." *Journal of Multilingual and Multicultural Development* 38, no. 7 (special issue).

May, Stephen. 2015. "The Problem with English(es) and Linguistic (In)justice. Addressing the Limits of Liberal Egalitarian Accounts of Language." *Critical Review of International Social and Political Philosophy* 18, no. 2: 131–48.

Morales-Gálvez, Sergi. 2017. "Living Together as Equals: Linguistic Justice and Sharing the Public Sphere in Multilingual Settings." *Ethnicities* 17, no. 5: 646–66.

Nettle, Daniel, and Suzanne Romaine. 2000. *Vanishing Voices: The Extinction of the World's Languages*. Oxford, UK: Oxford University Press.

Oakes, Leigh, and Yael Peled. 2018. *Normative Language Policy: Ethics, Politics, Principles*. Cambridge: Cambridge University Press.

Patrão, André. 2018. "Linguistic Relativism in the Age of Global Lingua Franca: Reconciling Cultural and Linguistic Diversity with Globalization." *Lingua* 210: 30–41.

Peled, Yael. 2014. "Normative Language Policy: Interface and Interfences." *Language Policy* 13, no. 4: 301–15.

– 2017. "Language and the Limits of Justice." *Journal of Multilingual and Multicultural Development* 38, no. 7: 645–57.

– 2018a. "Language Ethics and the Interdisciplinary Challenge." In *The Oxford Handbook of Language Policy and Planning*, edited by James W. Tollefson and Miguel Pérez-Milans, 140–62. Oxford, UK: Oxford University Press.

– 2018b. "Toward an Adaptive Approach to Linguistic Justice: Three Paradoxes." In *Language Policy and Linguistic Justice: Economic, Philosophical and Sociolinguistic Approaches*, edited by Michele Gazzola, Torsten Templin, and Bengt-Arne Wickström, 173–88. Berlin: Springer.

– 2018c. "Language Barriers and Epistemic Injustice in Healthcare Settings." *Bioethics* 32, no. 6: 360–7.

– 2019. "The Political Ethics of Linguistic In-Betweenness." In *Language Politics and Policies: Perspectives from Canada and the United States*, edited by Thomas Ricento, 45–59. Cambridge: Cambridge University Press, 2019.

Peled, Yael, and Matteo Bonotti. 2016. "Tongue-Tied: Rawls, Metalinguistic Awareness and Political Philosophy." *American Political Science Review* 110, no. 4: 798–811.

– 2019. "Sound Reasoning: Why Accent Bias Matters for Democratic Theory." *Journal of Politics* 81, no. 2: 411–25.

Petrovic, John E. 2014. *A Post-Liberal Approach to Language Policy in Education*. Clevedon, UK: Multilingual Matters.

– 2019. "Alienation, Language Work, and the So-Called Commodification of Language." In *Language Politics and Policies: Perspectives from Canada and the United States*, edited by Thomas Ricento, 60–77. Cambridge: Cambridge University Press.

Ratcliffe, Matthew. 2015. *Experiences of Depression: A Study in Phenomenology*. Oxford, UK: Oxford University Press.

– 2019. "Language Nausea." Unpublished paper.

Rawls, John. 1999. *A Theory of Justice* (revised edition). Oxford, UK: Oxford University Press.

Réaume, Denise, and Meital Pinto. 2012. "Philosophy of Language Policy." In *The Cambridge Handbook of Language Policy*, edited by Bernard Spolsky, 37–58. Cambridge: Cambridge University Press.

Ricento, Thomas. 2000. "Historical and Theoretical Perspectives in Language Policy and Planning." *Journal of Sociolinguistics* 4, no. 2: 196–213.

Ricento, Thomas, Yael Peled, and Peter Ives, eds. 2014. "Language Policy and Political Theory." *Language Policy* 13, no. 4 (special issue).

Riera-Gil, Elvira. 2019. "The Communicative Value of Local Languages: An Under-
    estimated Interest in Theories of Linguistic Justice." *Ethnicities* 19, no. 1: 174–99.
Sandel, Michael. 1988. *Liberalism and the Limits of Justice*. Cambridge: Cambridge
    University Press.
Schiffman, Harold. 1996. *Language Policy and Linguistic Culture*. London and New
    York: Routledge.
Schmidt, Ronald, Sr. 2006. "Political Theory and Language Policy." In *An Introduc-
    tion to Language Policy: Theory and Method*, edited by Thomas Ricento, 95–100.
    Oxford, UK: Blackwell.
– 2014. "Democratic Theory and the Challenge of Linguistic Diversity." *Language
    Policy* 13, no. 4: 395–411.
Shorten, Andrew. 2018. "Justice in the Linguistic Environment: Narrow or Wide?"
    In *Language Policy and Linguistic Justice: Economic, Philosophical and Sociolinguis-
    tic Approaches*, edited by Michele Gazzola, Torsten Templin, and Bengt-Arne
    Wickström, 153–72. Berlin: Springer.
Taylor, Charles. 1985a. *Human Agency and Language: Philosophical Papers 1*.
    Cambridge: Cambridge University Press.
– 1985b. *Philosophy and the Human Sciences: Philosophical Papers 2*. Cambridge:
    Cambridge University Press.
– 1989. *Sources of the Self: The Making of the Modern Identity*. Cambridge: Harvard
    University Press.
Tonkin, Humphrey, ed. 2015. "Linguistic Equality." *Language Problems and
    Language Planning* 39, no. 3 (special issue).
Van Parijs, Philippe. 2011. *Linguistic Justice for Europe and for the World*. Oxford,
    UK: Oxford University Press.
Wee, Lionel. 2011. *Language without Rights*. Oxford, UK: Oxford University Press.
Wright, Sue. 2015. "What Is Language: A Response to Philippe van Parijs." *Critical
    Review of International Social and Political Philosophy* 18, no. 2: 113–30.

1

What Is (or "Are") Language Ethics?

DAN AVNON

The word-pair "*language ethics*" seems to refer to something familiar. Yet when focusing on it, using imagination and thinking, one cannot say that it is indeed readily recognizable or knowable. "Language" implies a number of different phenomena, and as for "ethics" ... well, there is an active scholarly interest in examining and re-examining ethics, whether in the singular (as a single sphere of activity) or in the plural (implying numerous, different ethics, pertaining to distinct areas of human conduct). Considering the initial perplexity, and then the scope, range, and diversity of possible referents, I will begin by clarifying what I have in mind when considering language ethics in the context of this volume.

Language communicates moral codes by establishing, preserving, and transmitting through the ages certain key concepts, metaphors, idioms, and phrases. That is why language, ethics, and morality are profoundly and immanently interrelated.[1] The immanent pairing of language and morality constitutes a principled justification for establishing language ethics as an idiom that refers to a particular field of human activity and scholarly enquiry. What remains is to determine the contexts that merit consideration as meanings (issues concerning conceptual analysis) and manifestations (as a sphere of activity) of "language ethics."

Discussion of language will be limited to its everyday sense as a native language ("mother tongue") such as English, Hebrew, Arabic, and so forth. Such languages are recognizable, and have specific "phonological, syntactic, and semantic/conceptual structure" (Jackendoff 2002, 278). Their function is communicative, and their various forms of expression are the basis for the creation of cultures and communities. This approach to language is age-old, and is found in diverse cultural traditions.

The choice to limit the discussion of language to native languages is heuristic, as it enables separation of this object of enquiry from language in general, or from the human language faculty (Trask 2007, 130).[2] Similar considerations guide my understanding of what is implied when the notion of "ethics" is joined to "language" to form an image of "language ethics": I will refer to ethics in its use as granting direction and justifications for human intentions and actions. Applied to language, ethics pertains to considerations guiding our understanding of the purposes and benefits of language for individual and communal well-being, and the conduct that comes in the wake of such understanding.[3]

At least two developments give rise to the contemporary need to consider ethical principles to guide action (and thinking) regarding the relation between language and human well-being. The *first* is increasing linguistic diversity within well-established liberal-democratic states. This development undercuts prevalent assumptions about ethical commonalities that are bases of social and political order in established (nation-)states. A growing plurality of language-based minority communities in erstwhile single-language social and political spheres within modern nation-states gives rise to a diversity of ethical codes. The coexistence in one political order of diverse ethical codes undermines the shared ethical foundations that are embedded in a dominant national language. The distance from ethical fragmentation to social (and then political) fragmentation is short. This is particularly true in instances where liberal respect for the right to develop individual and communal identities is perceived as a challenge to shared public narratives "by which people make sense of their condition and interpret the common life they share" (Sandel 1996, 350).

This development points to the practical need to develop a language ethics that would assist in deliberating appropriate balances between competing ethical codes, those stemming from diverse linguistically-based cultural communities. For example, if tensions in society and state are related to an increase in linguistic diversity (due to the diversity of cultural codes embedded in language), then language ethics would provide ways of thinking about and then addressing the challenges created by diverse ethical systems competing for precedence in clashes over the contours and practices of shared public spheres. From this perspective (which is merely one example of the need for language ethics in this day and age), language ethics would have to provide principles to guide issues of inclusion or exclusion of languages within a political community accustomed to an authority that stems from one dominant language (and its attendant ethics).[4]

A *second* development that exemplifies the need to develop language ethics, or a language ethics, is the steady decrease in the overall number of spoken languages.[5] If we keep in mind the aforementioned claims regarding the potentially negative effects of a diversity of languages on political and social stability, then the overall decrease in the number of languages would actually seem to be a positive development. Such an interpretation would rest on the assumption that the decrease in the number of languages implies fewer competing moral codes (Lauring 2008, 343–61). Consequently this development would seem to heighten the prospects for moving beyond the nation-state to a global civilization that shares universal moral codes by virtue of a shared language. However, the transition to a less linguistically heterogeneous human community has potentially troubling side effects (Romaine 2015; Skutnabb-Kangas, Maffi, and Harmon 2003). For example, a decrease in cultural diversity may weaken conditions conducive to creativity (Skutnabb-Kangas 2002). So whatever we may think about these developments and the sample of opinions regarding their potential for gain or loss, we do need a morality that will guide our thinking and our actions as we experience such profound changes in our political communities and in our global civilization.

The first section of this chapter will offer some instances of using language ethics as an analytical category within the discourse of political thought. The second section will consider the need for language ethics in the context of my practical experience in creating programs that advance a shared civic language for Israel's diverse cultural and linguistic communities: Jewish and non-Jewish, Hebrew and non-Hebrew (primarily Arabic) speakers. Consequently, the discussion of language ethics – as an analytic tool on the one hand and as a frame of reference for creating a shared civic language on the other hand – will demonstrate possible uses of this notion both in conceptual analysis and in the context of seeking ethical guidelines for actual (not merely imagined or theoretical) social circumstances.

1. LANGUAGE ETHICS IN POLITICAL THOUGHT:
FOUR LEVELS OF ANALYSIS

There are four different levels of analysis within which the notion of language ethics may be relevant to political philosophy, to politics, and to social life:

1. language ethics as it pertains to the development of individual minds and lives (regardless of specific culture or native tongue);
2. language ethics as it pertains to tensions between majority and minority groups in contemporary nation-states;
3. language ethics as it pertains to the development of policies in matters regarding the role of language in shaping public spheres;
4. language ethics as it pertains to the steady decrease in the number of spoken languages on this planet.

The *first* level of analysis addresses the issue of language ethics from the perspective of our child-rearing practices. For example, it is considered natural and normative that the need to acquire a language is initially satisfied by exposure from birth to the mother- or parent-tongue of those who raise the child. Yet one may ask whether it is beneficial for the newborn to be raised *solely* in the particular language spoken by his parents. Perhaps his or her life prospects will be enhanced by being raised in two or more languages?

There are rather banal utilitarian justifications for advancing such a possibility. For example, if the newborn is a member of a linguistic minority within a public sphere shaped by the language of a political majority, then for all practical reasons it is beneficial to have this future citizen learn the language of the political majority as early as possible. In this instance, it is clearly to the advantage of the newborn to master a language that would enhance her prospects for making a living. This reasoning could support programs to add English to the habitat of a child born into impoverished societies with little prospects for economic opportunity, or to add Chinese to the linguistic environment of a child born in an industrial society keen on "developing markets" in China.

But wait. If we consider these kinds of justifications for championing early childhood bi- or pluri-lingualism, we should ask whether the examples just cited indeed address the welfare of a human being just born into this world. A language ethics approach would ask what is good and advantageous for the individual, what is right and beneficial for the community, and what is the appropriate balance between individual and communal well-being. Such musings would probably lead to consideration of a child's upbringing in terms of her particular cognitive capacities[6] and potential for autonomous development. Seeing the particular child and her unique capacities would then be prior to molding the child according to political or economic configurations. Language ethics thus emerges as a set of propositions that can guide parental and communal behaviour at a basic point of entry into social life: that of language acquisition. The ethical stance seems to be clear: as a species we have a shared interest in furthering our development through the betterment of individual minds. Language is central to developing our minds/brains. So language acquisition is a central (although certainly not sole) factor in actualizing our innate potential.

Findings in mind science support such a principled stance, and may be a basis for the claim that it is (or may be) advantageous for *all* children (not only those in need of economic betterment) to be raised in two or more languages (Macnamara and Conway 2014, 520).[7] From this perspective, sensitivity to principled and well-grounded justifications for enabling language acquisition at an early stage of development is supported by a different form of justification, the well-established fact that there is a critical period, between the ages of approximately two and twelve, when language acquisition is relatively effortless (Elman 1993; Hurford 1991; Jackendoff 1993). At this stage of her life, the child is dependent on parental or communal support in developing her innate capacities. It won't help her to learn later in life that as a child she had a ten-year-long mental window of opportunity to acquire languages. She needed a responsible adult or community who knew the facts and helped her develop her potential when the available knowledge was relevant to her realizing her latent potential. In turn, the adult or the political community needs a language ethics that articulates and then guides the social implementation of such knowledge.

In addition to the self-evident benefits that come with the ability to move with ease between languages (and consequently between cultures, communities, and economic spheres), it is claimed that polyglots have an enhanced capacity to respond to complexity. For example, recent research suggests that children who are bi- or pluri-lingual develop neuronal circuits that are also beneficial for managing complexity in general, not only for the processing of different languages (Ibrahim et al. 2013).

But before we get carried away and articulate a language ethics that draws upon scientific findings, we should note that the previous discussion assumes probabilities based on a certain area of scientific research, without considering equally forceful alternatives from other areas of science. For example, when a parent suppresses his own natural language in order to communicate with a child in a language that scientists claim is beneficial, he may find himself acting in an artificial manner.[8] He does this for the sake of human betterment, which is a worthy moral justification. Yet one may ask whether the benefits of creating neural circuits stimulated by the introduction of a second language at early stages of development indeed outweigh the possible emotional harm caused by parents who communicate with their children through the mediating prism of utilitarian calculations rather than from the immediate reaction articulated in the parent's intimate language. When we factor in the possible emotional impact of mandatory bi- or pluri-lingualism, then it may be that justifying the imposition of bilingualism in terms of material necessity may overlook the impact of such social engineering on a child's emotional development.

The point is clear: these competing and perhaps conflicting rationales illustrate the need for a language ethics to guide our thinking and our actions as we advance into an era in human evolution that may change the way we understand the role of natural languages in the course of human development. A responsible and coherent language ethics for the twenty-first century would be greatly enhanced by the adoption of cross-disciplinary research. Such scholarly cooperation would include combining, matching, pairing, and/or confronting findings in cognitive science and genetics with assumptions guiding philosophy, normative social theories, political theory, and so forth.

For example, if research that cross-cuts cultures and academic disciplines repeatedly proves that early-age bi- or pluri-lingualism expands the mind's capacity to understand complexity and navigate within it, then such research could be the basis for an ethics promoting bilingualism (Bialystok and Viswanathan 2009; Hilchey and Klein 2011; Barac and Bialystok 2012). Similarly, if studies that track the impact of bilingualism on individuals, families, communities, and cultures indicate that such practices may harm their emotional health, then we might offer other, perhaps opposing, ethical guidelines for addressing initiatives to change language acquisition practices.

The first level of analysis focused on the individual mind. The issues at stake are immanently social, as they deal with the meeting of minds: the mind of the newborn and the minds of those who nurture and prepare her for life in the human community on this planet. The ethics at stake are specifically and significantly concerned with a certain understanding of language as an essential, innate human capacity that we are accustomed to develop through a unilingual approach to child-rearing. Language ethics would help think about other, bi- or pluri-lingual, alternatives to ingrained custom.

Let's now move to a *second* level of analysis. Contemporary societies are ordered in political associations called "nation-states." The development of nation-states is intertwined with the development of national languages. We all know that in the first quarter of the twenty-first century, very few developed states live up to the image of one homogeneous nation associated in one state. Given that current demographics are stronger than eighteenth- or nineteenth-century social theories, the idea of a single national language dominating the public sphere, once widely perceived as empirically factual and normatively reasonable, is under attack. Indeed, the idea of granting minority groups rights to conduct their affairs or to raise their children in bilingual public school systems is spreading in democratic states where the growth in numbers of minority groups enables voters to change well-entrenched norms that oppose public funding of bilingual schools.[9]

The rise in the legal status of minority languages in contemporary democracies is not developing in a theoretical bubble. It is commensurate with a weakening of the immanent connection between language and civic identity. The emergence of linguistically plural political spaces may be pointing toward a shift away from nation-states to other forms of political association, such as states, regions, communities, federations, or unions. If this is indeed the case, then how does this development influence our notions of language-based identity, widely assumed to be a necessary foundation of the nation-state's political order? Should the transition from nation-states to states and from states to regionalism on the one hand, and to trans-national organizations on the other hand, lead to new conceptions of the role of language in the development of civic identities?

These issues are not primarily about individual well-being, but rather about the cohesion and stability of the originally (imagined as?) homogeneous nation-state. Nations are intertwined with language, and nation-states are identified with national tongues. To either change or enforce this political habit necessitates an ethics that would offer moral, utilitarian, or other ethically pertinent justifications for upgrading (or downgrading) minority languages within the greater body politic.

A *third* level of analysis remains within the sphere of the nation-state, yet is analytically distinct, and therefore merits separate consideration. It addresses a different area of public and scholarly discourse, a different language-game. What I have in mind is the field of public policy and the potential role of language ethics in providing principled and universally applicable guidelines for public policies that pertain to the development of language skills (the first level of analysis) or political order or cohesion (the second level of analysis).

From this perspective, language ethics would provide the ethical rationale for – or ethical challenge to – administrative decisions regarding the role of language in public systems or spheres.[10] For example, should the public school system enable, tolerate, promote, and actively establish schools that teach in the language of a local, minority cultural community? Conversely, should state-funded schools be required to teach solely or primarily in the language of the majority national group?[11] Language ethics would provide thinking that is prior to political contingencies or expediencies. Such principled deliberation would include ways to consider questions related to the loci of effective decision-making in matters relating to language policy in educational systems or in shared public spheres.

A *fourth* and final level of analysis that I consider political is the rapid decrease in the number of spoken languages on the globe, referred to by some as "the death of languages" (Romaine and Nettle 2000, 4–5). The data about the diminishing number of human languages implies the disappearance of a variety of cultures that wither away with the death of their last speakers. Should we care? Is there anything to say or do about this phenomenon beyond being sentimental about, outraged about, or indifferent to it? If humanity is converging toward a limited number of languages, then we may be transforming ourselves into a homogeneous form of life. What does this imply for the continued diversity necessary for our survival? The development of a world of apparent homogeneity may stifle individual creativity and the joy of life. Indeed, the loss of a culture is for many a form of acute existential pain. And what is life worth if we do not care for its joy? Surely these are questions that ought to concern attentive and educated citizens wherever they may happen to reside.

A neat division of language ethics into four areas of political discourse is convenient. Limiting it to liberal-democratic nation-states is also convenient. It reflects a democratic, perhaps a liberal-democratic, frame of academic mind: I assume nation-states; I assume sensitivity of the majority to minorities; I assume that the development of nation-states comes hand-in-hand with the development of a common language; I assume that a common language refers to a specific tongue and is the basis of (or "for") shared ethics. But such convenience is deceptive. It enables a sense of order that is prior to engaging in the messiness and disorder of political existence. I now turn to the messy aspect, to the application of language ethics to actual social and political circumstances. I will draw upon my experience as a citizen of a particular nation-state, the State of Israel (this capitalization is its official name).

2. LANGUAGE ETHICS IN ISRAEL: SOME CONSIDERATIONS

In the founding years of the Israeli polity (1950s), Arabic was granted formal status side-by-side with the dominant ethnic group's language, Hebrew (Spolsky 1999). A central effect of this policy was to create a separate school system for Arab-Israelis, taught in Arabic. From a liberal perspective, this may seem to be a "*kosher*" way to grant equal status to minorities and thus protect their unique traditions and forms of life. Similarly, Ultra-Orthodox Jews (*charedeem*) were granted the right to establish their own independent school system where teaching was predominantly in Yiddish. Israeli Hebrew was taught only in the national-religious and national non-religious school systems.[12]

The establishment of separate schools for Arab/Palestinian-Israelis and for Ultra-Orthodox Yiddish-speaking Jews effectively prevented the development of an Israeli civic identity that would evolve around a common civic language (Avnon 2006). By "civic language" I mean a set of moral codes that constitute the do's and don'ts of the Israeli public sphere. Such codes can be articulated in Hebrew or Arabic idioms (in both cases, Hebrew and Arabic idioms are further delineated by their respective religious and non-religious vernaculars). However, prior to separate translations of the common language of the public sphere into separate dialects, there should have been a common language from which such translations would emanate. The absence of such a shared language implies that unlike French Republicanism, the first generations of Israelis were not raised on a shared ethos grounded in a shared language. Israeli republicanism developed among and for those parts of the Jewish Israeli polity who were raised in Israeli Hebrew.[13]

The dire effects of this policy came to bear fruit in the 1990s and the early 2000s, years of intense political and civic strife: the Oslo agreements of the early 1990s exposed the distance between liberal-democratic and religious-nationalistic interpretations of Israel's raison d'être as a nation-state; the enactment in 1992 of two Basic Laws ensuring constitutional protection to individual rights proved to be a source of contention between the liberal-democratic constitutional values upheld by the supreme court and the values originating in Jewish sources and their rabbinic interpreters;[14] the assassination in 1995 of Israel's Prime Minister Itzhak Rabin uncovered the disparity between the basic ethics underlying democratic forms of government and certain (not all) rabbinic and Jewish-messianic guides to political action; the killing in 2001 by police forces of thirteen Arab/Palestinian-Israeli citizens who participated in demonstrations against Israel's policies in the West Bank revealed the depth of alienation, antagonism, and distrust between Israel's government and a significant percentage of its citizenship.

These are just a few dramatic examples of schisms within Israeli society that reflect a public sphere within which groups challenge the authority of the State or the legitimacy of claims brought forth by significant minorities. One common denominator of these sets of issues is the diversity of moral codes reflected in these conflicts: the challenges to the state and to its public sphere were voiced in Jewish-messianic, Jewish-Halachic,[15] Arab-Palestinian, Western liberal-democratic, and additional ethical systems. These challenges to a liberal-democratic civic culture revealed the paucity of democratic or liberal education in Israel, and the consequent absence of a shared civic language. In the words of Michael Walzer, factions who abide by particular moral codes may finally stand on opposing sides "of a chasm like that which opens between men who no longer speak the same language" (Walzer 1967, 204).

The absence of sensitivity to the role of language in creating a dialogical political culture was in the background of our establishing in 2001 a research and teaching centre at the Hebrew University of Jerusalem that was committed to establishing theoretical and practical foundations for a shared Israeli civic language, the Gilo Center for Civic Education & Democracy.[16] The goal of the Center was to develop a "shared civic language," which would be prior to separate native languages and ethical systems. Since the goal of the project was to have all children in Israel learn the same code of conduct, we defined civic language in terms of a shared civic ethic (Avnon 2006, n23). To this end, we initiated the research and curriculum development necessary for creating a national civics policy that would be implemented in all school systems.

Although we did have a clear sense of our overall purpose and of activities that we hoped would lead to attainment of the goal of creating a shared civic language across the entire Israeli secondary-school system, we did not have a language ethics to guide us through the issues and programs that we initiated. The justifications for our programs were articulated in terms of democratic principles and theories of civic education. The Center initiated a series of interrelated academic programs: an MA program for teachers and social activists who specialize in civic education; research grants for students and faculty interested in preparing textbooks, programs, and research pertaining to the Center's mission; special three-year classes for high school students from the Jerusalem municipal district who came on a weekly basis to our campus and studied the enhanced civics that we developed in our research and graduate courses; and extra-curricular courses in civic ethics and activism for Jewish (Hebrew) and Arab/Palestinian (Arabic) schools in Israel.

We advanced quite quickly in implementing our goals. Working closely with a broad coalition of educators, academic institutions, teachers, and Education Ministry officials, we contributed to the upgrading of civics in the school curriculum. Parallel to our participation in lobbying for this administrative change, we worked on the preparation of materials for an enhanced high school curriculum that would impart a shared civic ethics through the national school system.

The mainstay of our curriculum development projects was classes for high school kids studying in the Jerusalem municipal district. We hosted these classes at our Center. Teachers who had graduated from our MA program implemented the curriculum developed in our other programs. Our ambition to change the system from within led us to prepare materials for teaching civics at the highest possible level of study, on par with mathematics, English, or similarly prestigious core subjects. We assumed that in order to create a shared civic language for all branches of state-funded schools, we needed a common national curriculum that would make sense to all teachers and children – be they Hebrew, Arabic, Yiddish, or other native-language speakers or systems.

A committee that developed the curriculum for these classes worked for two years. The most contentious issue was that of the language of teaching. Should it be Hebrew? Simultaneously Hebrew and Arabic? The proponents of Hebrew as the language of teaching argued that since Israel's primary language is Hebrew, the business of the Israeli public sector is conducted in Hebrew, and educational and financial opportunities are available in Hebrew, then the teaching should be in Hebrew. These are utilitarian justifications for the principled position. But we also had additional reasons. Our long-term goal was to have the shared behaviour encoded in a language that we all speak, read, and understand. In Israel that language is the language of the dominant national majority: Hebrew.[17] After many discussions in the steering committee of the program, this principled position – to teach in Hebrew – was accepted.

The decision to teach in Hebrew a class of native Hebrew and Arabic speakers proved to be an ongoing issue. Since each class was co-taught by Jewish Hebrew-speaking and Arab Arabic-speaking teachers, the status of Arabic was continually debated and renegotiated by each cohort's set of teachers. After two years of experimentation, new incoming classes switched from Hebrew as the language of instruction (and of assignments) to bilingual teaching. All teaching was conducted in both languages, by two teachers addressing the one, mixed group of Hebrew and Arabic pupils. The Arab-Israeli teachers who initiated this change justified the move in two principled terms.

First, they claimed that Arab speaking pupils were at a disadvantage vis-à-vis their Jewish Hebrew-speaking co-learners. This led to an unjustified disparity between their understanding (in Arabic) and the evaluation of their understanding (in Hebrew language assignments). Then the claim was that the use of Hebrew in the classroom led to an exacerbation of the dominant, hegemonic status of Jewish-Israeli children in relation to their Arab-Israeli co-learners, for in actual classroom settings Hebrew grants Jewish kids more power and authority, and this fact relegated most Arab kids to silence on the sidelines.[18] So the teaching staff moved to bilingual co-teaching, alternating between Hebrew and Arabic explanations.

The basis for the decision to teach in Hebrew was not articulated in terms of a language ethics, which today I realize was clearly lacking. It reflected vectors of political power: the positions of scholars and practitioners who had shaped the program, of donors, of ministry officials, of partners in the Jerusalem municipal department of education, of the teachers, of the pupils. Some of the participants in the debate were Arab/Palestinian Israelis, others Jews. Since we did not have a language ethics as an external referent for our discussions, debates, and arguments, we negotiated according to our beliefs and convictions.[19] The formal result was that the language of teaching would be Hebrew, and that kids coming from the Arab-speaking school system would be granted special support to augment their Hebrew-language skills. The practical result was that within a year the classes reverted to bilingual teaching. The original position – that it would be beneficial for the purposes of the national curriculum to develop a program in Hebrew and thus open the public space to those whose minority tongue was Arabic – was taken over by different agendas and pedagogical approaches.

The above example referred to formal policy and structured teaching that adhered to national guidelines and therefore constituted a path for institutional reform. Parallel to this mode of operation were other programs in civic education that sought ways to inculcate a shared civic language that would take into account diverse linguistic backgrounds. These programs were not part of the official, national curriculum and therefore could reflect more accurately our intention to overcome the distances created by the absence of shared mother tongues. The absence of state or other official guidelines enabled us to put at the centre of our considerations and programs the individual child, teacher, school, or community. In those programs we sought to impart a sense of identity that comes from experience rather than from propositions, deriving from self-understanding rather than from the need to succeed in national matriculation. These non-official programs gave rise to numerous situations that would have merited consideration in terms of language ethics. I will present two.

The first situation involved a year-long after-school program aimed at teaching eighth graders values that would lead to an appreciation of tolerance and more acceptance of others.[20] Contrary to the formal program that assumed Hebrew as the primary language of learning, this program was based on the assumption that each community should retain its native tongue prior to learning a common civic language. So we developed a curriculum that imparted basic democratic and humanistic values in Hebrew and Arabic. One group came from an Arabic-speaking Palestinian East Jerusalem school, kids whose sense of identity was, to say the least, under severe stress; a second group was from a Jewish town of Hebrew-speaking children, most of whom were first-generation Israelis born to immigrants from many Jewish communities; a third group were Arabic-speaking Bedouin Israelis who reside in the southern desert of Israel, in towns and huts that are not recognized by the State (although we worked with a school that was recognized and funded by the State).

This was extra-curricular activity, in all instances conducted in cooperation with and under the auspices of local schools. We trained and supported the guides. While operated in local sites and conducted in native languages, the program did provide participants in the groups pre-designated opportunities to meet and to interact. In one memorable situation, groups from different Jewish and Arab/Palestinian-Israeli schools met to share a day of joint activities. One of the activities was to write whatever graffiti they desired on a giant banner. The Hebrew kids wrote in Hebrew, the Arabs in Arabic. The Jewish kids wrote innocuous graffiti about an affair between two Israeli teenage heartthrobs. The Arab/Palestinian kids conducted a graffiti war between various factions of Palestinian society – Fatah, Hamas, and so forth – with some nationalist undertones. The variety of colourful slogans were written on one huge, shared banner. Most of the adults and all of the kids were oblivious to the meanings of words and symbols of the "other" groups.

If one did not read the words, the scene was joyous and friendly. Hebrew-speaking Jewish children who did not read Arabic would not have known that the words on the banner could imply criticism of the national dimension of their identity.

What should we have done? Should we have stopped everything and discussed the potential insult that might be felt by Jewish-Israeli kids who were part of the entity being trashed in Arabic graffiti? Should we have let it be, and enjoyed the sense of joyous activity that did not reflect the words written on the banner?[21] Had we been part of a culture that had a sense of language ethics, would we have had a guide to setting up the situation differently? Would language ethics have helped us in real time, as this banner situation was unfolding? Perhaps a language ethics pertinent to circumstances of conflict such as this would teach us that sometimes words do not matter *that* much. After all, the cheerful activity shared by most of those present seemed to be a more significant experience than the cultural and political undertones. A language ethics that would justify such a response would perhaps articulate the proposition that direct contact and interaction do wonders to enhance interpersonal trust, curiosity, and willingness to see one another prior to judgment based solely or primarily on words or written statements. An opposite ethics would decry mutual ignorance of languages spoken in shared public spheres. This language ethics would probably point to such moments as illustrative of the necessity of bi- or pluri-lingual education. The justification would focus on the claim that one should have a basic knowledge of the "other's" language in order to engage in a meaningful manner with what other people express through their words and symbols.

Consider an additional situation from the same project, yet during a different year of activity with different projects and consequently different "moments" (the schools and the core staff running the program remained the same). Having learned from the experience of the graffiti incident and its a posteriori analysis, we ensured that in all points of contact between groups of Hebrew- and Arabic- speakers there would be at least one adult proficient in both languages to ensure that we knew what was going on.

That year the kids studied what it may mean to identify and articulate one's sense of self and communal identity. At a certain point in time kids from the three communities met in mixed groups, where they introduced themselves to one another. This was done by screening PowerPoint presentations that re-flected their individual sense of who they were and where they came from. Everything seemed fine and we (the responsible adults) left the area of activity with the sense that the day had been successful in terms of enabling direct con-tact between kids. That night I was deluged by telephone calls from parents of children from the Jewish town. It turned out that on the bus home, some of the Jewish kids told others that in their classroom they were exposed to a presentation by an East Jerusalem Palestinian boy whose image (it seemed to them) was an expression of hope that one day he would be a suicide bomber (this occurred in 2006, when suicide bombers claimed hundreds of Israeli lives on a terrifyingly regular basis).

To say that we were surprised and shocked by this claim would be an un-derstatement. The preparation of these PowerPoint presentations had been supervised by our staff members. At the moment of presentation our guides and teachers were in each and every room. But the Jewish kids were so upset, their parents so outraged, the schools we worked with so embarrassed that we had to temporarily suspend the program until we figured out what had hap-pened and how to continue.

I won't delve into the details of our intensive enquiry and attempt to re-construct the moment that the Jewish kids claimed represented a suicide bomber. It is sufficient to say that we had to deal with a perception that this event had indeed occurred, without being able to determine whether it had occurred in actual fact. Needless to say, perceptions of reality matter. They are or become "reality." Indeed, that was the entire point of the program: to in-troduce all of us – staff and children – to the tension and occasional disparity between events and perception of events. In the course of our enquiries we learned that what one sees is based on one's experience and consequent ex-pectations. These are present in the mind prior to the event itself (Deutscher 2011, 241–9). We should have known that. We should have had a language ethics that took into account such findings in cognitive science that are rel-evant to complex and emotionally charged situations, when fears and deeply ingrained predispositions determine what is "seen." A well-thought-out lan-guage ethics that is based on such up-to-date scientific knowledge would have been a basis for setting up the program, training our staff, and fine-tuning the relations between our ethics and our actions.[22]

3. CONCLUDING COMMENTS (NOT CLEAR-CUT CONCLUSIONS)

In this chapter we used the notion of "language ethics" in diverse ways and perspectives. By using the term we set up a basis for realizing that it is something to identify, contemplate, and articulate. If you are now thinking about language ethics and are using it as you ponder meaning or experience, then we have advanced in our understanding. Yet the play of meanings between language ethics in the singular and in the plural has not been resolved. Indeed, if I am an entity that accommodates numerous, at times conflicting, values,[23] how can I ever expect to articulate one overriding ethic that will be sensible and practical for the multitude of particular cases?

Similarly, the notion of language ethics as pertaining to language in the sense of "native tongue" may also be questioned. The examples from the Israeli experience suggest that a shared ethic may not necessitate as a precondition a shared native language. One may claim that it does not matter whether a Hebrew speaker, Yiddish speaker, Arabic speaker, Russian speaker, or Amharic speaker continues to think and act in his/her native tongue(s). What matters is that they share a common civic language and attendant habits of behaviour in the public sphere (i.e., share and uphold civic ethics through whichever native first language they have acquired).[24] In this respect, language ethics will promote principles that address 'language' in terms of its enabling human well-being, in all spheres of interpersonal relationships. Whatever the perspective may be, it seems to me that language ethics is a way of thinking and of judging that awaits articulation, use, and ongoing honing.

NOTES

I thank Daphna Saring and Daphna Avnon-Amit for their valuable comments on an earlier draft of this essay, and Netta Galnoor for her research assistance.

1 For similar perspectives see Chowers 2012, 180. Examples of such interrelations between language and ethics include "Have you murdered and also taken possession?" (1 Kings 21:19), an example of Hebraic morality in the Hebrew Bible, and "But I tell you, love your enemies and pray for those who persecute you" (Matthew 5:44), an example of Christian morality in the New Testament.

2 I have reflected upon language from significantly different epistemological

and ontological perspectives in Avnon 1995, and in Avnon 1998a, 128–39. In those works, I refer to language in relation to contemplation and thinking, a perspective that I have kept out of this study (although it is inevitably in the background, so to speak).

3   Aristotle noted that "language serves to declare what is advantageous and what is the reverse, and it therefore serves to declare what is just and what is unjust … It is the peculiarity of man … that he alone possesses a perception of good and evil, of the just and unjust … and it is association in these things which makes a family and a *polis*" (1962, Book 1:10, 6). Evidentially, this is a secular understanding of ethics. See a discussion of the two kinds of secular ethics (in contrast to religious ethics) in Leibowitz 1995, 18–19.

4   Matteo Bonotti and Yael Peled take this concern into an additional, important dimension. Their notion of "aural morality" address inter- and intra-linguistic effects of the co-existence of diverse accents (and hence of diverse hearings) of identical terms. How do we – as a particular society or community – deliberate the effects of accent on perceptions of speech-acts performed in the same public language (in democratic polities) yet interpreted according to diverse responses to sensory data? (Peled and Bonotti 2019).

5   See a personal and thought-arousing account in Abley 2003.

6   Following Lakoff and Johnson, the meaning of "cognitive" goes beyond reasoning or formulating propositions. It implies "aspects of our sensimotor system that contribute to our abilities to conceptualize and to reason" (Lakoff and Johnson 1999, 12).

7   The bilingual advantage hypothesis is hotly contested. For example, see De Bruin, Treccani, and Della Sala 2015.

8   The example does not address instances where the child's natural habitat is a bilingual household (bilingual parents or other caretakers), without needing to introduce language as an implementation of social theories grounded in scientific findings.

9   For example, the ongoing debates in California, where in 1996 61% of the electorate voted into law Proposition 227 which barred teaching academic subjects in any language other than English. The California Multilingual Education Act, passed in November 2016, overturned this law by a 73% majority (Hopkinson 2017).

10 Language ethics would then be related to Educational Neuroscience, which

"draws its empirical strength from its sister discipline, Cognitive Neuro-science, which combines decades of experimental advances from cognitive, perceptual, and developmental psychology with a variety of contemporary technologies for exploring the neural basis of human knowledge over the life span" (Petitto and Dunbar 2009, 185).

11 See Stephen May's comprehensive discussion (2012).

12 For the notion of Israeli Hebrew see Zuckermann 2009.

13 For a comparison of French and Israeli republicanism see Porath 1998.

14 See discussion in Avnon 1998b.

15 Halacha is the collective body of religious laws by which observant Jews abide.

16 For a rich discussion of the "dialogical self" and the implications of its under-standing for liberal-democratic theory and consequent educational practices see Peled 2017.

17 I may add that modern Israeli Hebrew includes words in Arabic (and in Yid-dish). In a perfect pluralistic civic world, all Israeli Hebrew-speakers would study Arabic as a second language, and this would strengthen the basis for a deeper understanding of the minority language and the way that the codes of the speared languages intertwine and create the cognitive basis for a shared "civic language."

18 The ethical implications of ways classroom dynamics are structured according to the relative power or hegemony of language are discussed in detail in Yael Peled's work, where she observes that disparities such as those mentioned above "reflect on existing power relations in language, [identify] the moral wrongs that they may exhibit, and call for developing alternative structures that are capable of righting them" (Peled 2018, 142).

19 For an example of such Israeli conundrums in the context of legal rights talk, see Pinto 2009.

20 For circumstances leading to the development of this project see Avnon 2010, 22–3.

21 We ended up doing nothing. But this was because the Hebrew-speaking staff were oblivious to the words being written in Arabic, and the Arabic-speaking staff did not intervene or say anything to enlighten their Hebrew-speaking partners.

22 Some intriguing developments in the background of the emergence of language ethics are findings in the fields of cognitive science and genetics.

Those fields of research are offering scientific data that may radically impact our assumptions about how our capacity for language is activated within our individual brains, and what that may mean for our overall cognitive abilities. In my field of expertise, the most interesting and controversial summary of the challenge posed to traditional philosophy and to contemporary political theory is in Lakoff and Johnson 1999, and in Lakoff 2008.

23   For discussion of plurality of self and consequent plurality of ethics see Avnon 2010, n30.

24   This principle addresses to a certain extent issues related to the political status of languages of significant immigrant communities, such as the Russian immigrants to Israel. See discussion in Pinto 2007.

REFERENCES

Abley, Mark. 2003. *Spoken Here: Travels Among Threatened Languages*. London: Arrow Books.

Aristotle. 1962. *The Politics of Aristotle*. Edited and translated by Ernest Barker. New York: Oxford University Press.

Avnon, Dan. 1995. "'Know Thyself': Socratic Companionship and Platonic Community." *Political Theory* 23, no. 2: 304–29.

– 1998a. *Martin Buber: The Hidden Dialogue*. Lanham, MD: Rowman & Littlefield.

– 1998b. "The Israeli Basic Laws' (Potentially) Fatal Flaw." *Israel Law Review* 32, no. 4: 535–66.

– 2006. "Why Israeli Democracy Lacks a Developed Civic Tongue." In *Civic Language in Israel*, edited by Dan Avnon, 1–22. Jerusalem: Magnes Press (Hebrew).

– 2010. "Plurality of Self and Pluralism: A View from Jerusalem." In *Plurality and Citizenship in Israel: Moving Beyond the Jewish/Palestinian Civil Divide*, edited by Dan Avnon and Yoram Benziman. London and New York: Routledge.

Barac, Raluca, and Ellen Bialystok. 2012. "Bilingual Effects on Cognitive and Linguistic Development: Role of Language, Cultural Background, and Education." *Child Development* 83, no. 2: 413–22.

Bialystok, Ellen, and Mythili Viswanathan. 2009. "Components of Executive Control with Advantages for Bilingual Children in Two Cultures." *Cognition* 112, no. 3: 494–500.

Chowers, Eyal. 2012. *The Political Philosophy of Zionism: Trading Jewish Words for a Hebraic Land.* New York: Cambridge University Press.

De Bruin, Angela, Barbara Treccani, and Sergio Della Sala. 2015. "Cognitive Advantage in Bilingualism: An Example of Publication Bias?" *Psychological Science* 26, no. 1: 99–107.

Deutscher, Guy. 2011. *Through the Language Glass: Why the World Looks Different in Other Languages,* 1st ed. New York: Picador.

Elman, Jeffrey L. 1993. "Learning and Development in Neural Networks: The Importance of Starting Small." *Cognition* 48, no. 1: 71–99.

Hilchey, Matthew D., and Raymond M. Klein. 2011. "Are There Bilingual Advantages on Nonlinguistic Interference Tasks? Implications for the Plasticity of Executive Control Processes." *Psychonomic Bulletin & Review* 18, no. 4: 625–58.

Hopkinson, Ashley. 2017. "New Era for Bilingual Education: Explaining California's Proposition 58." *EdSource,* 6 January. https://edsource.org/2017/a-new-era-for-bilingual-education-explaining-californias-proposition-58/574852 (accessed 19 February 2019).

Hurford, James R. 1991. "The Evolution of the Critical Period for Language Acquisition." *Cognition* 40, no. 3: 159–201.

Ibrahim, Raphiq, Reut Shoshani, Anat Prior, and David L. Share. 2013. "Bilingualism and Measures of Spontaneous and Reactive Cognitive Flexibility." *Psychology* 4, no. 7A: 1–10.

Jackendoff, Ray. 1993. *Patterns in the Mind: Language and Human Nature.* New York: Basic Books.

– 2002. *Foundations of Language: Brain, Meaning, Grammar, Evolution.* Oxford, UK: Oxford University Press.

Lakoff, George. 2008. *The Political Mind: Why You Can't Understand 21st-Century American Politics with an 18th-Century Brain.* New York: Viking.

Lakoff, George, and Mark Johnson. 1999. *Philosophy in the Flesh: The Embodied Mind and Its Challenge to Western Thought.* New York: Basic Books.

Lauring, Jakob. 2008. "Rethinking Social Identity Theory in International Encounters: Language Use as a Negotiated Object for Identity Making." *International Journal of Cross Cultural Management* 8, no. 3: 343–61.

Leibowitz, Yeshayahu. 1995. *Judaism, Human Values, and the Jewish State.* Edited by Eliezer Goldman. Cambridge, MA: Harvard University Press.

Macnamara, Brooke N., and Andrew R.A. Conway. 2014. "Novel Evidence in Support of the Bilingual Advantage: Influences of Task Demands and Experience on Cognitive Control and Working Memory." *Psychonomic Bulletin & Review* 21, no. 2: 520–5.

May, Stephen. 2012. *Language and Minority Rights: Ethnicity, Nationalism and the Politics of Language*. New York and London: Routledge.

Peled, Yael. 2017. "Language and the Limits of Justice." *Journal of Multilingual and Multicultural Development* 38, no. 7: 645–57.

– 2018. "Language Ethics and the Interdisciplinary Challenge." In *The Oxford Handbook of Language Policy and Planning*, edited by James W. Tollefson and Miguel Pérez-Milans. Oxford, UK: Oxford University Press.

Peled, Yael, and Matteo Bonotti. 2019. "Sound Reasoning: Why Accent Bias Matters for Democratic Theory." *Journal of Politics* 81, no. 2: 411–25.

Petitto, Laura-Ann, and Kevin Niall Dunbar. 2009. "Educational Neuroscience: New Discoveries from Bilingual Brains, Scientific Brains, and the Educated Mind." *Mind, Brain and Education: The Official Journal of the International Mind, Brain, and Education Society* 3, no. 4: 185–97.

Pinto, Meital. 2007. "On the Intrinsic Value of Arabic in Israel – Challenging Kymlicka on Language Rights." *Canadian Journal of Law & Jurisprudence* 20, no. 1: 143–72.

– 2009. "Who Is Afraid of Language Rights." In *The Multicultural Challenge in Israel*, edited by Ohad Nachtomy and Sagi Avi, 26–51. Boston, MA: Academic Studies Press.

Porath, Yehoshua. 1998. "A State of All Its Citizens?" In *The Arabs in Israeli Politics: Dilemmas of Identity*, edited by Elie Rekhes, 117–24. Tel Aviv: Dayan Center Tel Aviv University (Hebrew).

Romaine, Suzanne. 2015. "The Global Extinction of Languages and Its Consequences for Cultural Diversity." In *Cultural and Linguistic Minorities in the Russian Federation and the European Union*, edited by R. Toivanen, H. Marten, M. Rießler, and J. Saarikivi, 13: 31–46. Cham, Switzerland: Springer.

Romaine, Suzanne, and Daniel Nettle. 2000. *Vanishing Voices: The Extinction of the World's Languages and the Erosion of Human Knowledge*. Oxford, UK: Oxford University Press.

Sandel, Michael. 1996. *Democracy's Discontent: America in Search of a Public Philosophy*. Cambridge: Harvard University Press.

Skutnabb-Kangas, Tove. 2002. "Why Should Linguistic Diversity Be Maintained and Supported in Europe? Some Arguments." In *Communication Studies 2003: Modern Anthology*, edited by Olga Leontovich, 44–54. Volgograd, Russia: Peremena.

Skutnabb-Kangas, Tove, Luisa Maffi, and David Harmon. 2003. *Sharing a World of Difference: The Earth's Linguistic, Cultural and Biological Diversity*. Paris: UNESCO.

Spolskey, Bernard. 1999. "Language in Israel: Policy, Practice, and Ideology." In *Language in Our Time: Bilingual Education and Official English, Ebonics and Standard English, Immigration and the Unz Initiative*, edited by James E. Alatis and Tan Ai-Hui, 164–74. Washington, DC: Georgetown University Press.

Trask, Robert L. 2007. *Language and Linguistics: The Key Concepts*, 2nd ed. Edited by Peter Stockwell. Oxon, UK, and New York: Routledge.

Walzer, Michael. 1967. "On the Role of Symbolism in Political Thought." *Political Science Quarterly* 82, no. 2: 191–204.

Zuckermann, Ghil'ad. 2009. "Hybridity Versus Revivability: Multiple Causation, Forms and Patterns." *Journal of Language Contact* 2, no. 2: 40–67.

2

Language: Rights and Claims

JOHN EDWARDS

1. INTRODUCTION

This chapter is built around the clarification of a simple point: claims are not the same thing as rights. Within the sociolinguistic literature, this is virtually never addressed. A recent collection of articles devoted to language rights (see May 2005) discussed the plight of "at-risk" languages in many different contexts – but only Grin (2005) pointed out that the "linguistic human rights" perspective is weakened by its virtually exclusive reliance upon *claims* resting upon moral considerations alone. No mention of this central matter was made by the other authors; see, however, my references to Blommaert (2001a; 2001b; 2005), below. Even Wee – whose recent book (2011) discusses many of the difficulties attaching to the concept of language rights, and whose general perspective is (as mine is here) a critical one – does not delve at all into the substratum of the matter (see also Wee 2007).

While, as we shall see, there is increasing attention being given to questions of language rights in specific quarters, the topic has yet to substantially penetrate the mainstream linguistics literature. In Hogan's *Cambridge Encyclopedia of the Language Sciences* (2011), no consideration of language rights is made in its thousand pages.[1] At a more focused level, the *Cambridge Handbook of Sociolinguistics* (Mesthrie 2011) has nothing specific to offer in its five hundred pages, and the equally expansive *Routledge Handbook of Applied Linguistics* (Simpson 2011) gives only one page (out of seven hundred) to language rights (and that is merely to point out that closer scrutiny is needed within the language-policy-and-planning literature). There is no coverage at all of relevant broader matters such as ethics and justice. In the popular introductory sociolinguistics text edited by Mesthrie et al. (2000), the matter of ethics arises only in connection with appropriate and inappropriate behaviour of fieldworkers, ethnographers, and others who interact closely with their informants; on this particular topic, see Edwards (1994).

Matters of rights, justice, and ethics *are* central to an important sector within the sociology of language, whatever the researchers and writers there may believe or acknowledge. It makes sense, then, that Spolsky's book on language "management" (a term he now prefers to "planning") makes some brief room for a discussion of language rights. Spolsky is largely content to remain at a descriptive level, although he does note that "I prefer to avoid the term 'language rights' and to talk about human and civil rights relevant to language, to avoid the deification of language and the consequent disregard for speakers that sometimes follows from using this term" (2009, 214). In this vein, he points to difficulties associated with the fair and appropriate distribution of language rights – among individuals versus groups, for example, or as applied in minority-majority contexts, or in settings in which multilingualism and not monolingualism is the norm. He also discusses the role of those "supranational" organizations – such as the United Nations (often via UNESCO) or the European Union (via institutions such as the European Bureau for Lesser-Used Languages) – whose charter-like pronouncements on rights are so closely parsed by language activists; see also de Varennes (2012). Spolsky reminds us, however, of something that committed advocates often choose to ignore: rather than directly participating in language management per se, these international bodies essentially "provide moral and rhetorical support" (222). Statements of support do not imply obligations "to implement them and face their practical consequences" – and, more pointedly, Spolsky writes that international organizations "can formulate utopian policies without the responsibility to enforce them" (224).[2] Support without obligation: this is a central theme throughout this chapter.

As I shall discuss here, the current discourse on "linguistic human rights" is centred almost entirely upon the desire to preserve and protect "small" or endangered languages; see, for instance, Freeland and Patrick (2004). The invocation of the "rights" attaching to them is meant to bolster what is, in essence, a *moral* case. There is, of course, nothing wrong with making arguments based upon shared principle – or, indeed, upon more personal ethical

or preferential analysis. But there *is* something amiss, something disingenuous, when these bases are described and presented incorrectly. The failure
of sociolinguistic scholars to consider the underpinnings of "rights" at
general levels is an intellectual failing – to say the least. At more immediate
or specific levels, however, investigators might also consider that proceeding
from inaccurate or poorly understood bases is unlikely to work to the benefit of those communities who are the focus of their researches, and the
alleged beneficiaries of their scholarly advocacy.

Appeals to language "rights" – despite the decontextualized and often
naïve ways in which the latter are treated by activists and advocates – are
best understood as specific invocations of just and ethical treatment. I take
it that contemporary approaches to justice now stress fairness in one sense
or another, a consequence of the substitution of human agency for divine or
closed-system imperatives. Justice can involve both distribution and retribu-
tion, both application and withholding, and, in broadest perspective, some
species of social utilitarianism. So, as Rawls famously observed, "justice is the
first virtue of social institutions" (1971, 3). If this is so, then a pre-existing
moral philosophy – an ethics – must inform and underpin the application
of fairness.

Consideration of ethics in contemporary social science is rarely explicitly
acknowledged as such, but much can be mapped onto the common terms of
"descriptivism" and "prescriptivism." Most social scientists are concerned
with descriptive ethics, because they believe it is outside their remit to venture
into prescriptive or "normative" territory. This terrain they leave to others,
whose attention is focused on questions involving "oughts" and "shoulds,"
whose interests lie in broad conceptions of values, of rights and wrongs –
either in specified contexts or, indeed, across settings. The logical first task
here involves meta-ethical concern with those terms (right, wrong, good,
bad), a thorough understanding of which must precede any application of
them along normative or prescriptivist lines. At such a broad level, the social
scientists are correct: meta-ethics is indeed the province of philosophers. And
most philosophers would agree: where moral philosophy is concerned, their
most appropriate work is at the level of meta- or theoretical ethics.

The descriptivism of modern social science and its dislike of coming to
normative judgments is closely allied to adherence to cultural or moral rel-

ativism. As an antidote to the universalism that – while it can of course fuel honest Kantian quests for cross-cultural moral normativity – has more typically undergirded narrow and unpleasant ethnocentrism, relativism surely has much to commend it.[3] But it is a part of my argument in this chapter to suggest that today's social scientists are not always as relativistic in their posture as they imagine, and that prescriptivist leanings are evident – particularly in matters of language and, even more particularly, in matters of language rights. Further comment must rest upon a brief and more general consideration of rights per se.

2. RIGHTS ... NATURAL AND OTHERWISE

Rights are today most closely associated with conceptions of normative ethics. People are often considered to be entitled to certain things by virtue of their membership in groups in which some code of morality obtains: the scope of these groups can range from all of humanity to the smallest describable divisions. Rights are thus seen to rest upon shared understandings of what is just – and earlier views holding that there are inherent or "natural" underpinnings to these remain powerful in many quarters. Indeed, they support many contemporary claims having to do with language in particular. Commonly seen as "natural," for example, are rights to life and to freedom – seen as inalienable and indefeasible in the sense that they require no legislated backing but are, instead, basic to the human being. The American Declaration of Independence made the famous claim that these rights are simply "self-evident," and I imagine that most people in the world would support as "natural" the right to life, once you have it, and to a liberty that stops only at the point at which it infringes on the freedom of someone else.[4]

Conceptions of "basic" rights, considerations of what human beings are "naturally" entitled to, have steadily enlarged over the years.[5] Where, roughly speaking, seventeenth- and eighteenth-century ideas of such basic prerogatives rested upon freedom from unwanted restraints, modern suggestions involve positive benefits. Thus, in 1948 (the two hundredth anniversary of the birth of Jeremy Bentham, to whom I shall shortly turn), the United Nations Universal Declaration of Human Rights observed that everyone had the right to a "social security" that involves food, medical care, and adequate housing – but rights to education, to both work and leisure time, and even to enjoyment of the arts were also specified. The formal preamble to its thirty articles pointed out, however, that it was a "common standard of achievement for all peoples" that was being outlined – not, that is to say, an enforceable directive (an important proviso to which I shall return under a more specific heading). What all such modern "additions" have in common with the most basic principles of life and liberty is that they are conceived to be *rights*. This is a central point, for, as Benn (1972, 198–9) pointed out, "a man with a right has no reason to be grateful to benefactors; he has grounds for grievance when it is denied. The concept presupposes a standard below which it is intolerable that a human being should fall." Benn concluded his succinct but useful treatment by observing that "human rights are the corollary ... of the equally modern notion of social justice."

In the very first sentence of his book on rights, Waldron (1987, 1) emphasizes the recency of current concerns: "the idea of human rights is taken more seriously now than it has been for centuries" (see also Sen 1999 – and Arendt 1967, on the lack of seriousness with which declarations of rights were taken until relatively recently). Attention to language rights is quite new; see Neier (2012) for a general historical account of rights. Focusing more specifically on language matters, McRae (1970, 212) also noted that "the notion of linguistic rights is relatively recent," something he attributes to such factors as the emergence of minority groups as a factor in politics, the force of nationalism, and increasing liberal concerns for the situation of threatened varieties. He adds that "it has seldom been argued that language rights are a universal human right, or a natural right of mankind" (213) and, at a more practical level, that such rights "should be kept conceptually distinct from 'classical' human rights ... because the problems of full-scale implementation ... may be far more complex and subtle" (214).

Some general attention to the rights-claims distinction now becomes necessary, because it is a differentiation essential to informed discussion in the area – including, therefore, to the specific language matters to which I shall turn later on. It is at least arguable that even the most basic of "natural" rights are, ultimately, only claims of what ought to be – claims that, indeed, we have seen regularly violated throughout history, claims that the endorsements of

important individuals, organizations, and even governments have often failed
to protect. Blackburn (2009, 180) points out, simply, that we should understand "talk of natural rights as part of the vocabulary of advocacy." He also
notes, however, that such advocacy – essentially, making a *claim* to a right – is
not in itself an unreasonable course of action. So does Sen (1999, 229), when
he remarks that the essence of the human-rights exercise is a demand ("no
more than just that – a demand"), based upon ethical considerations, for
alleged entitlements to be enshrined in law. This is a point central to current
debates about language rights: there is nothing at all wrong with making
claims, but there *is* something wrong when scholar-advocates write as if claims
are rights *tout court*. The appeal, of course, of such a blithely and simplistically
constructed equation is obvious: as Bentham observed in 1776: "we [then]
have no matter of fact to encumber ourselves with. When you have said [a
man] has a right – insist upon it: it is a plain case, all proof is needless. The
business is thus settled in a trice by the help of a convenient word or two, and
without the pains of thinking" (Schofield 2003, 25).

To suggest that a quite particular argument is the only one open to enlightened thought is an ideological statement rather than a scholarly one (see also
Blommaert 2001b); when enforced, it shuts down intellectual debate. In this
connection, Blackburn (2009, 185) notes that "the language of rights occupies
something of the role of a new, proselytizing religion, impatient of the existence of infidels." And, as is often the case with zealotry, cases are sometimes
made without much nuance. Thus, Sen (1999, 227): "the suspicion is that there
is something a little simple-minded about the entire conceptual structure that
underlies the oratory on human rights." (For Bentham, the matter is effectively countered by bringing *utility* into the picture, for any appeal to *that*
requires proof.)

It is important, I think, to accept that, when applied to human rights, the
word "natural" can only have meaning within the human context – unless, of
course, one wishes to invoke some extra-human agency revealed to us through
religion. With the growth of secularism, this invocation has become much less
common, of course. Indeed, most of those who endorse some sort of extension of the rights outlined in the UN Declaration – and, more specifically here,
many who would add language rights to the list – clearly do *not* make such an
invocation. And yet the force of their arguments often seems to rest upon the

notion that there are, after all, some imperatives that do not emerge from collective human agreement, some principles that exist above and beyond secular reality, some "natural" entitlements that are universal, timeless, and independent of social context. They haven't read their Bentham.

2(a). Jeremy Bentham and Human Rights

Written in 1795, first published (in French) in 1816, and disseminated in English only in 1834 (two years after the author's death), Bentham's famous *Anarchical Fallacies* summarized his examination of the French Revolution's several declarations of human rights. It is now easily consulted as part of his collected works, edited by his friend and executor, John Bowring, between 1838 and 1843; see also Schofield et al. (2002). Bentham's basic argument is that "natural" rights – that is to say, universal, or inalienable, or "self-evident" human rights – are illusory. Indeed, the term "natural right" is, he writes, a "perversion" of language; it is ambiguous, sentimental, and figurative. At one level, he adopts the Hobbesian view that since any right "anterior to law" is not logically subject to legal limitation, and since human motivation is largely underpinned by self-interest, the result would ("could" is more apt here) be anarchic. The only real rights are those created by law, which means that the idea of "natural" rights is "nonsense" – which, with the addition of imprescriptibility, becomes "nonsense upon stilts."[6] Extra-legal "rights," Bentham adds, are at best, *hopes* for rights – but desires and aspirations for rights are not rights.

As David Hume famously pointed out – in his "law" or "guillotine" – one cannot logically jump from what *is* the case to what *should* be the case: description is not prescription. In essence, this was Bentham's criticism of Blackstone's famous legal "commentaries" (1765–69). Having endorsed the idea of "natural law" – "co-eval with mankind," and knowable through the "due exertion of right reason and through divine revelation" (Schofield 2003, 4) – Blackstone thus confused the roles of "expositor" and "censor." That is, he went beyond the reasonable mandate of describing what the English law *was*, and attempted a justification of established practice by arguing that "every thing is now as it should be" (Schofield 2003, 3). Panglossianism is, among other things, an abrogation of Hume's injunction. One might add here that scholar-advocates of various stripes, including those who argue on behalf of "small" or endangered languages, are in effect lobbying for a sort of reverse Humeanism – they want their ideas of what *ought* to apply to become actual and official.

As implied above, recent stronger and more specific arguments have often presented *claims* rather than "hopes"; see Kukathas (1992) and below. Bentham foreshadows the notion; as Schofield (2003, 26) paraphrases him: "[t]he best that might be said regarding a statement about natural law or natural rights was that it amounted to an expression of opinion on the part of the speaker that such a law or such a right *ought to* exist – in other words, the statement was a moral claim ambiguously expressed."

For Bentham, specific legal rights – often correlated with specific duties and obligations – are desirable to the extent to which they contribute to the "general mass of felicity."[7] Otherwise, they should be abandoned. And so, he summarizes: "[r]ight ... is the child of law; from real laws come real rights; but from imaginary laws, from laws of nature, fancied and invented by poets, rhetoricians, and dealers in moral and intellectual poisons, come imaginary rights, a bastard brood of monsters" (Bowring 1838–43, II: 501).[8]

In his discussion of the force (or lack of it) of unlegislated rights, Sen also touches upon the concern that "rights" without corresponding obligations seem rather hollow: entitlements whose fulfilment is left uncertain have little meaning. In this sense, he continues: "human rights ... are heartwarming sentiments, but they are also, strictly speaking, incoherent. Thus viewed, these *claims* are best seen not so much as rights, but as lumps in the throat" (Sen 1999, 228, my italics). He does not entirely agree with this rather Kantian position of necessary obligation, but his disagreement rests, again, upon the power of moral *claim*, on the basis of "benefits ... which everyone *should* have" (230).[9]

These are tough words. In Bentham's case, we must of course remember that they were occasioned by his strong reactions to the words (and deeds) originating across the Channel. The fear of revolution, of the unruly crowd, was a constant throughout most of the nineteenth century, for all of the ruling classes of Europe. While Burke proclaimed some ultimate solidarity with the poor and the oppressed, it is hardly surprising that he also wrote that their "reason is weak; because when once aroused, their passions are ungoverned" (Waldron 1987, 90). In literature, we find Dickens's famous depiction of the French Revolution – and its strongly implied warning to the English aristocracy – in his *Tale of Two Cities* (1859), with its vivid scenes of mob violence.[10] And the classic piece of reactionary non-fiction was Le Bon's popular study in collective psychology, *Psychologie des foules* (1895).

So, Bentham's philosophically interesting observations are, like most, products of a particular environment. But were they accurate then – and are they accurate now? In his critique, Bedau (2000) foreshadows the beliefs of those contemporary scholars who would like to see language rights placed firmly under the "natural" heading, and he adds that a lack of formal underpinning need not imply that such rights do not exist. He quarrels, then, with Bentham's "legalist thesis," arguing that *moral* rights can exist quite independently of legislated ones. He makes a curious case here, suggesting that "one does not need to invoke the law or a legal system to claim a right of self-defense" (275). It is curious because, of course, most legal systems *do* make allowance here. And, drawing upon the work of Nickel (1987) and Thomson (1990), he makes this still more curious observation: "there are human rights norms, and … therefore human rights exist to the extent and in the sense that justified moralities contain such norms regardless of what legal norms a given legal system may provide … there are moral rights apart from the law and any legal system because we are creatures subject to the moral law and because we have inherently individual interests" (276). He returns to rather firmer ground, I think, when advocating the use of "our moral rights to criticize a legal system for its failure to turn those rights into legal rights" (275). If we parse Bedau's argument here, we find that he endorses – with vague usages such as "human rights norms," "justified moralities," and "creatures subject to the moral law" – the existence of a range of rights which, regardless of legal buttressing, have a moral basis. Yet part of Bentham's argument was that we can only escape from the frightful subjectivity and *parti pris* that these usages reflect or imply by insisting upon the firm basis that only a translation from what may be thought desirable to what has achieved legal force – with the reasoned backing that that entails (or should entail) – can establish.

Bedau notes that many declarations of rights are meant to protect minority interests of one sort or another, acting as protection against "neglectful or tyrannical majorities." This is correct. A corollary is that most language rights with the force of legislation behind them emanate from majority populations. Many states and regions within states, for instance, enshrine a language as "official" or "national" (sometimes more than one, of course), and the enabling laws reflect the dominance of particular ethnonational communities. Within those dominant groups, such official status has generally attracted little attention (why would it?), but declarations that endorse one or more official varieties inevitably leave others unauthorized. Such statements are looked upon unfavourably, then, by those concerned with "smaller" or minority-group linguistic interests. A recent discussion by Kristinsson and Hilmarsson-Dunn (2012) provides an illustration. They describe a Nordic language declaration which proclaims all languages to be equal, asserts "a democratic language policy for the multilingual Nordic community" (224) – and then emphasizes Norwegian, Danish, and Swedish. The implication is that other, minority languages have been shunted aside.[11]

Bedau (2000, 278) makes the point that, if it is the case that rights, for Bentham, are to be legally enshrined "only if it is to the advantage of some majority to do so, then it appears that rights cannot play the anti-majoritarian function that is so crucial." This is not simply curious, it is quite wrong-headed. First, the declarations to which Bedau refers – the French and UN assertions, with their support for minority or disadvantaged groups at risk from those "neglectful or tyrannical majorities" – are of course drawn up and endorsed by those in power; they show, in other words, some "majority" concern that apparently goes well beyond its own advantage. I use the word "apparently," however, because it may in fact be quite advantageous for majority groups to treat minorities more equitably. Nonetheless, while motivations here may be more self-serving than self-effacing, outcomes for subaltern populations may yet be favourable. Second, Bedau has misrepresented Bentham at base. The utilitarian philosopher did not suggest that rights should become legal only when useful for the majority; he argued, rather, for such protection when it contributed to that "general mass of felicity" which I have already noted. Such a process does rely, of course, upon suitably enlightened legislators – usually (but not at all always, of course) representatives of the majority – but this is precisely part of Bentham's treatise; and see the comment I have just made.

It may be, as Bedau (2000) points out, that fears of anarchy prompted by declarations of rights – in France and elsewhere – are not well-founded. Blackburn (2009, 185), too, suggests that Bentham's case for anarchy was overstated – but he reminds us that "thinking of a calculus of rights, unique and visible to people of reason everywhere, is dangerous in many directions ... it is certainly a recipe for self-righteousness, and it substitutes a kind of arid scholasticism for any fully human and multi-dimensioned thought."

We might also bear in mind that, as Brown (2010) has recently argued, declarations of rights are routinely endorsed by the most vicious and intolerant regimes, and great violence has been done in the name of human rights. This journalistic observation is hardly novel, of course. A more academic assessment was provided by Minogue (2001, 27). While it might be imagined that a regime that accords rights more readily than others – which has, perhaps, erected them in some constitutional form – is a just or liberal one, he demurs, writing that "your average demagogue now loves rights; they have become devices for taking control of subjects who can easily be persuaded that being given a right is always a benefit. In fact, it is a device for creating a static and servile society."[12]

He adds that the "current passion" for social engineering via rights is a form of "legal fundamentalism." An important point about this "current passion," this modern "movement," is one that might not have suggested itself to Bentham and other early critics. It has to do with a sort of double standard. Here is Minogue once again: "[t]he ideology of the human-rights movement oscillates between a denial of objectivity as merely a cloak of power and privilege, on the one hand, and an insistence on moral and legal objectivity of rights on the other."[13]

This succinct statement seems to me a well-aimed arrow, one that strikes to the heart of a profound and intrinsic problem – and one of particular relevance where language rights are under discussion. For example, as May (2012, xiv) correctly points out, *all* perspectives on linguistic and minority-group rights involve moral attitudes: "ideology is not the sole preserve of minority-language proponents ... all research is value-laden." Fair enough, perhaps, but we should also acknowledge the Orwellian observation that some studies are more heavily freighted than others. More pointedly, the "critical social research" that May claims for himself – and, no doubt, for other scholar-advocates who write on behalf of the linguistic and cultural rights of "small" groups – views "reality" (his quotation marks) as a social construction; situations cannot be merely "described" as they "really" are since this would imply an "objective 'commonsense' reality where none exists" (xiv).[14]

It is bad enough, perhaps, to encounter such a cavalier dismissal of the possibility of objectivity; it is worse when proponents of an unfettered social constructionism decide, themselves, that *some* things – linguistic human rights, say – apparently possess an undeniable objective reality. But such a posture is, of course, to be expected when discussions of rights are discussions of a "movement"; as Nathan (2012, 51) points out, "human rights has become a new world ideology, even a kind of secular religion." And, as a "sizeable sociolinguistic industry and … an emblem of the sociolinguistic establishment," *linguistic* human rights has become (in some circles, anyway) "good politics." However, Blommaert (whose words these are) then goes on to say that "radical rhetoric and a firm belief in one's cause are not a substitute for critical analysis" (2001a, 541; see also Blommaert 2001b; 2005). Just so.

3. LANGUAGE RIGHTS IN CONTEMPORARY PERSPECTIVE

In contemporary social-scientific discussion, and in the sense of them that I emphasize here – that is, with a specific focus on the protection of "small" varieties – language rights are almost always treated within an "ecological" framework. This has several pivotal features which not only contextualize the specific attention given to language rights but, as well, are all complementary to and supportive of that attention.[15] I cannot go into much detail in this section, but see Edwards (2002a; 2002b) for fuller details.

As a term and a focus of study, ecology is a nineteenth-century coinage of Ernst Haeckel – Darwin's "German bulldog" – and, as its Greek root (οἶκος = home) implies, the emphasis is upon the holistic study of environments within which lives are lived and intertwined: the "web of life" that includes both the beneficial and inimical interrelationships among plants, animals, and even inorganic surroundings. Ecology is about adaptations, then, whose necessity arises from inevitable linkages.

The extension to an "ecology of language" is particularly associated with the work of Haugen (e.g. 1972). His intent was to emphasize the interconnectedness of languages with their environments, with particular regard to status and function, and he produced a list of contextualizing questions – about who uses the language, its domains, varieties, written traditions and family linkages, the degree and type of support it enjoys, and so on. Beyond this, Haugen also expressed a preference for linguistic diversity, seeing in it – as, I imagine, any educated person would – part of the richness of the human experience; see Haugen (1987).

Despite the fact that any undertaking styling itself as an "ecology" should have a very wide and expansive focus, despite Calvet's (1999, 17) view that the specifically linguistic variety consists of all "les rapports entre les langues et leur milieu" [the linkages between languages and their settings], the breadth of the ecology-of-language view has in fact been progressively reduced. Nelde (2002) may have put things a little too bluntly when he argued that there is no language contact without conflict, suggesting a struggle among languages – with a range of outcomes from sturdy health to extinction. Still, current ecological arguments mean to play down the fiercer features of social Darwinism. Indeed, it is interesting that "même parmi les fondateurs ... de la recherche moderne en contact des langues ... le terme "conflit" apparaît rarement" [even the pioneers of modern research in language contact rarely mentioned 'conflict'] (Nelde 2002, 266). The reason for this rests, as we shall see, upon a more "pacific" view of interactions among languages – or, rather, an argument that successful resistance to English "imperialism" could and should lead to a more equitable linguistic landscape for all and, particularly, to a fairer and more "rightful" treatment of "small" and endangered varieties.[16]

This view has been most clearly expressed by Mühlhäusler (2000, 308): "functioning ecologies are nowadays characterized by predominantly mutually beneficial links and only to a small degree by competitive relationships ... metaphors of struggle of life and survival of the fittest should be replaced by the appreciation of natural kinds and their ability to coexist and cooperate." This is certainly a kinder and gentler picture, but it is also a confused and inaccurate one. Some brief consideration of the major emphases of the contemporary ecological thrust will flesh out the general picture – and reveal some important inadequacies.

3(a). Some Central Features of the Current Ecology-of-Language Model

Unfair Human Intervention

Human interference, we are told, is at the heart of contemporary linguistic injustice. Thus, while "healthy ecologies" are both "self-organizing" and "self-perpetuating," our inappropriate actions have unbalanced pristine balances (Mühlhäusler 2000, 310). The implication seems to be that otherwise "healthy" ecologies have been unfavourably penetrated by human incursions – as if, in other words, they were not exclusively and intrinsically human to begin with! The perspective here is illustrative of the curiously static and ahistorical quality of much ecological thinking: once some balance is achieved (or regained), some wrong righted, some redress made, then the new and more moral arrangements will exist in some "self-perpetuating" amber. But history is the graveyard of cultures. It is naïvely selective to pay attention to some – to those whose languages must now exist in the shadow of large and looming neighbours – and not to others. How many mourners are there, I wonder, for the Raj; how many would argue that because it once existed it had a right to continued existence?

Language Diversity as an Unqualified Good

From an ecological point of view, linguistic diversity is taken as an unalloyed good, to be defended wherever it seems to falter. Beyond the quasi-legalistic approach emphasized in formal proclamations (see below), there are other bases upon which defences of diversity have been built, and these can be summarized under moral, scientific, economic, and aesthetic headings (see Mühlhäusler 2000).

Assumptions of inherent *rights* obviously draw upon moral sources – and attention to these takes us back to the first sections of this chapter, on to the formal proclamations that remain to be considered and, ultimately, to the conclusions I shall draw here. But morally based arguments have also been made which stress the unconscionable loss of accumulated experience and knowledge that allegedly follows language attrition and loss. Second, it has been suggested that linguistically diverse societies reach higher levels of achievement, and that cross-language "encounters" aid scientific advance. This then suggests, third, that language diversity is economically beneficial. Finally, and, I would argue, quite uncontroversially, an aesthetic appreciation values all diversity, and regrets all loss. While I have again drawn upon Mühlhäusler here, any inspection of the current ecology-of-language literature will reveal the generality of these points. All are, of course, very debatable. While I must refer the reader again to earlier work for some substantiation here, it seems clear that arguments for linguistic diversity and its maintenance are not always as strong as their proponents would have us think. We might usefully bear in mind Ladefoged's (1992, 810) admonition that "statements such as 'just as the extinction of any animal species diminishes our world, so does the extinction of any language' are appeals to our emotions, not to our reason." Does this suggest that the case for diversity has no basis at all? Quite the contrary. But it is important to understand that the most substantial base on which it rests is constructed of perceptions of morality and aesthetic preference. These are the essential animating articles of faith that underpin all ecological expression.

Biological Analogies ... and More
A linkage has been suggested between language and biology – "un lien entre l'écologie biologique et l'écologie linguistique" [a link between biological and linguistic ecology] (Heller 2002, 175). In a world increasingly aware of environmental issues, the advantages of adding anxieties about language decline to concerns with endangered plant and animal populations are obvious. But how far can the analogy reasonably go? Not very far at all, I would suggest. Thus, Boudreau et al. (2002, 31) observe that "on doit prendre garde de ne pas investir le concept d'écologie linguistique de contenus trop biologiques ... les langues ne sont pas des organismes vivants" [linguistic ecology should not be understood as a biological entity ... languages are not living organisms]. And they add that, when discussing language ecology, Haugen himself "était bien

conscient qu'il s'agissait d'abord d'une métaphore" [understood very well that it was essentially a metaphor].

Recent ecological arguments, however, have attempted to make the link between linguistic and other types of diversity much more than metaphoric. In some parts of the world, biological and linguistic richness co-occur, and it has been argued that the two diversities are thus "mutually supportive, perhaps even coevolved" (Maffi 2000a, 175). More pointedly still, Maffi (2000b, 17) suggests that "the persistence of vigorous, thriving linguistic diversity around the world may afford us our best chance of countering biodiversity loss and keeping the planet alive and healthy." Faced with this bizarre point of view, we should again recall cautions about causation and correlation. There are now sophisticated biological investigations that bear on the matter; technical details may be found in the work of Pagel (2012a; 2012b) and Fincher and Thornhill (2008), for example. All of the biologically based hypotheses that they examine are as one in their implicit rejection of any simplistic "co-evolution" of languages, plants, and animals. The idea that protecting linguistic diversity may help in sustaining global flora and fauna – or, indeed, vice versa – is, to put it charitably, a little naïve. Blommaert (2001b, 140) writes, simply, that "the equation of languages and biospecies is a paralogism." See also Maffi (2005), however, for a somewhat more informed discussion.

Small Is Beautiful

It is not uncommon to find disparagement of the scientific culture and concern for the "privileging" of its knowledge over "folk wisdom" (see Rhydwen 1998). There is a special regard for "small" cultures and local knowledges, and it takes two forms. The first, a simple and straightforward desire for the survival of such cultures and systems, is unexceptionable. The second argument, however, is that the practices and values of small, indigenous societies are somehow more "authentic," and thus superior to those of larger, more technologically advanced, and more heterogeneous communities. While this view is generally expressed subtly, the mask occasionally slips: thus, "without romanticizing or idealizing the indigenous cultures, it is clear that they are superior to the mass culture because their members retain the capability of living in at least relative harmony with the natural environment" (Salminen 1998, 62). Despite the half-hearted disclaimer, this is romanticism *tout court*.

Or consider this dedicatory line in a recent anthology: "to the world's indigenous and traditional peoples, who hold the key to the inextricable link between [sic] language, knowledge and the environment" (Maffi 2001).

A dislike of the modern world is usually the background for arguments on behalf of "indigenous" cultures.[17] Polzenhagen and Dirven (2004, 22) thus discuss the "pronounced anti-globalisation, anti-Western and anti-Cartesian" stance of the romanticized ecology-of-language model. We find Mühlhäusler (2000, 338) emphasizing a "holism" uniquely associated with the small and the aboriginal, and citing with approval views that Western civilisation is particularly "artificial," consisting "almost overwhelmingly of lifeless, inanimate objects." The disdain here naturally extends to the scientific culture generally, indeed to the generalities which many would see as the pivots of progress. Fishman (1982, 8) endorses the notion that "the universal is a fraud, a mask for the self-interest of the dominating over the dominated" – this, in a paper defending those peoples who "have not capitulated to the massive blandishments of western materialism, who experience life and nature in deeply poetic and collectively meaningful ways." Or consider the view expressed by Chawla (2001, 118): "Indians have traditionally treated the inanimate and animate world with awe and concern in ways that do not indiscriminately damage the natural environment." In fact, as I have discussed elsewhere (Edwards 2009), there is a great deal of evidence that "indigenous" peoples can be as profligate as any contemporary urbanite when opportunity and circumstance permit. Yet again, space restrictions do not allow me to present the many easy rebuttals to these strange conceptions, but I ask readers to think about the sorts of societies and lifestyles that people leave behind, and those that attract them – romanticization notwithstanding.[18]

3(b). The Enshrinement of Language Rights

As already discussed, important facets of the contemporary ecology-of-language paradigm all bear upon the central matter of *rights*. The general area is fuelled largely by two broad concerns. The first is that the "big" languages of the world (notably English, of course) are running roughshod over the smaller ones. This is sometimes attributed straightforwardly to the vicissitudes of social and historical evolution; as well, however, the global penetration of English is often seen as greatly assisted by active and conspiratorial policies (see Edwards 2011). The argument for the manipulated power of large languages such as English is only the broadest-brush treatment of allegedly unfair human intervention in the linguistic ecology of the planet. The second involves an often uncritical allegiance to the idea that the maintenance of linguistic diversity is – always and everywhere – an unalloyed good. These two concerns are the animating articles of faith in the ideology of the new ecology. The just and rightful positions of endangered languages are further underpinned, it is argued, by *necessity* – that is, by the intertwining of biological and linguistic fortunes. And there is an ever-present strain of anti-modern romanticism.

Official and Semi-Official Declarations

There are several useful overviews of language-rights claims and legislation, the most exhaustive being that of de Varennes (1996; see also 2012); other relevant commentaries include the collection edited by Kontra et al. (1999), Ruiz Vieytez (2001), and the rather more pointed contributions by Phillipson (1992; 2000; 2009). The on-line journal *MOST* provides many useful linkages to both European and non-European language-rights legislation; its issue 3:2 (2001) is devoted to minority-language rights (see http://www.unesco.org/most), as is issue 20:1 (1998) of *Language Sciences.*

If we return, first of all, to the Universal Declaration of Human Rights (1948), we find that language is mentioned only in the second of its thirty articles: here, the applicability of the charter to everyone, without any distinction as to language (among other things), is stated. Articles 10, 19, and 26 relate to fair trials, freedom of expression, and educational rights, respectively, but rights of individual language use are not explicitly provided for.[19] An accompanying United Nations document, the International Covenant on Civil and Political Rights (1966), came into force in 1976. Its own Article 2 repeats the general injunction found in the earlier, post-war declaration, and the point is reiterated in Articles 4, 24, and 26. Its Article 19 refers to freedom of expression, as does the earlier paragraph of that number. With regard to trials and tribunals, the Covenant's Article 14 is more explicit, noting that people must be informed of charges against them in a language that they understand, and that interpretation should be provided where necessary. Finally, its Article 27 states that linguistic minority groups should not be deprived of the right to use their own language. A third UN document – the Declaration on the Rights of Persons Belonging to National or Ethnic, Religious and Linguistic Minorities (1992) – draws upon the Covenant's Article 27 in a series of statements endorsing various protections for minority groups. Countries are enjoined to protect the linguistic identities and usages of group members, and to provide opportunities for mother-tongue education "wherever possible" (Article 4:3). In a similar vein, and two generations earlier, a group of scholars under the auspices of UNESCO also recommended early mother-tongue education for all children, wherever feasible, in their report *The Use of Vernacular Languages in Education* (published in 1953).[20] Another UNESCO document, the Convention for the Safeguarding of Intangible Cultural Heritage (2003), has now been ratified by the great majority of member states (although Canada initially refused agreement, and the United States remains a non-signatory). Its Article 2.2(a) makes specific mention of language as a "vehicle of the intangible cultural heritage." Similar in intent and phrasing to the UN's 1992 declaration is the Council of Europe's (1995) Framework Convention for the Protection of National Minorities.

These documents and declarations – not all of which have received either overall or partial approval in all states, by the way – argue that people *should* have freedom of expression, including in a minority language, and that the necessary linguistic accommodations *should* be made in legal tribunals. They do not explicitly recognize any right to education in a particular language.

Small languages have received further attention in the European Charter for Regional or Minority Languages (1992) – most but not all states have signed, although some signatories have not yet ratified the agreement. It aims to protect the languages of indigenous minorities only, and in some cases application has hinged upon the outcome of discussions of dialect-language distinctions. Paying special attention to one population, the United Nations Declaration on the Rights of Indigenous Peoples (2007) notes (in its Article 13.1) that states should ensure that these populations have the right to use, develop, and revitalize their languages. Article 14.1 discusses indigenous control of education, and the language used therein – and states, indeed, that even children living outside their communities ought to have access (when possible) to education in their own culture and language. Article 16.1 deals with the establishment of indigenous-language media. Again, while almost all countries are now signatories, the United States is not. Canada initially refused to join, but then did so in 2010. There are one or two aspects of their endorsement, however, which are rather telling (and which have been criticized in some indigenous quarters). Referring to the Declaration as "aspirational" and "non-legally binding," the Canadian ratification statement goes on to say that it "it does not reflect customary international law nor change Canadian laws." This sort of qualification is found in many of the ratification protocols.

Of special interest is the Convention Concerning Indigenous and Tribal Peoples in Independent Countries (ILO-169), published by the International Labour Organization in 1989. While, like all the other declarations, it is "not particularly enforceable" (as Grenoble [2015, 4] points out), it *is* presented for ratification as a legally binding instrument. Following a Preamble which recognizes "aspirations" to control and development of identities and languages, Article 1.1(b) actually spells out what the Convention understands as "tribal" and "indigenous" – the criteria here are "descent from the populations which inhabited the country, or a geographical region to which the country belongs, at the time of conquest or colonisation or the establishment of present state boundaries" and the retention of "some or all" social and cultural institutions. Article 1.2 adds that "self-identification as indigenous or tribal" is also a "fundamental criterion." Article 28 pays close attention to both the provision of education in indigenous languages, and the development and use of these varieties. At the same time, the attainment of fluency in national or official languages is not to be neglected. And Article 30 deals with the governmental duty to ensure that indigenous peoples are kept fully abreast of all important political and cultural matters.

Since it *is* a more strongly worded document, and since its signatories agree to be legally bound by it, it is perhaps unsurprising that few countries have endorsed it. Survival International (formed in 1969 to help indigenous people) points out on its website that ILO-169 – the "only international law designed to protect [the rights of] tribal peoples" – has, to date, been ratified by only twenty-two countries. At this rate, "it will be another 170 years before every country has ratified the Convention." (Australia, Canada, New Zealand, and the United States are among the very many non-signatories.) Referrring specifically to the Arctic countries – but in a statement that many would no doubt find of much broader applicability – Alfredsson (2013, 195) laments the re-markable and unfortunate lack of endorsement of "human rights standards that concern the indigenous peoples who live in their northernmost areas."[21] It may be unfortunate, but it is hardly remarkable that official ratifications of documents having to do with rights decrease when something beyond unen-forceable recommendations is involved.

Unofficial Declarations

Non-governmental statements are also to be found, of course, and the most specific of these is the so-called Universal Declaration of Linguistic Rights (1996). Approved in Barcelona, this statement makes some now-familiar and often jejune assertions: its Article 25, for example, states that "all language communities are entitled to have at their disposal all the human and material resources necessary to ensure that their language is present to the extent they desire at all levels of education within their territory: properly trained teachers, appropriate teaching methods, text books, finance, buildings and equipment, traditional and innovative technology." Despite its title, this Barcelona proclamation is essentially the child of some interested parties: elements of PEN International, some NGOs, language "experts," and so on; see http://www.linguistic-declaration.org. Of similar stature is the Declara-tion of Oegstgeest (Netherlands). Approved at an international academic conference held in 2000, its twelve articles argue for greater recognition of and support for the regional, minority, and immigrant languages of Europe (Extra and Gorter 2001). A very recent example – and, like others, relating itself to the Barcelona declaration – is the Donostia Protocol to Ensure Lan-guage Rights, presented in San Sebastián in 2016 by the Euskararen Gizarte Erakundeen Kontseilua (a non-profit organization usually known in English simply as the Basque Social Council). There are of course others of like kind.

Organizations formed expressly for the protection of endangered lan-guages – the American Terralingua society, for example, or the Foundation for Endangered Languages, based in England – typically have a charter or a statement of intent stressing linguistic rights. The former, for instance, ob-serves that "deciding which language to use, and for what purposes, is a basic human right" (Terralingua 1999). As well, existing language associations have argued for rights. Thus, Teachers of English to Speakers of Other Languages

(TESOL 2000) have advocated that "all groups of peoples have the right to maintain their native language ... a right to retain and use [it]." The other side of the coin, they argue, is that "the governments and the people of all countries have a special obligation to affirm, to respect and support the retention, enhancement and use of indigenous and immigrant heritage languages." (This last point raises a knotty question: while we might legislate rights to *use* a language, how can a right to be *understood* be effected? If it cannot be, then rights of usage surely remain rather empty – or, at least, of limited scope.)

A Synopsis

Formal provisions for language rights have been discussed by de Varennes (2001), and several important generalities emerge. The relevant documentation is generally not of a legally binding nature, reflecting rather the "political and moral obligations" that signatory states have acknowledged. There are no judicial remedies for sins of omission here. As well, the various charters often distinguish between rights to the private use of languages by individuals and the public use of such varieties in official or authoritative contexts. As the author points out elsewhere (de Varennes 1999), there currently exist no unqualified rights to use a minority language. Furthermore, while language rights are typically restricted to "national minorities," why shouldn't immigrant minority groups benefit, too? This distinction is of the greatest significance in many contemporary arguments over the allocation of rights (see Kymlicka 1995a; 1995b; Kymlicka and Patten 2003b) and requires much further attention. There are many complexities, and they do not always conform to expected patterns. We note, for instance, that when the French government endorsed the European Charter for Regional or Minority Languages, it rejected the restriction to national minorities, preferring to "recognize" minorities of all provenances. A big-hearted effort at inclusion, a desire to see rights extended to the furthest? Perhaps. Or perhaps, as cynics suggested, because the French strategy here was to widen the field so much that action for any would become impractical (see Wright 2001).

As I have implied throughout this piece, there are many problems associated with efforts to legislate linguistic rights. As Kymlicka and Patten (2003a) note, most official or semi-official declarations of rights make little reference to language per se and, where they do, rather vague statements of tolerance predominate over arguments for active promotion. Even activist supporters of language rights thus find existing legislation to be inadequate, and no sort of guarantee of protection. Phillipson (1992, 95) notes, for example, that "existing ... declarations are in no way adequate to provide support for dominated languages" (see also de Varennes 1999). Simpson (2001, 29) writes that not only are "arrangements for the domestic protection of human rights" weak and inadequate, but "at an international level the situation is much worse: for most ill-treated people, most of the time, human-rights instruments are not worth the paper they are written on."

Of course, language conventions and the like are not always weak. Where they appear effective, however, they are inevitably a reflection of larger social trends and pressures, tending to add a particular linguistic endorsement to some broad *projet de société* – as in Quebec, for instance. Arguments for official neutrality in cultural and linguistic terms can hardly ignore the reality that in most societies this neutrality is clearly violated for at least one "mainstream" group. A government may refuse to endorse *any* religion, but it must – at least *de facto* – endorse a given language (or languages). States cited as counter-examples, countries where official recognition is extended to more than one variety, are typically ones in which territorial restrictions apply – the twinned monolingualisms of Belgium, for example. But these are not the sorts of settings of greatest interest to supporters of "small" languages – their concerns are with more or less threatened varieties, and their aspirations, therefore, are for legislation that is more "promotional." It is in *these* circumstances that legislation typically proves lacking in their eyes.

A final issue here has to do with the breadth of application of language rights. Their proponents are generally motivated by the plight of small groups whose languages and cultures are considered to be at risk – and this may sit uneasily with traditional liberal-democratic principles that enshrine rights in individuals, not collectivities. For some, of course, the liberal core *can* be reconciled with differential group treatments; the work of Kymlicka and his colleagues is central to this question. And, for those who argue that language rights are in essence individual rights, the need for some reconciliation never arises (de Varennes 1999; 2001). But it is surely the case that language rights, in any but the most rarefied of contexts, involve more than the individual; language itself generally presupposes a social context. A more nuanced position might be that language rights necessarily comprise a sort of "hybrid" category. On the one hand, language may be considered an individual characteristic, arguably of some importance to personal identity; on the other, it is group membership that leads to demands for language rights, and language is seen as a pivotal marker of group identity (see Coulombe 1993; Edwards 2009; MacMillan 1982; 1983; Waldron 1987).[22]

4. CONCLUSION

The first sentence of this chapter suggested simplicity: consequently, this conclusion can be very brief. I have tried to show, first, that discussions surrounding human rights in general, and language rights more specifically, are often flawed or incomplete. Second, I have contended that it is within a contemporary ecolinguistic paradigm that language rights find their most prominent and pointed treatment. Third, I have attempted to flesh out the oddly restricted perspective of this paradigm – which should, if its name means anything at all, be alive to *all* facets of language-in-context – demonstrating that all the features treated under its rubric are essentially summoned to the service of its centrepiece: the maintenance and promotion of linguistic diversity. I do not suggest here that such an undertaking is inappropriate or unworthy, but I do submit that it is disingenuous to emphasize a quite specific thesis under an apparently general and wide-ranging heading. And fourth, I hope to have shown that, when it comes to matters of alleged *rights*, ecology-of-language arguments are essentially *hopes* and *claims*. I am of course aware that what are claims today may be officially sanctioned tomorrow and, furthermore, that arguing for the legal fulfilment of aspirations is a legitimate avenue for attempting to effect this transition; see also Blackburn (2009).[23] But the passionate arguments of scholar-advocates are, again, disingenuous in the manner of their presentation; and, quite apart from the specific complaint I make here, they reveal the hazards involved when intellectual discussions become intertwined with deeply felt preferences, and with unshakeable convictions of where the moral high ground is to be found.

Even the most committed of scholar-advocates might consider that contemporary treatments of rights run the real risk of cheapening the currency.[24] Something as important as *rights* should not "be taken for granted in moral and political discussion. Few of us want the language of rights to degenerate into a sort of lingua franca in which moral and political values of all or any kinds may be expressed" (Waldron 1987, 2).

Where Waldron writes "language of rights," we might well read "rights *to* language" as well. In a similar vein, Blackburn (2009, 179–80) refers to the dangers of an "uncontrolled expansion of rights," adding that "rights claims seem peculiarly adapted to generate heat." And, as I have already noted, he also observes that "we should see talk of natural rights as part of the vocabulary of advocacy." Nathan (2012, 51), too, suggests that overextending conceptions of human rights can reduce "the sacrosanct quality of the original idea." And Neier (2012; see Nathan 2012, 49–50) is perhaps more pointed still, when he argues that "only civil and political rights can be considered real human rights" – that is, only those pointing to what authorities *cannot* do. These are justiciable, while social and cultural "rights" – statements of what governments and officialdom *should* do – are not. Preserving the "quality of rights" means not confusing the two categories here.

I don't know that I completely agree with Neier's position here, but I do think that it – along with the other explanatory and cautionary notes that I have touched on in this piece – suggests the need for a more deeply informed approach to language rights. Such an approach implies going beyond what is often a narrow and decontextualized sociology-of-language literature, which now often finds itself positioned somewhere between a simple lack of awareness of or attention to necessary underpinnings, on the one hand, and outbreaks of special pleading, on the other. Such an approach also implies a more rigorous and accurate placement of language rights within the larger domain of human rights – necessarily giving rise to fuller and more inclusive discussions bearing upon just and ethical treatment. Such an approach must ultimately lead to more appropriate and less ephemeral language-management undertakings.

NOTES

1   There *is* an entry on "ethics and language," by Hilary Putnam: its title recalls
    the now-classic treatment by Charles Stevenson (1944), an author admired but
    not always agreed with by Putnam. Both, however, deal with propositional
    logic, values, truth, and ethics in ways that – while not entirely outside its
    scope – are not directly relevant to the thrust of this chapter.

2   Even Bentham, to whom I shall soon turn, felt that declarations were reaso-
    nable if understood as guidance or as advice (or, as we might then say, as
    claims). This is not unlike the position taken by Neier (2012) in his powerful
    summary of human rights.

3   There are difficulties, of course, with an out-and-out relativism, and most
    have to do with questions of where we might or should "draw the line" when
    confronted with extreme cultural variations. *Are* there some universal moral
    principles, some cultural yardsticks, that can measure all humanity? Diderot
    argued for these when searching for what we would now call cross-cultural
    consensus; see his article "Droit naturel" in the famous *Encyclopédie* (Diderot
    and d'Alembert 1751–72). Such a consensus might furnish a basis for universal
    rights – but even Locke had already shown what later anthropological work
    would confirm, and what cultural relativism would champion: what is self-
    evident in one community need not be in another. Among other things,
    the failure of a "consensus" underpinning for human rights was seen to
    strengthen the case for one based upon utilitarian principles; see also
    Waldron (1987).

4   John Locke had added property rights to those of life and liberty, while the
    Declaration of Independence plumped for the "pursuit of happiness" instead.

5   Nathan (2012, 48) tells us that "the website of the U.N. High Commissioner for
    Human Rights lists about a hundred conventions, protocols, and statutes …
    by which sovereign states undertake commitments to one another about how
    they will – and especially, will not – treat their own citizens." Of course,
    "whether states actually implement these commitments" is another matter.

6   "Nonsense upon Stilts" was Bentham's original and preferred title for what
    Étienne Dumont – the editor of the original French publication – called
    Un traité des sophismes politiques. It was Bowring who made the translation
    into "anarchical fallacies": see Bedau (2000) and Schofield (2003).

7 In both *Common Sense* (1776) and the *Rights of Man* (1791–92) – his famous
   response to Burke – Thomas Paine also wrote that declarations of rights implied declarations of obligations. He did not, of course, see eye to eye with
   Bentham on everything! Schofield (2004) points out that we await a close
   comparative study of the thought and works of Paine and Bentham.

8 We can imagine that Bentham, who argued that the establishment of once-
   and-for-all laws was a method "enabling the dead to chain down the living"
   (Schofield 2003, 9), would have made short work of the much-disputed second amendment to the American constitution – the one concerning the right
   to bear arms. See also Blackburn's (2009, 183) caustic comment about the
   "minute and pedantic care" here, the way in which a document now well
   over two hundred years old is treated as a "sacred text."

9 Sen also discusses another concern, a cultural critique: "is the idea of human
   rights really so universal? Are there not ethics, such as in the world of Confu-
   cian cultures, that tend to focus on discipline rather than on rights, on loyalty
   rather than on entitlement" (231)? This matter, which he discusses under the
   rubric of "Asian values," is an interesting one, but cannot be followed up here.
   See also Nathan's (2012) observation – citing the work of Neier (2012) – that
   contemporary human rights are a post-war creation, primarily intended to
   extend American and European values, and therefore perhaps of lesser
   attraction in other quarters.

10 Dickens's only other full-length work of historical fiction, *Barnaby Rudge*
   (1841), also takes place in a setting of mob violence: the Gordon Riots of 1780.
   As Orwell (1940) reminded us, Dickens was horrified at such violence,
   describing rioters as lunatic and bestial. This is of a piece, of course, with
   Le Bon's arguments about the irrationality of crowds.

11 The authors fail to note, however, that the official declaration (Nordic Council
   of Ministers 2007) appears in nine languages: Danish, Swedish, and Norwegian, of course – but also Faroese, Finnish, Sámi, Icelandic, Kalaallisut
   (Greenlandic), and English. Such a multilingual presentation might be a
   rather cynical gesture towards languages that are, after all, seen to be of
   subaltern status. On the other hand, perhaps it reflects at least some sense of
   tolerance and inclusivity. (It may be worth noting here that both authors work
   at an institute for Icelandic studies, and claim in their paper that the position

of Icelandic speakers in the Nordic community is analogous to that of non-native vis-à-vis native speakers of English.)

On a related point: members of *la francophonie* around the world may or may not accept the suggestion from *l'hexagone* that they constitute a coalition for the defence of *all* languages currently menaced by global English – but we might be forgiven for seeing the real linguistic thrust of the organization as rather narrower than that; see Edwards (2011).

12 The orthodox Marxist view was that declarations of the rights of *man* reflect bourgeois capitalist sentiment – the rights of "egoistic man," in fact. The rights of *citizens*, however, might be a different matter, were it not for the fact that "in the human rights tradition … the egoism of the former taints and over-whelms whatever communalism there is in the concept of the latter" (Waldron 1987, 132).

13 Minogue (2002, 333) makes a similar remark elsewhere: "rights are curious concepts, being imperious in what they demand and flabby in what holds them up."

14 We should be careful when engaging with any contemporary field of study that styles itself as "critical" – or, if not careful, at least aware that we are likely to encounter quite narrowly specific postures; see Edwards (2010a).

15 As may be imagined, meaningful treatments of the social life of language have *always* attended to the necessary contextualization, and careful scholars were *always* ecologically minded. As Roland Breton (2002, 238) observed, in his discussion of linguistic topography, "toute géographie intelligente repose sur une écologie" [all meaningful geography rests upon ecology]. Furthermore, I don't suggest that all modern work in language planning now takes place under this particular rubric. Nonetheless the "new" ecology of language seems to be increasingly attractive, and it is certainly the venue for the most pointed – and the most ill-considered – attention to matters of language rights.

16 Fuller treatment of linguistic imperialism can be found in Edwards (2011).

17 As with "authentic," the meaning of "indigenous" has acquired quite specific connotations in ecological circles.

18 We recall here both Bentham's "poetical fancies" and Fishman's admiration for those who continue to live their lives in "deeply poetic" ways (both cited above).

19   McRae (1970, 215) notes that, during the proceedings leading up to the UN
     Declaration, "the question of incorporating a specific clause on linguistic and
     other minority rights was debated at some length." He discusses why this did
     not occur.

20   With regard to caveats such as "where possible or feasible," I hope it won't
     seem crass to mention, merely in passing, the question of money. The Indian
     poet and politician Sarojini Naidu once wrote that "it costs a great deal of
     money to keep Gandhiji living in poverty." The translation services of the
     European Union cost a great deal of money. It is expensive for taxpayers to
     subsidize the maintenance of the remaining Celtic languages, to say nothing of
     Māori, Moksha, or Mi'kmaw. And so on. Of course, many worthwhile things
     cost a lot of money – I simply note here that it would be unwise to imagine
     that expanding the currency of language rights would not create, *inter alia*,
     currency problems of another sort.

     The works of Abram de Swaan (2001; 2004) and Philippe van Parijs (2003;
     2011) provide detailed discussions of another controversial question in which
     economic matters are deeply implicated: the spread of English, its place vis-à-
     vis other languages, and ways in which non-native speakers of English might
     be compensated – economically and otherwise – for the disadvantage of
     having to learn something that comes free to Anglophones.

21   Alfredsson is cited in Grenoble (2015), whose discussion of language declara-
     tions and conventions is particularly useful.

22   The nature of the linkage between language and identity is something I have
     addressed in some detail; see Edwards (2009; 2010b; 2011), and the brief but
     useful commentary of Coulmas (1998).

23   Nathan (2012) suggests that states may not always honour the commitments
     made in the many conventions and declarations that they agree to; conse-
     quently, little may change on the ground, as it were. Nonetheless, he echoes
     Blackburn when he writes that international and "soft law" can at least pro-
     vide an "opening wedge" pointing to firmer action.

24   Activists might also consider what Heini Gruffudd – the chairman of Dyfodol
     I'r Iaith (A Future for the Language), founded in 2012 – said about one endan-
     gered language, that "campaigners have been 'dazzled' by 'easy victories' in
     areas such as language rights, but have been diverted away from the core task

of maintaining and reviving the use of Welsh" (Williamson 2014). It is the thrust of this chapter, of course, that those "easy victories" typically take the form of declarations that are largely unenforceable, of rights that are not justiciable.

REFERENCES

Alfredsson, Gundmundur. 2013. "Good Governance in the Arctic." In *Polar Law Textbook II*, edited by Natalia Loukacheva, 185–98. Copenhagen: Nordic Council of Ministers.

Arendt, Hannah. 1967. *The Origins of Totalitarianism*. London: Allen & Unwin.

Bedau, Hugo Adam. 2000. "'Anarchical Fallacies': Bentham's Attack on Human Rights." *Human Rights Quarterly* 22: 261–79.

Benn, Stanley. 1972. "Rights." In *The Encyclopedia of Philosophy: Volume Seven*, edited by Paul Edwards, 195–9. New York: Macmillan.

Blackburn, Simon. 2009. *Philosophy*. London: Quercus.

Blackstone, William. 1765–69. *Commentaries on the Laws of England*. Oxford, UK: Clarendon.

Blommaert, Jan. 2001a. "Review of *Linguistic Genocide in Education, or Worldwide Diversity and Human Rights?* [by Tove Skutnabb-Kangas]." *Applied Linguistics* 22: 539–42.

– 2001b. "The Asmara Declaration as a Sociolinguistic Problem: Reflections on Scholarship and Linguistic Rights." *Journal of Sociolinguistics* 5: 131–42.

– 2005. "Situating Language Rights: English and Swahili in Tanzania Revisited." *Journal of Sociolinguistics* 9: 390–417.

Boudreau, Annette, Lise Dubois, Jacques Maurais, and Grant McConnell. 2002. "Problématique." In *L'écologie des langues*, edited by Annette Boudreau, Lise Dubois, Jacques Maurais, and Grant McConnell, 23–32. Paris: L'Harmattan.

Bowring, John. 1838–43. *The Works of Jeremy Bentham*. Edinburgh: Tait.

Boswell, James. 1924. *The Life of Samuel Johnson*. London: Navarre Society.

Breton, Roland. 2002. "La géographie des langues face à son facteur central: l'état." In *L'écologie des langues*, edited by Annette Boudreau, Lise Dubois, Jacques Maurais, and Grant McConnell, 237–55. Paris: L'Harmattan.

Brown, Andrew. 2010. "Do Human Rights Exist?" *The Guardian*, 20 October.

Calvet, Louis-Jean. 1999. *Pour une écologie des langues du monde*. Paris: Plon.

Chawla, Saroj. 2001. "Linguistic and Philosophical Roots of Our Environmental Crisis." In *The Ecolinguistics Reader*, edited by Alwin Fill and Peter Mühlhäusler, 115–23. London: Continuum.

Coulmas, Florian. 1998. "Language Rights – Interests of State, Language Groups and the Individual." *Language Sciences* 20: 63–72.

Coulombe, Pierre. 1993. "Language Rights, Individual and Communal." *Language Problems and Language Planning* 17: 140–52.

Dickens, Charles. 1841. *Barnaby Rudge: A Tale of the Riots of Eighty*. London: Chapman & Hall.

– 1859. *A Tale of Two Cities*. London: Chapman & Hall.

Diderot, Denis, and Jean le Rond d'Alembert. 1751–72. *Encyclopédie, ou dictionnaire raisonné des sciences, des arts et des métiers*. Paris: Briasson.

Edwards, John. 1994. "Review of *Researching Language: Issues of Power and Method* [by Deborah Cameron, Elizabeth Frazer, Penelope Harvey, Ben Rampton, and Kay Richardson]." *Ecumene* 1: 402–5. (*Ecumene* became *Cultural Geographies* as of volume 9, 2002.)

– 2002a. "Old Wine in New Bottles: Critical Remarks on Language Ecology." In *L'écologie des langues*, edited by Annette Boudreau, Lise Dubois, Jacques Maurais, and Grant McConnell, 299–324. Paris: L'Harmattan.

– 2002b. "Linguistic Ecology and Its Discontents." Paper to round-table discussion on *L'écologie des langues: mélanges William Mackey*. Moncton, NB: Université de Moncton.

– 2009. *Language and Identity*. Cambridge: Cambridge University Press.

– 2010a. *Language Diversity in the Classroom*. Bristol, UK: Multilingual Matters.

– 2010b. *Minority Languages and Group Identity*. Amsterdam: John Benjamins.

– 2011. *Challenges in the Social Life of Language*. New York: Palgrave Macmillan.

Extra, Guus, and Durk Gorter, eds. 2001. *The Other Languages of Europe*. Clevedon, UK: Multilingual Matters.

Fincher, Corey, and Randy Thornhill. 2008. "A Parasite-Driven Wedge: Infectious Diseases May Explain Language and Other Biodiversity." *Oikos* 117: 1289–97.

Fishman, Joshua. 1982. "Whorfianism of the Third Kind." *Language in Society* 11: 1–14.

– 1991. *Reversing Language Shift*. Clevedon, UK: Multilingual Matters.

Freeland, Jane, and Donna Patrick, eds. 2004. *Language Rights and Language Survival*. Manchester, UK: St Jerome.

Grenoble, Lenore. 2015. "Leveraging Language Policy to Effect Change in the Arctic." In *Policy and Planning for Endangered Languages*, edited by Mari Jones, 1–17. Cambridge: Cambridge University Press.

Grin, François. 2005. "Linguistic Human Rights as Source of Policy Guidelines: A Critical Assessment." *Journal of Sociolinguistics* 9: 448–60.

Haugen, Einar. 1972. "The Ecology of Language." In *The Ecology of Language: Essays by Einar Haugen*, edited by Anwar Dil, 325–39. Stanford, CA: Stanford University Press.

– 1987. *Blessings of Babel: Bilingualism and Language Planning*. Berlin: Mouton de Gruyter.

Heller, Monica. 2002. "L'écologie et la sociologie du langage." In *L'écologie des langues*, edited by Annette Boudreau, Lise Dubois, Jacques Maurais, and Grant McConnell, 175–91. Paris: L'Harmattan.

Kontra, Miklós, Robert Phillipson, Tove Skutnabb-Kangas, and Tibor Várady, eds. 1999. *Language: A Right and a Resource*. Budapest: Central European University Press.

Kristinsson, Ari, and Amanda Hilmarsson-Dunn. 2012. "Unequal Language Rights in the Nordic Language Community." *Language Problems and Language Planning* 36: 222–36.

Kukathas, Chandran. 1992. "Are There Any Cultural Rights?" *Political Theory* 20: 105–39.

Kymlicka, Will. 1995a. *Multicultural Citizenship: A Liberal Theory of Minority Rights*. Oxford, UK: Oxford University Press.

– ed. 1995b. *The Rights of Minority Cultures*. Oxford, UK: Oxford University Press.

Kymlicka, Will, and Alan Patten. 2003a. "Language Rights and Political Theory: Context, Issues and Approaches." In *Language Rights and Political Theory*, edited by Will Kymlicka and Alan Patten, 1–51. Oxford, UK: Oxford University Press.

– eds. 2003b. *Language Rights and Political Theory*. Oxford, UK: Oxford University Press.

Ladefoged, Peter. 1992. "Another View of Endangered Languages." *Language* 68: 809–11.

Le Bon, Gustave. 1895. *Psychologie des foules*. Paris: Félix Alcan.

Mackey, William. 1978. "The Importation of Bilingual Education Models." In *Georgetown University Round Table on Languages and Linguistics*, edited by James Alatis, 1–18. Washington, DC: Georgetown University Press.

Macmillan, Michael. 1982. "Henri Bourassa on the Defence of Language Rights." *Dalhousie Review* 62: 413–30.

– 1983. "Language Rights, Human Rights and Bill 101." *Queen's Quarterly* 90: 343–61.

Maffi, Luisa. 2000a. "Language Preservation vs. Language Maintenance and Revitalization." *International Journal of the Sociology of Language* 142: 175–90.

– 2000b. "Linguistic and Biological Diversity: The Inextricable Link." In *Rights to Language*, edited by Robert Phillipson, 17–22. Mahwah, NJ: Erlbaum.

– ed. 2001. *On Biocultural Diversity: Linking Language, Knowledge and the Environment*. Washington, DC: Smithsonian Institute Press.

– 2005. "Linguistic, Cultural and Biological Diversity." *Annual Review of Anthropology* 34: 599–617.

May, Stephen. 2005. "Language Rights: Moving the Debate Forward." *Journal of Sociolinguistics* 9: 319–47. (This is the introductory essay in a collection of six articles on language rights.)

– 2012. *Language and Minority Rights: Ethnicity, Nationalism and the Politics of Language*. New York: Routledge.

McRae, Kenneth. 1970. "The Constitutional Protection of Linguistic Rights in Bilingual and Multilingual States." In *Les droits de l'homme, le fédéralisme et les minorités*, edited by Allan Gotlieb, 211–27. Ottawa: Institut canadien des affaires internationales.

Mesthrie, Raj. 2011. *The Cambridge Handbook of Sociolinguistics*. Cambridge: Cambridge University Press.

Mesthrie, Raj, Joan Swann, Ana Deumert, and William Leap. 2000. *Introducing Sociolinguistics*. Amsterdam: John Benjamins.

Minogue, Kenneth. 2001. "Bang to Rights." *Times Literary Supplement*, 9 February, 26–7.

– 2002. "Review of *Language and Minority Rights* [by Stephen May]." *Journal of Multilingual and Multicultural Development* 23: 333–4.

Mühlhäusler, Peter. 1996. *Linguistic Ecology: Language Change and Linguistic Imperialism in the Pacific Region*. London: Routledge.

– 2000. "Language Planning and Language Ecology." *Current Issues in Language Planning* 1: 306–67.

Nathan, Andrew. 2012. "The New Ideology." *The New Republic*, 6 December, 47–51.

Neier, Aryeh. 2012. *The International Human Rights Movement: A History.* Princeton, NJ: Princeton University Press.

Nelde, Peter. 2002. "La linguistique de contact, la recherche sur le conflit linguistique, et l'aménagement linguistique." In *L'écologie des langues*, edited by Annette Boudreau, Lise Dubois, Jacques Maurais, and Grant McConnell, 257–80. Paris: L'Harmattan.

Nickel, James. 1987. *Making Sense of Human Rights.* Berkeley, CA: University of California Press.

Nordic Council of Ministers. 2007. *Deklaration om nordisk språkpolitik.* Copenhagen: Nordiska ministerrådet.

Orwell, George. 1940. *Inside the Whale, and Other Essays.* London: Gollancz.

Pagel, Mark. 2012a. "War of Words." *New Scientist*, 8 December, 38–41.

– 2012b. *Wired for Culture.* New York: Norton.

Paine, Thomas. 1776. *Common Sense.* Philadelphia, PA: Bell.

– 1791–92. *Rights of Man.* London: Jordan.

Van Parijs, Philippe. 2003. "Linguistic Justice." In *Language Rights and Political Theory*, edited by Will Kymlicka and Alan Patten, 27–44. Oxford, UK: Oxford University Press.

– 2011. *Linguistic Justice for Europe and for the World.* Oxford, UK: Oxford University Press.

Phillipson, Robert. 1992. *Linguistic Imperialism.* Oxford, UK: Oxford University Press.

– ed. 2000. *Rights to Language.* Mahwah, NJ: Erlbaum.

– 2009. *Linguistic Imperialism Continued.* Hyderabad, India: Orient Black Swan.

Polzenhagen, Frank, and René Dirven. 2004. "Rationalist or Romantic Model in Language Policy and Globalisation." Paper presented at the LAUD (Linguistic Agency, University of Duisburg) Conference, Landau, Germany.

Putnam, Hilary. 2011. "Ethics and Language." In *Cambridge Encyclopedia of the Language Sciences*, edited by Patrick Hogan, 290–2. Cambridge: Cambridge University Press.

Rawls, John. 1971. *A Theory of Justice.* Oxford, UK: Oxford University Press.

Rhydwen, Mari. 1998. "Strategies for Doing the Impossible." In *Endangered Languages*, edited by Nicholas Ostler, 101–6. Bath, UK: Foundation for Endangered Languages.

Ruiz Vieytez, Eduardo. 2001. "The Protection of Linguistic Minorities: A Historical Approach." *MOST* [Management of Social Transformations Programme] *Journal on Multicultural Societies* 3, no. 1. https://unesdoc.unesco.org/ark:/48223/pf0000 143789.page=7 (accessed 6 July 2019).

Salminen, Tapani. 1998. "Minority Languages in a Society in Turmoil: The Case of the Northern Languages of the Russian Federation." In *Endangered Languages*, edited by Nicholas Ostler, 58–63. Bath, UK: Foundation for Endangered Languages.

Schofield, Philip. 2003. "Jeremy Bentham's 'Nonsense upon Stilts.'" *Utilitas* 15: 1–26.

– 2004. "Jeremy Bentham, the French Revolution and Political Radicalism." *History of European Ideas* 30: 381–401.

Schofield, Philip, Catherine Pease-Watkin, and Cyprian Blamires, eds. 2002. *Rights, Representation, and Reform: Nonsense upon Stilts and Other Writings on the French Revolution*. Oxford, UK: Clarendon.

Sen, Amartya. 1999. *Development as Freedom*. New York: Knopf.

Simpson, Alfred. 2001. "In Rights We Trust." *Times Literary Supplement*, 8 June, 17.

Simpson, James, ed. 2011. *The Routledge Handbook of Applied Linguistics*. Oxford, UK, and New York: Routledge.

Spolsky, Bernard. 2009. *Language Management*. Cambridge: Cambridge University Press.

Stevenson, Charles. 1944. *Ethics and Language*. New Haven, CT: Yale University Press.

de Swaan, Abram. 2001. *Words of the World: The Global Language System*. Cambridge: Polity.

– 2004. "Endangered Languages, Sociolinguistics and Linguistic Sentimentalism." *European Review* 12: 567–80.

Terralingua. 1999. *Statement of Purpose*. Hancock, MI: Terralingua.

TESOL. 2000. *TESOL Board of Directors Reaffirms Position on Language Rights*. Alexandria, VA: TESOL.

Thomson, Judith. 1990. *The Realm of Rights*. Cambridge, MA: Harvard University Press.

de Varennes, Fernand. 1996. *Language, Minorities and Human Rights*. The Hague: Martinus Nijhoff.

– 1999. "The Existing Rights of Minorities in International Law." In *Language: A Right and a Resource*, edited by Miklós Kontra, Robert Phillipson, Tove

Skutnabb-Kangas, and Tibor Várady, 117–46. Budapest: Central European University Press.

– 2001. "Language Rights as an Integral Part of Human Rights." MOST [Management of Social Transformations Programme] *Journal on Multicultural Societies* 3, no. 1. https://unesdoc.unesco.org/ark:/48223/pf0000143789.page=17 (accessed 6 July 2019).

– 2012. "Language Policy at the Supranational Level." In *The Cambridge Handbook of Language Policy*, edited by Bernard Spolsky, 149–73. Cambridge: Cambridge University Press.

Waldron, Jeremy. 1987. *'Nonsense Upon Stilts': Bentham, Burke and Marx on the Rights of Man*. London: Methuen.

Wee, Lionel. 2007. "Linguistic Human Rights and Mobility." *Journal of Multilingual and Multicultural Development* 28: 325–38.

– 2011. *Language without Rights*. Oxford, UK: Oxford University Press.

Williamson, David. 2014. "The Death of the Welsh Language Is a Reality in Many Communities, a Leading Campaigner Will Warn Today." *Wales Online*, 17 June. http://www.walesonline.co.uk/news/wales-news/death-welsh-language-reality-many-7277055.

Wright, Sue. 2001. "Language and Power: Background to the Debate on Linguistic Rights." MOST [Management of Social Transformations Programme] *Journal on Multicultural Societies* 3, no. 1. https://unesdoc.unesco.org/ark:/48223/pf0000143789.page=46 (accessed 6 July 2019).

3

Language Ethics
Keeping Linguistic Freedom from Becoming Linguistic Free Riding

DAVID ROBICHAUD

1. INTRODUCTION

Normative aspects of language diversity have been explored and discussed by many scholars from different fields of enquiry. New knowledge about the rate at which languages "die," the formation of supranational entities such as the EU, the emergence of a global *lingua franca*, the rise of the number and proportion of Spanish speakers in the United States, and the daily linguistic challenges in federations such as Switzerland, Belgium, Canada, and India are but a few reasons that have prompted this kind of research. Scholars have mainly tried to get a better understanding of what was happening, of who was suffering, of the moral problems of this suffering, and have attempted to come up with solutions to improve the situation. A large debate emerged where the proper regimes of language rights were discussed, and a compelling account of language justice was sought. Most of these research results proposed institutional solutions, legal and/or political. They offered arguments built on the value of languages or language diversity; they condemned some constitutional or legal dispositions being favourable to some linguistic communities and individuals, or being in tension with some individual rights. The debates so far have mostly highlighted political problems and have suggested legal and political measures as possible solutions.

Of all the debates on language justice, very few voices have raised the issue of *language ethics*, that is, the evaluation of morally problematic behaviours in individual interactions. This probably has to do with the fact that many liberal thinkers are in favour of unconstrained linguistic freedom. Many argue in favour of a "politics of indifference" (Kukhatas 1998) when it comes to language and culture, and argue in favour of freedom of choice in their linguistic interactions. The only constraint on linguistic choices should be rational constraints in the search for individual interest. We could then consider that an "ethics of indifference" is also desirable when it comes to individual linguistic behaviours, arguing that when laws are silent we can speak the language we want. I do not discuss the *content* of the message transmitted through a language – which of course can be immoral if one lies or demeans someone – rather, I concentrate on the *code* in which this message is expressed. Here I also leave aside the question of the moral duty of State officials or people's representatives to address the population in any official language, for example. I rather ask the more provocative and less debated question: Can it be morally wrong to use a certain language in a certain social context outside of any political institution?

Of course this "ethics of indifference" is intuitively interesting. How could the simple fact of expressing ideas in a given language be considered morally problematic? Who could come up with a legitimate moral objection since apparently no cost is imposed on anyone? This could explain the silence of scholars on *language ethics*. No matter what the reason is for this silence, I will argue that some of our free linguistic behaviours *are* imposing costs on others in various linguistic interactions. I will then propose an argument according to which we have some moral duties, unrelated to our political or legal duties, to behave in certain ways in our language interactions. I will argue that in order to have linguistic freedom without linguistic free riding, it is necessary to constrain individual behaviours using moral (or political and legal) norms.

2. FIRST VISIT TO THE MONK

Thanks to "globalization" and the rise of English as a *lingua franca*, it is now easier than ever to have goods or people travel across State and language borders (Crystal 1997). This creates unprecedented opportunities, but it also creates unprecedented linguistic encounters presenting new moral issues.

When I studied in Louvain-la-Neuve, I visited many amazing Flemish cities. I quickly realized that in order to get positive reactions from people in coffee shops, in restaurants, and on the streets, addressing people in (less than rudimentary) Flemish was best, English was fine, and French was only an option if I managed to explain that I was from Quebec in the very first moments of our exchange. It felt naturally like a kind, nice thing to do to try to address people in their language, and I could understand the frustration of being addressed in French in a Flemish community pressured by a regional French majority. Most people were able to speak French, at least better than I could speak Flemish, and certainly enough to do their job, do some small talk, or give directions. They nonetheless reacted as if it was wrong of me to impose a conversation in French on them, and they often refused to switch to French until they learned I was from Quebec. They reacted negatively to a behaviour they visibly thought was morally problematic.

I intuitively understood their reaction, and the moral emotion at its basis, since I experience something similar when I have to switch to English for my (informal) interactions in Montreal. This feeling is made worse when I learn that the person unable to understand French is not someone who arrived recently but someone who was born in Montreal. Two questions then emerge: Is it a moral sentiment that is understandable and legitimate, or is it a simple frustration closer to jealousy, bigotry, or to a refusal to face (minority) reality? Also, why does it make a difference when we speak French in Flanders or English in Montreal, whether we are tourists or locals? Before I went to Belgium, I thought that my sentiment was one of mere frustration. It is only once I was the person imposing a language upon others that I was able to see more clearly the moral problems implied by some linguistic behaviours.

The fact that many people experience negative moral feelings when they face people speaking a language they consider inappropriate in a particular social context seems widespread. This doesn't mean that this feeling is legitimate or justified, but it offers a starting ground to address the question of language ethics in this chapter. I think it is possible to offer an interpretation of some moral reactions we have when addressed in a language we judge inappropriate in a given context, using a moral justification of some linguistic duties grounded in individual interests. I will try to argue that some linguistic behaviour can be seen as free riding and abuse of others' investments in language skills.

Many of our behaviours impose costs on others, and usually such behaviours are considered immoral if those assuming the costs haven't freely agreed to do so. Moral norms against stealing, killing, or lying serve the purpose of prohibiting behaviours that are beneficial to the agent but whose costs are imposed on others. I will try to demonstrate that using a particular language can maximize the agent's utility but can also impose some costs on others. I will show that our linguistic behaviours create externalities and are subject to market failures, making it impossible to leave individuals free to choose whatever language they prefer to use and expect the result to be moral or optimal.

I will start from a situation considered desirable by many proponents of an ethics of indifference: total linguistic freedom. In such a situation, people try to maximize their utility using the more promising language they have mastered. I will show that such a situation is not morally neutral and doesn't produce optimal results due to collective action problems and the presence of market failures. These market failures are responsible for the transformation of an efficient and morally free zone of language interaction into an inefficient and morally problematic one. In order to reconcile individual behaviours and optimal results, we need the introduction of exogenous constraints such as moral norms. Norms are sometimes thought to be means to compensate for market failures and to produce optimal results (Arrow 1970). From there, we can interpret negative moral reactions as being produced by the violation of a collectively beneficial norm.

3. MORAL PROBLEMS WITH LINGUISTIC INTERACTIONS

When moral problems related to linguistic interactions are examined, many scholars turn their attention to the identity dimension of language. When trying to make sense of the moral reactions presented above, an obvious line of argument would then be to relate the negative reaction with the misrecognition of their identity. Many versions of the politics of recognition have been defended and they capture a fundamental aspect of our identity formation and the problems that can occur in the process (Taylor and Gutmann 1994; Honneth 1996; Fraser and Honneth 2003). According to such a theory, some behaviours are morally problematic since they reflect a negative image of some people's identity. Identity formation being the result of a dialogical process, one suffers when some dimension of his identity is reflected negatively by others (Taylor and Gutmann 1994; Honneth 1996). It could then easily be argued that we feel a moral harm from situations described above because we feel like our language is unworthy of other people's time and attention. They send us a signal that our language is negligible, that the culture, the people, and the scientific knowledge it gives access to are of little value. Many people see their language as an important aspect of their identity, so we could understand the negative feeling many of them get from some linguistic interactions like those presented earlier.

This line of argument is interesting and captures a part of our moral reactions, but it is an incomplete story. Of course, if people ridicule our language, it can create a negative moral reaction on our part. But even if someone seems to respect and recognize the value of our language, there is still a moral problem in certain interactions in which a speaker imposes a language upon others. Some say that they have no particular attachment to a given language, but still consider it rude for some "non-speakers" to address them in any other language, or at least to feel the necessity to justify themselves. It also remains to be explained why there is a difference in our reaction depending on the origin of our interlocutor.

What I want to propose is an account of the immorality of some linguistic behaviour grounded in the *instrumental dimension of languages* (Robichaud and De Schutter 2012). It is therefore compatible with any conception of the identity value of languages. I want to show that moral duties can derive not only from the identity dimension of languages, but also from their instrumental dimension. The argument will not rely on a strong principle of substantive equality, on a duty of due recognition, or on the intrinsic value of languages or linguistic diversity. It will be grounded only on the instrumental value of languages.

The argument is that languages and *language repertoire* are collective goods, and that when individuals contribute to produce collective goods, it opens up opportunities for free riding – that is, abusing other people's production of a good from which we benefit. Free riding can then be described as morally wrong, since one uses others and unilaterally imposes costs on them in order to improve one's own situation (Robichaud 2017). The solution we should turn to when we are faced with market failures such as this is to adopt mutually beneficial norms constraining our social behaviour (Arrow 1970; Gauthier 1986).

4. A DEFENSE OF TOTAL LINGUISTIC FREEDOM

The best way to justify moral constraints on our linguistic behaviour is by showing why linguistic freedom is problematic. The idea that nothing should constrain people's freedom in their language behaviour can be grounded in a powerful argument inspired by *laisser-faire* approaches in economics. Promoting freedom and rejecting moral or political constraints on linguistic choices can offer appealing positions. It could be argued that language freedom is too important, that it should not be constrained for the pursuit of collective goals such as the survival of a language or a collective desire to use an "unpopular" vernacular language. If people really wish to preserve a language, a simple way to guarantee its survival is to use and transmit it. If they don't, the language won't be used and may be abandoned, something that could be seen as regrettable, but not as morally relevant since the victims chose to abandon it. Nobody should have a duty or an obligation to learn, use, or transmit a language if this is not their desire. As Helder De Schutter puts it: "[t]he problem with survival policies is that to protect those who wish survival, the choice of those who wish to assimilate must be restricted, and the latter must be forced to remain within their original language. But to use some as means to satisfy the interests of others is morally problematic. While there is a right to speak your own language and to receive language recognition, there is no right to have your language spoken by others" (De Schutter 2011). This linguistic freedom argument is appealing but it gets much stronger if we take into account the idea that linguistic freedom is not only morally important for individuals but also the best way to produce optimal collective results.

To understand the large appeal of laisser-faire economics, we must understand the assumption according to which in a perfect market, the best way to produce optimal collective results is to let individuals make free rational choices maximizing their utility. When each and every individual makes the choices that are best suited to promote their individual interest, taking into account their preferences, the probabilities of success, and the expected be-haviours of others, the collective result is necessarily as desirable as possible. Any action and transaction beneficial to those involved is conducted, and the less desirable ones are discarded. It is therefore impossible to intervene in order to improve the situation of one actor without worsening the situation of another. By doing so, we would force someone to agree to a transaction they judged unsatisfactory or prohibit people from concluding mutually beneficial transactions. Public subsidies, protectionist policies, commercial prohibitions, and political or moral obligations are examples of exogenous interventions that would ruin the coincidence of rational individual choices and optimal results for everyone if people were interacting in an ideal mar-ket. Such measures should therefore be avoided both because they would arbitrarily constrain some individuals' liberty and they wouldn't produce an optimal result.

So *laisser-faire* doesn't condemn any constraint on individual freedom without consideration for the collective results that would be produced. The market is sometimes presented as the institution best able to coordinate in-dividual preferences and *respect individual liberty* (and the result of liberty: diversity). But it can also be presented as the best way to coordinate individual projects in order to obtain *optimal collective results*. The best way to produce satisfaction in a population is then to leave every individual free to pursue his own vision of the good life in each rational choice that he makes.

The genius idea of the invisible hand is that individual interests and collec-tive interests are served simultaneously when we let rational agents pursue their goals within the strict limits of their sphere of liberty. In other words, *equilibrium of choices* coincides with *optimality of results* when free rational agents choose to use, learn, or transmit the language that offers the best ex-pected utility in the context of interaction that is available to them.

A choice is in equilibrium if it offers the most interesting payoff to an agent *considering the social context and other people's preferences and beliefs*. This may not realize one's most important preference, but it realizes the highest prefer-ence that can possibly be realized in a given context, considering other people's preferences and beliefs. Applied to languages, it would mean that an individual would choose to use, learn, or transmit the language(s) that maximizes its util-ity in the context offered by the aggregation of everyone's language choices.

The chosen language may not be the one he prefers, but it will be the one offering the most interesting benefits.

A result is optimal if it is impossible to improve anyone's situation without worsening another's. For instance, in a context where everyone speaks English because it is the only language mastered by everyone, if what everyone prefers is mutual understanding, the result is optimal. No other choices made by individuals would have made any individual better off without worsening another's situation.

It follows that any exogenous intervention, from the State or from morality, would break this coincidence of equilibrium and optimality. If the State prohibits the use of English in our example, or if some individuals feel that they should use another language for moral reasons, the results won't be as beneficial to all the agents involved, and some will end up in a worse situation than the one that would have prevailed under freedom of choice.

According to *laisser-faire*, exogenous interventions could only be legitimate in circumstances where individual rational choices do not lead to optimal results, that is, where we are facing *market failures*. In a situation where equilibrium of choices and optimality of results coincide, there is no place for morality and a free market is the best way to coordinate free choices in order to produce collectively desirable results. Nobody can complain about his situation since everyone chose a free course of action, and the results are as beneficial as possible to all. Some may find themselves in a situation deemed undesirable when compared to others, but there is no moral problem with one's own situation since it is the best available considering everyone's preferences. For example, imagine that a small linguistic community is considering the possibility of a language switch to a vehicular language (a lingua franca). If every speaker but one prefers to switch to another language, the only speaker having a preference for language maintenance could consider that he is being treated unjustly since he is now forced to abandon his language. But there is nothing immoral in the situation. Every speaker chose rationally what seemed to be the most promising option, the result being satisfactory to every speaker but one. Any intervention to improve the situation of our poor speaker would involve worsening the situation of the others. This could be done, for example, by granting more weight to its utility, or by granting value to the preservation of a language without taking into account the speaker's interests and preferences. Both justifications sound morally problematic. So if every agent chose the best course of action made available by other agents' choices, if nobody was coerced to act in such a way, the result should be the best one available collectively. We should then consider that the situation is morally acceptable and that nothing can justify an intervention or a moral constraint on people's linguistic behaviour.

The *laisser-faire* approach then seems like a strong justification for linguistic freedom. The best way to realize people's linguistic interests would be to let individuals' free choices shape the linguistic landscape and consider that the result is morally acceptable, whatever it is. If a language community is too small to offer some prospects of a good life, people will turn to second languages; if someone wants plenty of communication partners he will learn some vehicular languages; and if they are happy with a handful of meaningful partners they might invest only in a vernacular language. Following these choices, if a language is abandoned, it will be because its speakers rationally switched to another language. They might think it is regrettable, the social context might disadvantage them, but we can still argue that it was the best choice available and that improving their situation, by introducing moral or political constraints, would necessitate arbitrarily worsening another individual's situation. *As long as everyone's liberty is respected, as long as no-one is forced to abandon, to learn, or to use a language, and as long as everyone assumes the costs of their choices without imposing them on others, the situation seems morally irreproachable.*

I now have to demonstrate that this vision of our linguistic choices and interactions is not accurate, and that free linguistic choices cannot be expected to produce optimal collective results.

5. LANGUAGE AND MARKET FAILURES: FROM LINGUISTIC FREEDOM TO LINGUISTIC FREE RIDING

What is true in economics is also true in the linguistic domain: free choices lead to optimal results *only under some very specific and demanding conditions*, namely a perfect competitive market. Unfortunately, due to the presence of market failures of different kinds, such an ideal market is impossible (Gauthier 1986). As soon as a simple market failure is present, free and rational individual behaviour in a market won't produce optimal results. François Grin identified six main forms of market failures that can be encountered in a linguistic environment that disrupt the coincidence of equilibrium and optimality (Grin 2006, 84):

1. Insufficient information for making rational choices
2. Transaction costs
3. Absence of markets for certain goods
4. Market imperfections
5. Presence of positive or negative externalities
6. Existence of public goods

As soon as one market failure is observed, we are not in an ideal market and therefore we cannot expect the best possible rational actions to lead to optimal collective results. We must correct those market failures, and one way to do so is by introducing constraints, moral or political, on linguistic behaviours. The slightest market failure can require massive interventions to reestablish the coincidence between equilibrium of choices and optimality of results (Lipsey and Lancaster 1956–57). Those interventions do not guarantee the re-creation of the coincidence, but without them we cannot expect individual choices to produce optimal results.

When we observe the "language market," we rapidly realize that most (if not all) of the above market failures are present. I will nonetheless concentrate on two forms of market failures: incomplete (asymmetry of) information and the presence of externalities. I will concentrate on these market failures in part due to space constraints but also because, in the case of externalities, they create problems that are obviously moral in nature. Other market failures on the linguistic market, such as transaction costs (Robichaud and De Schutter 2012; Barro 1996; Grin 2006), the absence of markets for certain goods (Robichaud and Turmel 2010; Grin 2006), the presence of monopolies (Carr 1985), and the definition of languages as (hyper)collective goods (De Swaan 2005; Grin 2006) have been discussed elsewhere.

First Market Failure: Incomplete Information

For individual choices to produce collectively desirable results, each individual must have all the relevant information to choose the best way to satisfy her preferences. When considering what language we should learn, use, or transmit, it is necessary to have access to others' linguistic preferences. These preferences represent variables necessary to make a rational choice. On most economic markets, people's preferences, both their content and their intensity, are made readily accessible to all through the mechanism of price. *Ceteris paribus*, the more a good is desired, and the more intensely it is desired, the higher its price will rise. This price mechanism makes available people's preferences to others so that we can make rational decisions as to where we should spend our money in order to maximize utility. The problem is that there is no such mechanism at work when it comes to languages.

Since languages are (hyper)collective goods, more demand for them won't change the cost of acquisition, transmission, or usage. It is therefore very hard to get precise information about what languages other speakers are learning and using. The problem is that the communicative value of any given language depends directly on the number of people speaking it and the particular contexts in which they speak it. In other words, it depends on the number of speakers and the quality of these speakers, that is, the value we find in communicating with them. Contrary to consumer goods, languages do not lose their value when they are used by someone, and contrary to collective goods, their value does not remain stable when used by many. Languages are hyper-collective goods, which means that they gain value each time they are used (De Swaan 2001). However, there are no signals of linguistic preferences available to individuals, no cues about how many people are using, learning, or transmitting a given language through a system of prices. Linguistic choices are then based on incomplete information, and the collective results of individual choices will necessarily be suboptimal: that is, some people could have been better off had they chosen otherwise, without harming anyone.

Learning or transmitting a language is an important and costly decision. It is one that will influence one's opportunities in a very significant manner throughout one's life. We are faced with options presenting different values in terms of identity and communicative potential. If the language most tightly related to our identity is also the one offering the most interesting communication perspectives, then the choice is easy. However, a problem arises when one is not sure of the communicative value of a language. In such a case, the worst situation we can find ourselves in is being one of the few still speaking a vernacular language when many others have chosen to switch to a vehicular language. In such a case, we invested in a language that has both very little communicative value, and a decreasing identity value since it is losing its status as the language of a proud and dynamic community. A slightly better solution then is to switch to a dominant language, offering better prospects on the instrumental dimension, even though it is not related to one's identity.

Doubting that others might prefer to switch languages or to transmit a dominant language can be enough to precipitate the fall of a language. Thomas Schelling encapsulated this collective phenomenon under the concept of "self-fulfilling prophecy": "The general idea is that certain expectations are of such a character that they induce the kind of behavior that will cause the expectations to be fulfilled …: [I]t is not, of course, the prophecy itself that leads to its own fulfillment, but the expectations that lead, through a chain of events and interactions that may be short or long, to an outcome that conforms to the expectations" (Schelling 1978, 115–16). The simple expectation that others might abandon a language, leaving one in a difficult situation, can motivate enough people to act in a way that will realize this expectation. The result may have been no-one's preferred outcome. It was only desirable as an alternative to a possible catastrophic situation. Had they known each other's preferences, supposing those preferences were to preserve the vernacular language and maintain the dominant language as a second language, they would have been able to realize their preference. It is not out of rational choice, as a way to produce the most desirable language situation, that people acted and produced a language shift. It was a prudent move, made rational only due to the lack of information about other people's motives and preferences. In cases involving such important investments, as in learning a language or transmitting it to the next generation, risk aversion is likely to be greater and also likely to dissuade people from making risky decisions. The result is then suboptimal for those speakers, since a better result, one preferred by most or all of them, was accessible.

One way to resolve this problem is for individuals to stop relying on individual maximizing strategies and to adopt a common strategy that will impose norms on individual behaviour and lead to a desired result. The linguistic landscape will then be determined by conscious decisions as to the preferred option instead of being left to individual decisions made in a situation of incomplete information. Those norms will orient individuals towards optimal results that they could rationally agree to. Such norms can be implicit or explicit; they can emerge naturally and become moral in nature, or they can be institutionalized, and have legal weight and political constraint added to them.

I will now turn to another type of market failure that is more explicitly problematic from a moral point of view: the production of externalities.

Second Market Failure: Positive and Negative Externalities

For equilibrium of choice and optimality of results to coincide, for an ideal market to be possible, all externalities must be internalized. That is, every agent must bear the costs and receive the benefits of every action. An externality can be positive, in which case we speak of the *external benefit* of an action, or negative, in which case we speak of the *external cost* of an action. "An externality arises whenever an act of production or exchange or consumption affects the utility of some person who is not party, or who is unwillingly party, to it" (Gauthier 1986, 87). When externalities are produced, utility functions are not independent, which means that one person's behaviour can impose costs on or offer benefits to others. They are "external" costs and benefits in the sense that they are not part of the calculation of costs and benefits agents do to choose the utility-maximizing action. Since these costs and benefits do not influence the expected payoffs for the agent performing the action, they do not influence the agent's decision. This leads individuals to produce more costs and fewer benefits than what would be collectively desirable. If we asked drivers of fuel-inefficient cars to pay for cleaning the air they polluted, they would probably reduce their use of those vehicles. In the present state of affairs, those drivers are free to impose some of the costs of their choice on every member of our society. Their freedom to drive their preferred car is in fact free riding, since we all suffer from the pollution produced and the costs of its cleanup will have to be assumed collectively. As for positive externalities, if we compensate people producing collective benefits, such as getting an education, driving an electric car, or growing flowers in their front yard, we will encourage such investments that are collectively beneficial.

When individuals maximize their utility through rational choices, the collective results of those choices cannot be optimal if externalities are present. This also applies to the linguistic domain. The freedom to pursue our projects freely and choose the language best suited to do it leads to linguistic free riding due to externalities. It is possible to free ride on someone in two distinctive ways. First, one can benefit from a (collective) good produced by others without contributing to it; second, one can transfer costs of his behaviour onto others and/or reduce the benefits others receive from the production of a (collective) good.

This problem is serious for both economists and moral philosophers. An economist would see a problem of efficiency: individual choices leading to suboptimal results. A moral theorist would see a moral problem: some individuals being free to unilaterally impose costs on other people in order to satisfy their preferences. For the situation to be efficient and moral, it is necessary to internalize the external costs and benefits produced. A radical way to intervene is to make some behaviours mandatory or forbidden by introducing rights and duties. As Ronald Coase demonstrated, this radical way of dealing with externalities is rarely the most efficient (Coase 1988). To internalize costs, we could ask for compensation from the individuals producing them; to internalize benefits, compensation could be offered to individuals producing them.

Languages, like any other communication tools, are subject to a particularly interesting type of market failure: network externalities. Positive externalities produced in the linguistic domain have been identified and discussed by many scholars, and some propose State interventions in order to internalize them (Dalmazzone 1999; Church and King 1993). Those externalities are peculiar to network goods, such as phones and faxes, operating systems on a computer, or DVD technologies. The idea is simple: the value of being part of a particular network is a function of the number of people who are also part of it. Being the only one using a phone or a Mac produces very little benefit. However, if a very large number of people are using them, we get important benefits from those goods giving access to the network and from economies of scale in the production of those goods (Katz and Shapiro 1985). The instrumental value of a language is, *ceteris paribus*, a function of the number of speakers it gives access to. When we join a particular network, when we get a phone or learn a language, for example, we do it strictly in order to maximize our private utility. We do not take into account that by entering the network we also increase the utility derived from the network by other members. Each time a new person joins a particular network, benefits are produced for every existing member. Those benefits are external since they are not part of the reasons why we decide to become part of a network. They are nonetheless immense since we produce as many new communication possibilities for existing members of a network as we obtain from becoming a new member.

The instrumental value of languages is then greatly influenced by individual decisions to learn, use, and transmit them. When we learn or improve our knowledge of a language, we produce benefits for ourselves but also for every speaker of this language. We also make the language even more attractive for non-speakers who might decide to learn it. Languages are, as mentioned earlier, hypercollective goods since their value increases with each usage (De Swaan 2001). This particularity of languages is in part responsible for the difficulty of producing optimal results from individual unconstrained choices.

6. SATISFACTION OF LANGUAGE PREFERENCES AND COLLECTIVE ACTION PROBLEMS

Individuals have complex language preferences. They have preferences for languages tied to their identity. These languages are felt as important identity markers and they offer privileged access to particular people, such as other generations or significant others, and meaningful objects, such as cultural goods and historical documents. The language associated with identity and culture is usually the mother language, that is, the one they are most comfortable using and in which they can express easily and clearly some complex and important matters such as emotional states and technical matters, or less important matters such as jokes. Most people feel intimately tied to these languages and care for their preservation.

So much attention has been directed to the identity dimension of languages that scholars often forget another important dimension: its instrumental dimension as a tool of communication (Weinstock 2003b). People have instrumental and communicative language preferences, and they want to learn and transmit a language that maximizes their opportunities of communication, or at least offers sufficient opportunities for them or their children to live a decent life. They want to have access to as many people as possible, but also to specific people, jobs, touristic places, bodies of literature, and other linguistically encoded goods. It is the value of languages as tools of broader communication that motivates and pressures individuals to learn vehicular languages. For some, those having an important vehicular language as a mother language, and most of all for those having English as their mother language, one language can satisfy all those preferences. They benefit from a privileged situation, since in many contexts they *must* learn only one language in order to satisfy all their linguistic preferences.

For everyone else, other than native Anglophones, language decisions are bound to be more difficult. The difficulty is in satisfying both types of preferences efficiently. Indeed, if we only cared for our vernacular language, for the preservation of our linguistic community, we would have a very easy and efficient strategy available: monolingualism in the vernacular language. If every member of the community spoke only the vernacular language, that would be the only language learned, spoken, and transmitted, and members would necessarily contribute to the maintenance of the language. This would also make it impossible for foreigners to settle and expect to integrate without learning the language. On the other hand, if all we cared about was maximizing language reach, the efficient strategy would be for all of us to choose to learn English as quickly as possible. This global *lingua franca* is already spoken by people all over the world, and is spreading fast – being the most popular individual choice for a second language. One generation would bear the costs of this desirable global language shift and then worldwide communication would be possible.

Obviously, individuals are not willing to protect their vernacular language at the price of an access to a broader community, and they are not willing to switch to English without any consideration for their vernacular language. This explains how bilingualism and multilingualism became the norm and not the exception. We may have preferences *for* languages, but we also have preferences that we satisfy *through* languages. Languages may have (intrinsic?) value as unique expressions of our identity (Réaume 2000), but they also have an important instrumental value as means to different ends (Robichaud and De Schutter 2012). We choose the languages in which to invest our time and energy on the basis of expected benefits. When more than one language is necessary to maximize our utility, we invest in language acquisition and we create a *language repertoire.*

The process through which we choose to learn and maintain a language is no different from the one used to make any other decision: we weigh the pros and cons, the expected costs and benefits. Learning a language requires a considerable investment of time and effort. If we consider that investing in learning English is the best way to improve our situation, we will have reasons to do it. If another language or another skill offers more expected benefits, we will rather invest elsewhere.

One thing is fundamentally important: we invest in language learning in order to master *complementary languages* and not to master *interchangeable languages.* For most people, the many languages they speak, more or less perfectly, are associated with different social domains or roles. They invest in second languages to expand their range of opportunities, to have access to new interlocutors and new goods. The best language to learn is the one that is the most complementary to the one(s) already spoken. We do not invest in languages in order to have more options to do the same things, but rather in order to have more options to do more and different things. We are not indifferent as to what language to use to accomplish particular tasks.

This complementarity and division of labour among languages makes it clear that what we invest in is not just a number of languages but a *language repertoire* (De Swaan 2001; Laïtin 1992). The good we produce when we invest in languages is not a loose web of languages to use indiscriminately, but rather a complex and structured linguistic good, where languages are associated with different roles and tasks and complement each other. We have preferences regarding which languages to invest in, but also preferences regarding which language to use in accomplishing what task. Each language is associated with a number of social roles, and to maximize preference satisfaction, this "division of labour" among languages or particular diglossia must be respected.

It could be argued that the best situation for most multilingual individuals is to remain in the comfort of their mother language for as many interactions as possible. This is the language they are most comfortable speaking, the one in which it is easiest to express complex emotional states, conduct business, and engage in strategic interactions involving communication, the one in which they are most likely to be clear and precise, funny and clever. We derive important benefits from studying, working, and socializing in a language we excel at. It is only when we *need* to reach out of our language community, when we benefit from opportunities unavailable through our vernacular language, that it becomes advantageous to switch to a second language. That is the reason why we make such a huge investment in our language repertoire; this linguistic collective good is composed of different languages, and each language is associated with different tasks and social roles.

7. THE POLITICAL AND THE MORAL SOLUTIONS TO COLLECTIVE ACTION PROBLEMS

This vision of language investments in *language repertoire* and not in simple languages makes a huge difference when it comes to the morality and efficiency of free linguistic choices. It highlights peculiar collective action problems and reintroduces opportunities for free riding in the linguistic domain.

If we consider only one language as being the good produced by a group of individuals coordinating in order to satisfy a language preference, free riding is impossible. The only way to benefit from the good produced, to communicate with those using it or to get access to cultural goods accessible through it, is to master it. In learning and using it, we contribute to the language, and therefore we are not free riding on others' investments. If we decide not to learn it, then the benefits produced by the language are restricted to those who did master it, and once again, free riding is not possible. If the public good contemplated is one language, no free riding is possible, and we could argue that any moral constraint on language behaviours is unjustified (Weinstock 2003a). But when we consider the collective good to be a linguistic repertoire, things are different: externalities can be produced and free riding is back in the picture.

When a large number of individuals, concentrated geographically, coordinate and invest in the learning of a language, when they invest in a particular language repertoire, this creates benefits for all those who have already mastered the language(s) learned. This is due to network externalities, as presented earlier. By getting linguistic access to such people, you also offer them access to you. Everyone mastering the newly learned language can now communicate, trade, and work with members of the community. They can also settle in those communities where it is now possible to live a decent life without mastering the vernacular language. They benefit from the creation of a collective good – a language repertoire containing a vehicular language they already know – and they have fewer incentives to learn the vernacular language since both languages give access to enough people and opportunities. For example, the fact that an increasing proportion of the population speaks English across the world, and especially in Western countries, makes it easier each year for Anglophones to settle in those communities and even to work, socialize, get an education, etc., without needing to learn the vernacular language. Globalization has made it necessary for businesses to hire people who have mastered English, and for schools to train people to master English.

Therefore, more and more people are fluent in English, and more and more schools and businesses are now accessible to Anglophones in many non-English regions. Since the costs of settling in an urban area without speaking the local vernacular language are decreasing for anyone speaking English, and since people respond to incentives, we can expect more and more people living on a given territory without mastering the vernacular language.

This may sound morally irrelevant. We could argue that it is unfortunate but that there is nothing immoral in the fact that some languages are abandoned or are losing ground to other languages. Once again, this would be true in a world of unilingual individuals. If individuals wanted to switch to another language, there would be no moral justification to constrain them or to condemn their choice. But our world is different. Indeed, the pressure on vernacular languages is made all the more intense since vehicular languages are learned as second languages by speakers of those "endangered languages." This learning is not motivated by subtractive bilingualism, a desire to switch language, in most cases, but by additive bilingualism (Lambert 1981), a desire to expand the range of opportunities available. The moral problem doesn't stem from the disappearance or the weakening of a language or a language community, as De Schutter argues (2011). It stems from the reasons for this disappearance, namely that speakers of vehicular languages get the opportunity to free ride on the linguistic investment of minority language speakers. They get benefits from a public good they didn't contribute to, and by doing so they reduce the benefits the members of the linguistic community can expect from their investment.

The problematic behaviours targeted are of two different forms: free riding and parasitism. First, people investing in a language repertoire and learning a language produce a public good from which people who have already mastered this language can benefit without contributing to it. They *free ride* on the good produced by others as soon as they benefit from the language repertoire without contributing to it. They do not contribute to it as long as they do not respect the social roles associated with each language, that is, as long as they do not use the appropriate language in the appropriate contexts.

From a moral point of view, things get worse due to parasitism: some people transfer the costs of their linguistic choices onto others. By not respecting the social roles associated with each language in a specific social context, they threaten the stability of the language repertoire produced by the local community and the division of language labour desired by members of the community. Every time a vehicular language is used in a context where a vernacular should have been used, the latter loses value and the former gains value as a communication tool. Therefore, it becomes easier for more vehicular speakers to use the language or to settle in areas where vernacular languages otherwise prevail. Users of vehicular languages also get the upper hand in many conversations where they have a better mastery of the vehicular language than the local people.

This decreases the satisfaction that members of the community can expect from their language repertoire. Not only do they bear the costs of the production of the language repertoire others benefit from by learning the vehicular language, but they also get less benefit from this public good because others transfer the costs of communication onto them. The moral problem is therefore that people settling there or people abusing the language repertoire in a way that is undesirable for members of the community are benefiting from the good produced while at the same time transferring the costs of their choices onto members of the community. The language repertoire in which a community invested was meant to realize preferences in a precise and structured way. By not respecting this linguistic division of labour, people are free riding on others; they are abusing the collective good that those others produced in a way that is detrimental to them. As soon as we have free riding, some linguistic behaviour can be described as morally problematic and as producing inefficient results.

For the language repertoire created by individual members of a community to be stable and produce optimal results, for them to get the expected returns on their investment, some constraints on individual behaviour are necessary. These are directed to individuals outside of the language community as well as individuals inside the community who have invested in the creation of a particular language repertoire.

Following this, newcomers shouldn't abuse this investment by settling without learning the vernacular language. Since the option of living there permanently without mastering the vernacular language is only made possible by the investment of the local community in a vehicular language, and since they would be using the good produced in a way contrary to the aim of the producers of that good, they would be free riding on members of the community if they started to increase the social situations in which the vehicular language is used. They should respect the social roles associated to each language in order to avoid transferring the costs of their decisions to members of the local community.

Also, local people should avoid acting in ways that are individually beneficial but collectively problematic. This includes any behaviour that threatens the stability of the language repertoire. As long as a speaker is satisfied with the social roles associated with each language, they should act in accordance with it even though sometimes it will not be in their immediate interest. They should contribute to maintaining the social roles associated with the languages composing the language repertoire. For example, they should refrain from hiring employees who can't speak the vernacular language. Of course, we cannot expect people to avoid any behaviour that is detrimental to the division of linguistic labour, since this would require them to be rude and refuse to reply to anybody addressing them in anything but the vernacular language. Philippe Van Parijs has the nicest way of expressing this: "the more kindly people behave towards one another, the more savagely languages treat each other" (Van Parijs 2011). The more people are willing to be nice and tolerate violations of the local division of linguistic labour, the more pressure they create on the vernacular language. It would be unreasonable to expect people to act in an "unkind" way so as to protect their language repertoire. Every time someone is faced with a situation where the division of linguistic labour is not respected, he faces a collective action problem: individually, the costs of acting unkindly are higher than the costs to his language repertoire; collectively, the costs of those kind behaviours become enormous and threaten the stability of the language repertoire.

This "kindness" shouldn't be interpreted as indifference regarding the language that should or can be used in a particular social context. The reality is that these people are forced into a situation where they must choose between acting in accordance with moral norms specific to the linguistic domain, or in accordance with broader moral norms of kindness. Therefore, we won't convince too many people to be rude with those who do not respect the social division of linguistic labour, but we can understand and justify those who, out of conviction and in order to contribute and protect the collective linguistic good produced in their community, refuse to speak the vehicular language in ways that threaten the stability of the language repertoire.

Two points must now be clarified. First, it isn't everybody speaking the vehicular language on the territory that poses a problem. Tourists, temporary workers, visiting students and scholars, etc. are not expected to master the vernacular language, and it is precisely in order to be able to communicate with these people that it made sense to invest collectively and individually in learning second languages. An interaction in our second language with such people doesn't amount to free riding on their part or to an abuse of our linguistic repertoire. It is rather precisely the type of interaction we want and expect when we add a new language to our language repertoire. This explains in part the different moral reaction one gets when speaking French in Flanders or English in Quebec. The tourist addressing us in the vehicular language doesn't force us to adopt a behaviour that threatens the stability and the efficiency of the language repertoire we produced, as opposed to a local person.

Second, it is not the simple fact of not mastering the language that poses a problem. De Schutter (2011) is right when he argues that "there is no right to have your language spoken by others." If someone decided to settle somewhere without speaking the vernacular language, and if he just abstained from communicating with local people, we would have no moral argument to criticize his behaviour. It is not the fact of not speaking the vernacular language that represents a moral problem; it is rather the use of a language repertoire in an inadequate and undesirable way. The moral problem occurs when someone benefits from others' language repertoire and unilaterally imposes costs on them.

The problem is made even more serious due to network externalities. The value of the vernacular language diminishes each time it is replaced by or shares a social role with the vehicular language. Every time the second language replaces the vernacular language in some social roles, or every time many languages can be used for the same task, it reduces the value of the vernacular language and increases the vehicular language's value.

When the *lingua franca* starts being used in vernacular domains, it reduces the expected return on the linguistic investment made by native speakers of this vernacular language. As long as many languages on a territory are associated with different social roles, as long as they are sovereign on a given "territory," they maintain their necessity and represent an asset for anyone settling there (Laponce 1987). This "territorial" imperative doesn't have to be geographic. For example, we could consider that all internal affairs in a firm must be conducted in the vernacular language, no matter where the meetings are held. Such measures are meant to maintain the necessity of mastering the vernacular language, even in contexts where a vehicular language could be used. Which social tasks should be accomplished using which languages should be decided by members of the community and not left to individual rational choices, mainly because of the many forms of market failures presented earlier.

8. CONCLUSION

As in many other domains, we tend to disapprove of behaviours unilaterally imposing costs on individuals. Social and moral norms can be interpreted as ways of compensating for market failures and restricting individuals from benefiting from others' behaviour or from imposing the costs of their decisions on others. I have tried to show that we can consider that there are and should be such norms in the linguistic domain, and therefore that there are some contexts in which we are morally justified to feel annoyed if someone addresses us in our second language in a linguistic context where another language should have been used. The argument presented explains both why we are annoyed by some language behaviours and why the identity of the speaker addressing us in our second language changes our moral reaction. If the speaker is one of those we wanted to get access to when we learned the second language, we won't feel "morally exploited." However, if the person is abusing our investment and efforts, if he is imposing a language of our repertoire in the wrong social context, then we will react negatively, feeling rightly that an implicit moral norm is being violated.

In this chapter, the above argument is applied to individual behaviours and it identifies some moral norms circumscribing acceptable behaviours, the ones promising individual benefits without imposing costs onto others. Justifications for a political theory of language rights and language policies could also be derived from such analysis, arguing in favour of some application of the linguistic territoriality principle (Robichaud 2011). The justification is the same: it is necessary to constrain individual behaviours in order to produce optimal results and satisfy as many language preferences as possible. Linguistic freedom leads inevitably to linguistic free riding, and this is benefiting speakers of vehicular (usually dominant) languages at the expense of minority language speakers. Morality and justice can justify restrictions to this linguistic freedom, not in order to promote language survival, nor in order to contribute to language diversity, but as a way to protect individual autonomy and avoid the externalization of some choices' costs. These restrictions are not arbitrary costs imposed on some people; they are ways of avoiding or internalizing costs that would be imposed on some individuals and language communities. It has been argued that such restrictions are unjust since they treat others as means (De Schutter 2011). All to the contrary, they impose restrictions intended to protect minority speakers from being treated as means by other vehicular language speakers. They contribute to producing efficient and morally acceptable results in the linguistic domain.

The norms that will prove desirable and justified will depend on the linguistic context and on the linguistic preferences people have, and those preferences can be diverse and complex (Ginsburgh and Weber 2011). Investing in a good can legitimize the protection of it through the exclusion of some individuals or some behaviours. It is necessary in order to guarantee that learning a vehicular language for a minority speaker comes with new opportunities, not new threats. Also, since every individual and every language community would benefit from such norms in some contexts, we can conclude that there is no problem of fairness or recognition. Indeed, all languages won't be recognized as "morally adequate" or as official in *all* linguistic contexts; however, each language will be considered "morally adequate" or official in *some* contexts. We can therefore justify protecting the investment made by individuals in a given area, as long as we also accept that every community investing in a language repertoire will also be protected on a given territory or in some given social contexts.

REFERENCES

Arrow, Kenneth J. 1970. "Political and Economic Evaluation of Social Effects and Externalities." In *The Analysis of Public Output*, edited by J. Margolis, 1–30. Cambridge: National Bureau of Economic Research.

Barro, Robert J. 1996. *Getting It Right*. Cambridge, MA: MIT Press.

Church, Jeffrey, and Ian King. 1993. "Bilingualism and Network Externalities." *The Canadian Journal of Economics* 26, no. 2: 337–45.

Coase, Ronald H. 1988. "The Problem of Social Cost." In *The Firm, the Market and the Law*, 95–156. Chicago, IL: University of Chicago Press.

Crystal, David. 1997. *English as a Global Language*. Cambridge: Cambridge University Press.

Dalmazzone, Silvana. 1999. "L'économie de la langue : méthode des externalités de réseau." In *Explorer l'économie linguistique*, edited by Albert Breton, 69–94. Ottawa: Patrimoine canadien, ministère des Travaux publics et des Services gouvernementaux du Canada.

De Schutter, Helder. 2011. "The Linguistic Territoriality Principle: Heterogeneity and Freedom Problems." In *The Linguistic Territoriality Principle: Right Violation or Parity of Esteem?* edited by Philippe Van Parijs, 22–7. Re-Bel initiative, https://www.rethinkingbelgium.eu/rebel-initiative-ebooks/ebook-11-linguistic-territoriality-principle-right-violation-or-parity-of-esteem (accessed 6 July 2019).

De Swaan, Abram. 2001. *Words of the World*. Cambridge: Polity Press.

Fraser, Nancy, and Axel Honneth. 2003. *Redistribution or Recognition?: A Political-Philosophical Exchange*. New York: Verso.

Gauthier, David P. 1986. *Morals by Agreement*. Oxford, UK, and New York: Clarendon Press / Oxford University Press.

Grin, François. 2006. "Economic Considerations in Language Policy." In *An Introduction to Language Policy. Theory and Method*, edited by Thomas Ricento, 77–94. Malden, UK: Blackwell Publishing.

Grin, François, and François Vaillancourt. 1997. "The Economics of Multilingualism: Overview and Analytical Framework." *Annual Review of Applied Linguistics* 17: 43–65.

Ginsburgh, Victor, and Shlomo Weber. 2011. *How Many Languages Do We Really Need? The Economics of Linguistic Diversity*. Princeton, NJ: Princeton University Press.

Honneth, Axel. 1996. *The Struggle for Recognition: The Moral Grammar of Social Conflicts*. Cambridge, MA: MIT Press.

Katz, Michael L., and Carl Shapiro. 1985. "Network Externalities, Competition, and Compatibility." *The American Economic Review* 75, no. 3: 424–40.

Laïtin, David D. 1992. *Language Repertoires and State Construction in Africa*. Cambridge: Cambridge University Press.

Lambert, Wallace E. 1981. "Bilingualism and Language Acquisition." *Annals of the New York Academy of Sciences* 379: 9–22.

Laponce, Jean. 1987. *Languages and Their Territories*. Toronto: University of Toronto Press.

Lipsey, Richard G., and Kelvin Lancaster. 1956–57. "The General Theory of Second Best." *The Review of Economic Studies* 24, no. 1: 11–32.

Réaume, Denise. 2000. "Official-Language Rights: Intrinsic Value and the Protection of Difference." In *Citizenship in Diverse Societies*, edited by Will Kymlicka and Wayne Norman, 245–72. Oxford, UK: Oxford University Press.

Robichaud, David. 2011. "Justice et politiques linguistiques : Pourquoi les laisser-fairistes devraient exiger des interventions de l'État." *Philosophiques* 38, no. 2: 419–38.

– 2017. "A Market Failure Approach to Linguistic Justice." *Journal of Multilingual and Multicultural Development* 38, no. 7: 622–31.

Robichaud, David, and Helder De Schutter. 2012. "Language Is Just a Tool! On the Instrumentalist Approach to Language." In *The Cambridge Handbook on Language Policy*, edited by Bernard Spolsky, 124–45. Cambridge: Cambridge University Press.

Robichaud, David, and Patrick Turmel. 2010. "La transmission intergénérationnelle du patrimoine: un problème de justice." In *Générations équitables*, edited by Dan Sylvain and Jeorg Tremmel, 221–38. Paris: Éditions Connaissances et Savoirs.

Schelling, Thomas C. 1978. *Micromotives and Macrobehavior*. New York: Norton and Company.

Taylor, Charles, and Amy Gutmann. 1994. *Multiculturalism: Examining the Politics of Recognition*. Princeton, NJ: Princeton University Press.

Van Parijs, Philippe. 2011. *Linguistic Justice for Europe and for the World*. Oxford, UK: Oxford University Press.

Weinstock, Daniel. 2003a. "Le paradoxe des droits linguistiques." In *Communauté de droits, Droit des communautés*, edited by Ysolde Gendreau, 43–83. Montreal, QC: Éditions Thémis.

– 2003b. "The Antinomy of Language Rights." In *Language Rights and Political Theory*, edited by Will Kymlicka and Alan Patten, 250–70. Oxford, UK: Oxford University Press.

4

Operationalizing "Diversity" for Language Policy
Meeting Sociolinguistic and Ethical Challenges

FRANÇOIS GRIN

1. TAKING DIVERSITY SERIOUSLY

Linguistic diversity has been attracting growing interest over the past decades, and a succession of historical developments has kept this interest going. The story is a well-known one: in the wake of the Second World War, diversity and difference tended to have bad press, largely because of the horrendous uses to which the very notion of ethnicity had been put in the Nazi era. Similar suspicion surrounded the notion of "minority" for a number of years, and in the post-war period, political and scholarly discourse laid emphasis on commonalities and universality rather than differences and diversity. This emphasis is eloquently reflected in the adoption by the General Assembly of the United Nations, in December 1948, of the Universal Declaration of Human Rights.[1]

The re-emergence of linguistic and cultural diversity as acceptable and normal features of modern societies has been a slow process, not least because of a deeply entrenched perception of diversity as the epitome of backwardness (May 2001). Joshua Fishman recalls that in the 1960s, a colleague dismissed as pleonastic the proposed title of a book he was then co-editing (Fishman, Ferguson, and Dasgupta 1968): by mentioning, in the book's title, the language problems "of developing nations," weren't the authors stating the obvious? For only "developing nations" could have "language problems," which would be solved by development – usually through the erosion of diversity and the attendant uniformization, at least at state level.

Since then, we have witnessed the "ethnic revival" of the late 1960s and 1970s (Fishman 1989, 530ff), the fall of the Berlin Wall with the reassertion and increased visibility of long-suppressed expressions of linguistic and cultural difference (Sanguin 1993), and, of course, large-scale migration. The importance of contemporary migration flows may have less to do with their size than with their increasingly multidirectional character, giving rise to what Hollinger (1995) has called the "diversification of diversity." The very word "diversity" now appears inadequate to some commentators, who recommend talking about "super-diversity" (Vertovec 2007), and one of the aims of this chapter is to assess the relevance of "super-diversity" as distinct from "diversity." As we shall see, there are many reasons, both positive and normative, for sticking to the term "diversity," making it clear, however, that it refers to the joint presence of various, fluid, and constantly evolving manifestations (Urry 2007).

Much has changed since the post-war years, and in present-day scholarly discourse about the sociological and political challenges confronting modern societies, references to diversity have become *de rigueur* – interestingly displacing references to "multiculturalism," a term which, at the time of writing, is surrounded by a distinct whiff of obsolescence.

Linguistic diversity has also become a policy object, with frequent references, in scientific and political discourse, to language policy or the management of linguistic diversity. This development raises two questions. The first, which will not be discussed here in detail, is that the interdisciplinarity such an endeavour demands is only rarely realized.[2] The second, which proceeds from the first, is that (possibly as a result of inadequate investment in interdisciplinary work) the very concept of diversity is underspecified, and its operational relevance for language policy selection and design, duly incorporating knowledge provided by a vast array of disciplinary approaches complementing each other, remains insufficiently explored. This is why this chapter proposes to re-examine some important implications of the concept of linguistic "diversity" and to assess its appropriateness for the selection, design, and evaluation of language policies.

This chapter attempts to pursue and expand a line of questioning first opened in a contribution to a book edited by Kymlicka and Patten (2003).[3] It is organized as follows.

In section 2, I argue that "diversity" offers a useful entry point for dealing with present-day social challenges because it enables us to consider jointly many components of diversity. These encompass not only indigenous minorities and diasporic groups, but also mobile groups of people including migrants in the traditional sense as well as "expats" (luxury migrants, as it were), foreign students, and retirees moving to more pleasant, but also linguistically different, surroundings for their sunset years (Gustafson 2008). What is more, diversity as understood here is not only constituted of stable groups made up of persons defined on the basis of their "linguistic attributes" – that is, the range of skills they possess in a first language (L1, which is often, though not necessarily, a "mother tongue") and other languages (L2, L3, etc.) picked up during their personal history. Linguistic diversity can be viewed as multidimensional and fluctuating, and encompass not just *skills*, but *use*. This opens up the possibility of including, in our characterization of linguistic diversity, eminently fluid communities of practice (McElhinny 2012). With this broad perspective, the "diversity" discussed here may be called "complex diversity," as proposed by Kraus (2012; 2018).

Traditionally, the literature on diversity has been focused on given types of established language groups, and was accordingly broken up into relatively separate lines of discourse produced by separate scientific circles with their distinct journals and conference circuits. One such line of discourse was devoted to "minorities" (with a further separation between "national minorities" and "linguistic minorities"), and another to migration issues – with the mantle of "multiculturalism" being largely hogged by the latter. Fortunately, the barriers between the professional subcultures characterizing these two (main) lines of discourse and research have partly been dismantled since the late 1990s. This change probably reflects the empirical realization that diversity, perhaps as a result of "globalization," is becoming increasingly multifaceted, encouraging researchers to consider these facets jointly rather than in mutual isolation. For the same reason, "diversity" may also serve to circumvent some limitations inherent to arguments couched in terms of rights (which tend to rely on established categories, even when such categories need to be questioned).

Whereas section 2 is concerned with overcoming conceptual divisions that are proving increasingly irrelevant (particularly from a policy standpoint), section 3 explains why it is useful to avoid what might be seen as the symmetrical risk: namely, that of muddling the questions at hand for the sake of their joint or integrated treatment. Some currently popular discourses about diversity (sometimes touting the "super-diversity" label) risk creating other problems with serious implications for diversity itself as well as for social justice. I shall try to show that one problematic implication of "super-diversity" – and associated notions such as "(poly-)languaging" – is that some forms of diversity, along with the associated policy questions, are disregarded. The policy priorities that this line of discourse, by exalting the notion of "languaging," tends to encourage may, paradoxically, endanger linguistic diversity and potentially defeat their professed purpose, while posing serious problems of human rights. A clear concept of diversity can help us prevent such regrettable omissions and their associated risks, whether in scientific analysis or in the formulation of policy responses.

Next, I argue in favour of an approach to policy analysis that goes beyond the mere quest of an "optimal" solution – or, to use a popular if hackneyed phrase, "best practice." I attempt to show, in section 4 of this chapter, that an expanded perspective on the use of policy analysis brings two interconnected advantages. The first advantage is that it offers an analytically consistent receptacle to accommodate findings from terrain research. Indeed, one of the likely reasons for the continuing disconnection between some strands of sociolinguistic research and actual policy development may have to do with the highly aggregated, macro-level positioning of policy analysis as a discipline. As we shall see, a proper use of the concept of diversity can in large part obviate this difficulty. The second advantage is political acceptability: instead of using policy analysis to identify the "best" solution and nudge social reality closer to it through well-designed policies, it can serve to operate the reverse movement – namely, to modify costs and benefits associated with existing diversity in order to increase the latter's net value. Policy, therefore, is not only about moving the existing towards the optimal, but also about moving the optimal towards the existing. This is directly relevant to the ethical issues with which language policy issues are necessarily bound up.

In section 5, I turn to the core of these ethical issues by discussing the perspective on diversity proposed in Van Parijs's influential work on linguistic justice (particularly Van Parijs 2011). Since the disciplinary background of this chapter is not normative political theory, the approach to ethical dimensions proposed here will seem crude to political theorists. However, the point of section 5 is, in a sense, to remain "a-ethical": it is not intended to characterize alternative policy scenarios as more or less conforming to ethical standards.[4] The focus of this chapter is on the development of a conceptual tool that can serve to identify (and, further down the line, to measure) the allocative and distributive implications of alternative language policies. Clearly, the distributive implications raise inherently ethical issues, but I leave it to specialists, in particular political philosophers, to transpose these distributive implications in formal ethical terms.

2. "DIVERSITY" AS THE CORNERSTONE OF AN INTEGRATED APPROACH TO POLICY

In an earlier exploration of the relevance of "diversity" (see note 3), I submitted that it should be more explicitly conceptualized as the centre of gravity of the management of multilingualism. The basic idea, by deliberately shifting the focus away from the concept of rights, was not to suggest that rights are irrelevant, but that a policy analysis approach emphasizing the identification of the benefits and costs of alternative policies should accompany the normative considerations of political theorists (e.g. Taylor 1994; Kymlicka 1995; Patten 2009; Robichaud and de Schutter 2012), or the closely related legal considerations (Henrard and Dunbar 2008) usually brought to bear on the matter. A policy analysis–based approach, fundamentally embedded in the discourse of advantages and drawbacks or, perhaps more bluntly, benefits and costs, could help break out of a common limitation of normative arguments (and legal ones as well, to the extent that the reach of legal instruments is also liable to be contested): namely, the risk of ending up preaching to the converted (Grin 2005).

This is why it seems reasonable to explore, through the prism of policy analysis, the question of what language rights should be granted to whom. This, in turn, requires looking at the granting of rights not as something mandated by ethical considerations, but as the logical consequence of the fact that the granting of rights has welfare effects. If it can be shown that aggregate welfare gains can be achieved, perhaps this avenue makes sense to garner support, as it were, among the unconverted – just as Van Parijs (2011, 191) puts it: "those who want to make a persuasive case for the value of linguistic diversity do realize that they need arguments that appeal to less factional interests [than those of professional linguists or translators]." In a sense, this approach can be seen as shifting the focus from a deontological to a teleological perspective.

The core feature of a public policy approach, also when applied to linguistic and cultural diversity, is that it thinks not in terms of "rights," but in terms of alternative scenarios in the handling of diversity. The alternatives can be described in quantitative or qualitative terms; the former, however, requires agreement on a metric to describe lesser or greater degrees of diversity. A back-up in terms of rights, themselves justified on ethical grounds, remains obviously necessary, but the selection and design of language policies will emphasize the allocative and distributive effects of alternative policies. Putting it differently, each proposed policy will be assessed in terms of its efficiency (in increasing aggregate welfare) and fairness (in terms of the acceptability of the resulting distribution of material and symbolic resources). Putting this in slightly different terms for the sake of clarity, we may say that instead of pondering the rights which, for ethical reasons, should or should not be granted to group X in context Y, or possibly, generalizing from this case, to any group having the characteristics of X in any context having the characteristics of Y, a policy analysis approach considers alternative scenarios (say, S1 and S2, possibly more) that imply the granting of rights to various groups, and asks two questions. First, what are the corresponding costs and benefits, in the aggregate, and how much do these costs and benefits amount to (thus operationalizing "efficiency")? Second, to whom do these benefits and costs accrue, and in what amounts (providing a form of metric for "fairness") (Gazzola 2014; Gazzola and Grin 2017)? Operating in this way is not pure speculation. It is, in fact, very practical, and this approach has already been implemented on a large scale in the case of the European Charter for Regional or Minority Languages.[5]

Rights-based perspectives tend to separate the rights granted to different types of groups at a relatively early stage of reasoning; it need not be so, but it is often the case. Typically, rights-based discourses begin by projecting a linguistic and cultural "other," and the process of projection often remains inadequately examined. It implies a recognition of the "non-other" as a norm, whose legitimacy is usually unquestioned. Work by Barry (2001) offers a well-known example of this type of omission.[6] The process of construction of the "other" can hardly escape falling back on established empirical distinctions between "autochthonous" vs. "immigrant" communities, thus quickly producing different types of "others" deserving different types of rights, or different levels of the same rights – something which hampers the production of a general theory of the treatment of "non-majorities."[7] By contrast, the public policy approach, while taking account of distinctions between majority and minority, as well as between autochthonous and immigrant communities, attempts to cut through these notions so that such labels do not imply a priori constraints on the nature of the policy response. Putting it differently, it aims to recast policies, at least at a general stage of the analysis, not as a matter of "minority v. majority," or "autochthonous communities vs. immigrant groups," but as a principled response to the challenges of linguistic diversity itself as a crucial feature of society. It makes it easier to propose language regimes based on the simultaneous consideration of rights to indigenous and migrant groups (Grin 1996; 2016).

The foregoing is in keeping with a modern vision of language policy as one whose actual object is to modify, in an efficient and fair direction, people's linguistic environment. Even if this expression has yet to gain wider currency, it cuts straight to the heart of language policy. Most of the general definitions of language policy are descendants of Cooper's (1989) discussion of the nature and scope of language policy, and they generally gravitate towards variants of the following: a systematic, rational, theory-based effort at the societal level to modify the linguistic environment with a view to increasing welfare (Grin 2003c). Against this backdrop, the granting of rights follows, but as a means to an end.

The reference to welfare in the preceding paragraph clearly requires the identification and measurement of the benefits and costs involved with alternative scenarios. However, it is worth repeating that these benefits and costs may be material, financial, or symbolic. There is no reason, at least from a policy analytical standpoint, to restrict the weighing of the advantages and drawbacks of competing scenarios to material and financial considerations. Contrary to a widespread belief, non-material and symbolic dimensions are a legitimate, even necessary, part of the economic assessment of policy choices.[8]

If the protection of diversity is the issue – adopting a teleological perspective which, oddly, wends its way in and out of the work of major contributors to this debate – some simple rules follow for the arbitration between potentially conflicting rights. In particular, "choices that favor relatively threatened components of diversity should take precedence over choices that favor less threatened components of diversity" (Grin 2003a, 185) – a decision rule reminiscent of John Rawls's third principle of justice.

The relevance of an approach that considers "diversity" in the aggregate increases with globalization and the attendant integration of hitherto distinct "linguaspheres," just like a form of world environmental governance may eventually be taking shape in the wake of the Kyoto protocols, and a world governance of human rights is progressively emerging with the increasing clout of the International Court of Justice. We may therefore envision, down the line, the emergence of a kind of world linguistic governance.[9]

3. QUESTIONING DIVERSITY: CURRENT CHALLENGES

The foregoing does not mean that "diversity," as an analytical construct and as a tool for action, is problem-free. It has been questioned from very distinct perspectives, and for the sake of brevity, I shall concentrate on two main lines of criticism.

The first is mostly political in its inspiration and concerns the sources and implications of elevating "(linguistic) diversity" (or the closely associated notion of "multilingualism") as a policy goal.[10] This criticism finds expression in what we might call a neo-Bourdieusian perspective, which stresses the roles that language (and, increasingly, pluri- and multilingualism) can play in the reproduction of the social order (Tollefson 1991; Duchêne 2007; Heller 2007; Duchêne and Heller 2011). Particularly in recent contributions, these authors take issue with the fact that (threatened) languages, and the overall diversity of which they are presented as components, are "recast as a matter of added value," and criticize the allegedly a-political nature of some of the work undertaken for the protection and promotion of endangered languages. Their line of argument has been neatly summarized by Muysken (2010, 96): "assumptions underlying the defense of minority languages are frequently concealed, and ... often there are interested parties that remain hidden. They [the authors] also criticize the commodification of minority languages, where language documentation is portrayed as creating a speaker-proof package of linguistic materials."

Up to a point, these critical observations are insightful and well-taken; their virtue is to keep us alert to our own conceptions and interests, as well as our implicit assumptions about language. But it is hard to see how far they practically matter, largely because the claims made are positioned at a very "meta" level. They usually offer commentary about discourse or purport to reconstruct discourse on language policies and their underlying motivations. In other words, this line of work is less about the actual management of linguistic diversity through policy than about the discourse of policy. However, this line of investigation, though fully legitimate, may well end up serving the very interests these criticisms set out to expose.

Let us take a closer look at the argument. It is of course useful to be reminded that language practices are always socially and politically embedded. But it is precisely a strong awareness of the social, political, and, one might add, economic embeddedness of language, and of the fact that language comes alive through its users (not only its "speakers"), that has animated important developments in sociolinguistics and language planning over the past thirty years. These renewed perspectives on language, which have arguably contributed significantly to the re-legitimation and reclaiming, as valid modes of social expression, of languages such as Welsh and Basque, may well, and relevantly so, rest on a questioning of the fact that some languages have been locked into radically un-economic roles.

The critical sociolinguistics approach warns against the "commodification" and occasionally the "reification" allegedly permeating language policy discourse. The term "commodification," which is unfortunately used in a rather vague fashion (and its application to language implicitly considered unproblematic), harks back to Marxian scholarship and usually refers to the treatment as marketable goods and services of objects, services, and ideas (and even, in the case of slavery, human beings) not normally regarded as marketable. This extends to (linguistic) "diversity," which may then also be "commodified." However, this criticism may be a crude example of the fallacy of composition: viewing language as a tool that communities may decide to recast as a "marketable" object and use with deliberate intent does not mean that language becomes only a commodity and stops being, say, a means through which social actors construct meaning, individually and collectively. If users of Irish find it useful, in order to increase the visibility and long-term prospects for the Irish language, to market the Irish character of the city of Galway, it is hard to see why (and on what authority) commentators should object.[11] Obviously, it is important to remain aware of the underlying interests in any language policy enterprise. However, this has been a well-established notion for a long time, and deriving its full implications (along with the necessary methodology) is precisely the task of distributive analysis, as part of policy selection, design, and evaluation: the very function of distributive analysis is to identify, under various policy scenarios, who wins, who loses, and how much.

A related though indirect criticism of the notion of diversity is that the "globalized new economy" presents specific characteristics connected with the processes of commodification and reification of the languages that make up this diversity. Let us note in passing that "the new economy" is a term which economists use very sparingly, recognizing that it may have different meanings.[12] Economists would generally contend that although we may witness new forms of consumption, production, and exchange, the core economic processes at hand remain much the same. Heller and Duchêne (2011) note that the linkage between state-backed processes of construction of "languages" as discrete entities on the one hand (to serve the political ends of state-building), and "commodification" on the other hand, challenges received notions of globalization, and that we are witnessing an "intensification of modernity." There again (and bearing in mind our earlier reservations regarding the notion of "commodification"), the point is well taken (in particular its implicit rejection of the notion of "post-modernity"): our construction of "diversity" as a policy object needs to be flexible enough to accommodate the full range of complex sociopolitical realities of globalization.

However, it does not follow that diversity is not a relevant policy object, and earlier sociological research (in particular Rossiaud 1997, extending the theory of social movements) has already provided us with some useful tools for approaching diversity in globalization: ongoing processes of subjectivation, a key marker of modernity, affect individual and collective identity creation. The deepening of the inner logic of modernity, therefore, brings about profound changes in the ways in which actors use language(s) in political action and in the construction of meaning. As such processes unfold at a global level, bringing in linguistic elements of diversity imported from well beyond the local pool of such elements, it is appropriate to view the reinvention of the role of language in subjectivation processes as an instance of *moNdernisation* – a compound, coined by Rossiaud, of the French words "mondialisation" (globalization) and "modernité" (modernity).[13]

The second line of criticism of diversity that I wish to discuss here comes from some strands of applied linguistics in which the emphasis is resolutely placed on the idea that "diversity" is *passé*, and that it has been decisively displaced by "super-diversity." Relatedly, some have claimed that as a result of the increasingly diverse forms that diversity takes (a point already mentioned in the first section of this chapter), the very notion that people use "languages" ought to be replaced by the notion that people are "languaging" (Jørgensen et al. 2011) – that is, they are using a linguistic repertoire in which languages such as "English," "French," "Swahili," and "Kurdish," far from being discrete entities, blend into each other; *ergo*, languages as they are used blend into each other to such an extent that it no longer makes sense to refer to "named" languages (Blommaert, Rampton, and Spotti 2011). Edwards (2011, 33–8), dismisses this approach as "pretentiousness and barren verbiage." Without meaning to enter this debate here, let me observe that if these pages were written in, say, Lezgin (a Caucasian language written using its own variant of the Cyrillic alphabet) or Burushaski (a linguistic isolate that can be written using the Urdu variant of the Arabic alphabet), there is a strong likelihood that most readers would no longer understand them. Thus, it seems quite likely that the concepts of "English," "Lezgin," and "Burushaski" are analytically relevant and practically useful. Interestingly, the "languaging" approach, whose predominant focus is face-to-face oral communication, has little to say about the written word, although the importance of the latter, if anything, has increased rather than declined with the spread of computer-based technological treatment of language and communication.

Yet even if we chose to ignore all written communication, the notion that actors are "languaging" rather than speaking (using, of course, their respective idiolects) variants of "named" languages such as English, French, or Urdu certainly strains credibility. It is of course true (and hardly novel) that "languages and language varieties, both across people and communities, as well as within individual linguistic repertoires, lack sharp boundaries" (Edwards 2012, 36), but if a speaker (say, at an internal work meeting taking place at the European headquarters of some multinational corporation) were to abruptly switch from English or French to Lezgin or Burushaski, she would no longer be understood by most – whether participants are "languaging" or not. Even if we allow for the highly diverse demolinguistic make-up of modern cities, the idea that "named" languages are no longer sufficient to describe oral face-to-face communication beggars belief.

Interestingly, this line of reasoning is based on no quantitative data whatsoever. Not only does an overwhelming proportion of total oral interactions on any given day take place between people who share one language (natively spoken or not), but most people do interact in recognizable variants of named languages.[14] Communicational situations are infinitely varied, and they certainly include duly documented situations where actors freely mix their own and each other's linguistic repertoires; but they are far outnumbered by communicational situations in which actors use perfectly identifiable "named" languages, and it is hard to see what precise or acute need is served by re-labelling "diversity" as "super-diversity."

The main point, however, lies elsewhere: the celebration of "super-diversity" seems to march hand-in-hand with neglect for, perhaps even dismissal of, the components of diversity: that is, languages themselves. Relatedly, the cultural experience (and future culture-related potential) with which these linguistic manifestations of diversity are connected gets short shrift. Advocacy of threatened languages, even by their very speakers, may suddenly be deemed politically suspect as embodying resistance to a shapeless but pervasive super-diversity. In their critical commentary of Martin-Jones, Blackledge, and Creese (2012), Phillipson and Skutnabb-Kangas (2013, 658) crisply summarize the unease that some facets of the discourse of super-diversity may inspire: "The impression is created that while social injustice regrettably occurs, sociolinguists of 'our times' should celebrate living in the best of all possible linguistic worlds, and produce academic theorization attuned to it" (see also Pavlenko 2019).

Dismissing languages to celebrate diversity or claiming that diversity ought to be dissolved in a "super-diversity" whose elements are made invisible does seem self-contradictory. After all, the very idea of diversity is meaningless if it is not made up of identifiably different elements – even if, obviously, the nature and extent of the differences between them do change over time. But more to the point, the discourse of super-diversity amounts to denying actors the right to linguistic and cultural maintenance, as well as the associated possibility of drawing on language and culture in the construction of individual and collective identity. The defense of (minority) language rights may then be dismissed as a form of essentialist resistance to a disembodied form of plurality, and so could, further down the line, the defense of bigger languages. This raises the uncomfortable question of whether proponents of "super-diversity" are sincerely interested in diversity. But beyond this ideological ambivalence, it also raises serious concerns for linguistic justice, because super-diversity is not neutral. Language is power, and if the protection and promotion of less influential languages is delegitimized in discourse – and subsequently weakened in practice – the dominance of other languages can only be reinforced. This applies in particular to English as the "hypercentral" language of globalization (De Swaan 2001), but of course the issue would be no different if Lezgin, Burushaski, or Urdu happened to occupy this globally dominant position.

Summing up, the discourse of "super-diversity" is not only conceptually and empirically problematic; it can also be an engine of disempowerment of the oppressed (Grin 2018). For all these reasons, sticking to "diversity" (defined on the basis of *identifiably different elements*) probably offers a safer basis for analytically and ethically sound language policies.

4. BROADENING THE FUNCTIONS OF LANGUAGE POLICY

This chapter is not concerned with establishing, either in a policy analysis perspective or on ethical grounds, whether linguistic diversity is good. Its point is to ascertain whether using the concept of "diversity" can help in the selection and design of efficient and fair language policy. Policy analysis crucially rests on the principle of comparison between competing scenarios carrying benefits and advantages, where the comparison is organized in terms of the criteria of efficiency and fairness. For the sake of the argument, let us assume that linguistic diversity can be measured along one simple quantitative dimension. In other words, there is "more" or "less" diversity," just like there can be "more" or "less" environmental quality, "more" or "less" gender equality, as measured by one or many – possibly compound – indicators. This does not exclude comparisons between scenarios that differ in terms of the quality or modalities of linguistic diversity characterizing them, but asserts, rather, that many such comparisons can be projected onto a quantitative scale. We only need indicators for them, and such indicators must be seen as relevant to the question of linguistic diversity. In general, the extent of the diversity of our "linguistic environment," which is the fundamental object of language policy, will be positively correlated to the degree of "diversitism" (or diversity-friendliness) of public policies, just like environmental quality, in the biophysical sense of the term, will, all other things being equal, be positively affected by environmentally friendly policies.

The state cannot *not* have a language policy, if only to decide in what language laws are written or how many languages will be used for tax collection purposes. It will also need to decide what formal status is given to various languages spoken by autochthonous minorities and immigrant communities. Hence, its language policy can be more or less "diversitist" and result in more or less diversity. Therefore, the function of policy instruments is analytically equivalent, whether they are used to identify and locate an appropriate degree of diversity or of "diversitism."

In general, more diversity can be assumed to generate more benefits and more costs. Benefits arise for at least some citizens, because given a certain demolinguistic makeup, the use of a wider range of languages will enable citizens speaking languages other than what would have been the default language (or languages) to have easier, more comfortable access to a wider range of information such as legal texts, official forms, product labels, instructions for product use, and safety notices. Respect for diversity is also, in Van Parijs's terms, a reflection of "parity of esteem" between linguistically different groups. Symmetrically, more diversity entails more costs, just like maintaining clean air or clean water, or protecting a region's flora and fauna, is not costless.

Benefits (B), Costs (C),
Net value (NV)

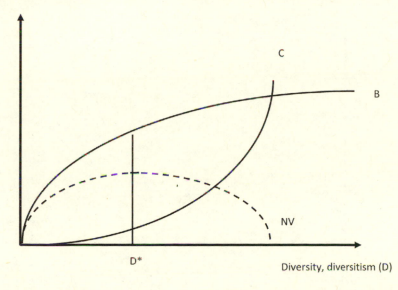

Figure 4.1 Diversity and optimality

The question, therefore, is how the benefits derived from living in a linguistically more diverse environment on the one hand, and the costs associated with this linguistically more diverse environment on the other hand, balance each other, because what matters, from a policy analysis standpoint, is the net value obtained by deducting costs from benefits. Let us bear in mind that both benefits and costs need not be material or financial, and should in fact include symbolic ones. The degree of diversity for which this difference (or "net value" NV) is highest is – in the most basic use of this analytical framework – the optimal solution, and the aim of public policy ought to be to nudge the degree of diversity towards this optimal level (D*).

In the absence of further information, there is no guarantee that D* is strictly positive.[15] However, even if it may be low, it is also unlikely to be zero, because a very general rule found throughout economics is that benefits rise at a decreasing rate, while costs rise at an increasing rate; this implies, in graphical terms, a concave benefits curve (B) and a convex cost curve (C), as shown in Figure 4.1 (already discussed in Grin 2003a). This very general (and

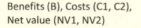

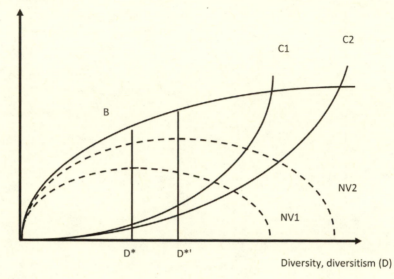

Figure 4.2 Diversity and optimality with downward shift of the cost curve

plausible) assumption is enough to ensure that optimum diversity will generally be positive, and that absolute uniformity will never be optimal.

Now, even if it has been possible to locate D*, it is not always possible or
desirable, including for political and ethical reasons, to enact policies that
move existing diversity (DE) towards D*. This problem is particularly likely
to arise if DE > D*. Forcing DE downwards might require a reduction in "diversitism," and hence in language rights, a course of action that could drift
dangerously close to xenophobia or ethnic cleansing and would most likely
be unacceptable from a normative standpoint.

The dialogue between the deontological, rights-based perspective and the
teleological, welfare-based perspective suggests another mission for language
policy. Its function is not only to locate D* and tell us how to reach it. It may
also be used to shift some of the curves in order to move D* closer to DE. Most
commonly, its mission may also be to shift the cost curve downwards, so that
the net value is maximized at a higher level of D, which we may call D*', as
shown in Figure 4.2: the principle, therefore, is not so much to make existing

diversity conform to some technically defined optimum, but rather to find ways to lower the costs of diversity so that existing diversity becomes optimal.

A downward shift of the cost curve is exactly what some forms of language policy are trying to achieve. One example is support for bilingual education. Bilingual education is, by comparison with traditional second-language instruction, a cheaper way to generate a linguistic environment characterized by a higher degree of (sustainable) multilingualism.

An upward shift of the benefits curve would result in a similar effect: the optimal degree of diversity would move to the right, and edge closer to existing diversity DE. To the extent that many benefits may be reinterpreted as "negative costs" (and vice-versa), it is not essential, for the purposes of this chapter, to devote a specific discussion to upward shifts of the benefits curve. Distinctions between the two types of shifts, however, are more important at the later stage where practical policy measures are designed.

The practical challenge, of course, is how to measure empirically the benefit and cost functions, which can then be plotted as curves. At this time, the problem defies general treatment, and only partial solutions have been devised, addressing specific parts of the problem of optimal diversity. For example, Ginsburgh and Weber (2011) end up recommending three, four, or five official languages for the European Union (instead of the current twenty-four), depending on the assumptions made regarding the nature and magnitude of benefits and costs, which imply that costs overtake benefits at different levels of diversity. Unfortunately, a typical limitation of this line of work is that the benefits of diversity taken into account are limited to communication, whereas other aspects ought to be considered, including esteem, direct enjoyment, or positive effects on creativity and innovation. Even if "communication" were sufficient, it is usually understood in the very narrow sense of information transfer, whereas communication theory shows that communication does not just pursue informational goals – that is, it is not just "informatory," but also "cooperative" (fostering team spirit, say) and "strategic" (persuading or charming others) (Paulré 1993).

One solution is to give up some of the ambition of generality in order to develop coordinated but theme-specific analyses devoted to different facets of language policy. This is the strategy adopted in a large-scale research project called MIME ("Mobility and Inclusion in Multilingual Europe," spanning four years from 2014 to 2018), supported by the European Union and combining eleven different disciplines (Grin et al. 2018).[16] Theme-specific approaches are used to (i) identify benefits and costs with respect to a given decision (such as choosing the number of official languages in an organization); (ii) formulate scenarios in which these benefits and costs appear, spelling out explicitly how they would manifest themselves in each scenario;[17] and (iii) evaluate costs and benefits. There is uneven experience across domains in such evaluations, particularly at an integrated level. A promising instrument for assessing less well-known advantages and drawbacks of diversity is *contingent valuation*, until now applied to environmental assets and other complex choices but never, to our knowledge, to language policy scenarios.

5. ON LANGUAGE DIVERSITY AND LINGUISTIC JUSTICE

Let us finally turn to quite a different perspective on diversity, presented in Van Parijs's book entitled *Linguistic Justice* (2011), which contains a chapter offering one of the most targeted discussions of linguistic diversity available in the literature to date.

There is no reason to object to the groundwork of Van Parijs's argument, namely, the distinction between three dimensions of diversity: richness (the number of components of diversity), evenness (the degree in symmetry in the relative importance of these components), and distance (the degree of non-resemblance between them). Operationalizing these dimensions in terms of the "complex diversity" discussed in this chapter opens up a vast field of research. Equally relevant is the distinction made between the levels at which diversity is perceived: within units $[\alpha]$, across units $[\gamma]$, or in terms of qualitative inter-unit differentiation $[\beta]$. Assuming agreement, on the basis of the foregoing concepts, on what we mean by diversity, I concur with much of the discussion in *Linguistic Justice* about whether linguistic diversity is a "curse" or a "treasure." I also by and large agree that among the arguments in favour of diversity, one of the strongest is that linguistic diversity is a condition of cultural diversity, and hence a guarantee of freedom.

Unfortunately, Van Parijs is not content with the argument that linguistic diversity, as a condition of cultural diversity, ultimately constitutes a guarantee of freedom, dismissing this notion as "speculative." However, the opposite view, which he holds, is at least as speculative. Indeed, it is not easy to make a watertight case backed up by sound econometric estimates for the argument that diversity *guarantees* freedom. But it is even more dubious to argue that cultures do not differ, and that linguistic difference is not a key part of that difference. In fact, it could even make up *most* of the content of that difference, but it still would not follow that linguistic diversity is *ipso facto* worthless or irrelevant.[18] Living in a multi-polar world does matter to those who fear uniformity, and linguistic diversity is, very plausibly, a key condition of *multi-polarity*. Multi-polarity may be desired for its own sake, or because of a dislike of the alternatives, which may take the form of caving in under the pressures of the powerful. Whether "power" speaks English, French, Mandarin, Lezgin, or Burushaski is of no importance; and Van Parijs's summary dismissal (2011, 31–6) of those who fear "Anglo-Saxon" ideological domination contains no argument whatsoever that could assuage such fears. Van Parijs then notes that linguistic diversity may defeat its own purpose because, by definition, it reduces access to the freedom-enhancing range of expressions of culture that would justify diversity in the first place. The argument is odd, because it completely ignores the possibilities of communication afforded by foreign language learning (including, but not confined to, a *lingua franca*), by translation and interpreting, and by another strategy which is entirely neglected in his book, namely, *intercompréhension*, or receptive skills in related languages (ten Thije and Zeevaert 2007; Conti and Grin 2008). No evidence is put forward to justify the claim that the costs of overcoming linguistic barriers (costs that would allegedly be spared by the adoption of a common language) would surpass the benefits from the generic diversity (whatever its nature) that is correlated with linguistic diversity. But as we have seen in the preceding section, it is in fact extremely unlikely that optimum diversity can ever be zero.

The heart of the matter is probably that Van Parijs discounts all too readily the widespread desire not to be overwhelmed or absorbed by bigger "linguaspheres," and actors' willingness to devote symbolic and material resources to the preservation of their difference from others. This willingness could in principle concern the preservation of diversity in the aggregate, but it is more likely to manifest itself with respect to the linguistic and cultural markers of one's group. Such markers are nonetheless part and parcel of aggregate diversity and they are a necessary condition of multi-dimensional "complex diversity." This desire may well trump many other concerns citizens might have, such as the wish to facilitate the financial transfers that encourage equality of welfare (Van Parijs 2004) and/or equality of opportunity across social groups. Even groups who are liable to suffer materially from such choices of diversity maintenance make them. A case in point is Quebec, where language legislation has arguably reduced the range of economic opportunities accessible to residents – or at least, so it has been stridently claimed in the 1970s and 1980s by opponents of this legislation. Social actors have nonetheless made this choice. Incidentally, their economic effects are probably much less than is often believed; economic estimates suggest a net effect of less than half a percentage point of GDP for the Quebec economy (Vaillancourt 1987).

Thus, the whole "anti-diversity" argument based on the fact that it would detract from actors' readiness to finance wider economic solidarity flounders for the same reason that Van Parijs has dismissed earlier arguments in favour of diversity: if actors do not care all that much about economic solidarity, and if they value difference no less, that should be enough, from a liberal perspective, to justify pro-diversity policies. Just like protesters opposing budget cuts to education have come up with the catchy slogan "If you think education is too expensive, try ignorance," we should ponder the relative attractiveness of continuing diversity on the one hand, and uniformity on the other hand. This sobering reminder, along with the observation that those who least seem to mind the perspective of uniformity are, more often than not, themselves native speakers (or occasionally highly fluent secondary speakers) of a dominant language, suggests that diversity should not be thrown overboard as lightly as some advocates of a single *lingua franca* would have us do.

Ultimately, we are left with an empirical question, very much along the lines of what Muysken (quoted earlier) writes. How much is a language worth – and, by implication, how much is diversity worth? There is, I believe, no way to avoid this question, along with all the conceptually complex, methodologically demanding, and sometimes also plain tedious work it entails. Diversity is, in conclusion, more than a relevant but ancillary concept for language policy; there is much to suggest that is an indispensable one. Therefore, we may have no choice but to try to operationalize it, even if this has to be done not in the form of a grand design answering once and for all the question of "how much is diversity worth?" but in the more pragmatic form of partial, but interrelated and mutually compatible, approaches to specific language policy decisions.

NOTES

1   See https://www.un.org/en/universal-declaration-human-rights/index.html (accessed 6 July 2019).

2   One would expect language policy research to import concepts and methods from policy analysis, also encompassing distributive considerations anchored in normative political theory. This type of development has been observed with respect to other issues such as health, transport, or the environment, or even in the broad range of "social policies," for which a robust policy analysis perspective has emerged (European Commission 2008). However, the interdisciplinary linkage often remains aspirational. Important tracts of socio-linguistic literature, while mentioning language policy and using the word "policy" in their titles, turn out not to address policy questions. Their focus, rather, is on neighbouring but distinct issues, with three theme areas receiving sustained attention: (i) at a fairly micro level, actors' language practices in oral interaction – the connection to policy narrowing down to how such practices respond (or, more to the point, fail to respond) to official, "top-down" language policies; (ii) at a more macro level, the sociological meaning and implications, in terms of production and reproduction of social stratification, of language policies; and (iii), on the basis of corpuses of written texts, the *discourse* about language policy emanating from the authorities, supra-national bodies included. In the main, however, these strands of research do not concern language policies so much as the *politics of language*. They nearly always stop short of using established instruments of policy analysis and applying them to language policy. Much of the policy analysis discourse on language policies, therefore, has been produced by economists and political scientists, and occasionally lawyers. Their conceptual apparatus, however, is not always sufficiently attuned to the complexities of language and multilingualism. Much work remains to be done to develop a genuinely interdisciplinary body of theory and method in language policy.

3   In that paper, devoted to a first assessment of the potential of the concept of diversity at three different levels (Grin 2003a), I explicitly pointed out that my starting point was not political theory, and that in particular, my goal was not to make a normative case in favour of, or against, linguistic diversity. Oddly, some reviewers chose to disregard this caveat and complained that normative questions were left unanswered. Let me therefore reiterate the warning: I am not chiefly concerned with this particular ethical question here. My goal is to deepen the assessment of "diversity" as a relevant concept for language policy, a topic which, however, raises ethical questions along the way.

4   The philosopher André Comte-Sponville (2004) proposes particularly clear criteria for distinguishing levels of discourse in his demonstration of the intrinsically a-moral, as distinct from immoral, nature of capitalism. The distinction between levels of discourse, however, also evinces their mutual complementarity.

5   At the time of writing (early 2017), the Charter had been signed by 33 member states of the Council of Europe and ratified by 25. In this document, the term "right" barely turns up at all – it does so only twice, and in a completely non-essential function (Grin 2003b).

6   This alone constitutes a reason for preferring to talk in terms of "diversity" rather than "difference." The latter term presupposes a norm; the former does not and is therefore more neutral.

7   The fragmentation of the issue is reflected, for example, in Van Parijs's discussion of territoriality, in which several issues are addressed in what turns out to be a relatively disconnected way: on the one hand, the rights of Belgium's linguistic minorities on either side of the language border (where Van Parijs advocates a fairly strong brand of territoriality); on the other hand, the management of large-scale language dynamics, exemplified by increasing encroachments of English in non-English-speaking parts of the world (where Van Parijs advocates strikingly weak forms of territoriality; see Van Parijs 2011). In Kymlicka's celebrated work on multicultural citizenship, the combination of external protections and internal restrictions is potentially able to deal with issues relevant to the situations of *both* autochthonous communities and immigrant groups; however, it is not adequately equipped to address issues of macro-language dynamics.

8   The economic analysis of public goods, including "environmental assets,"

provides a straightforward conceptual bridge to the economics of non-material values. In the same way, the distinction often made between "intrinsic" and "instrumental" motivations in language use, language learning, etc., though it may have some heuristic value, can be shown to be of limited analytical import.

9   Elements of a transnational governance of linguistic diversity are arguably already present in European legal texts. Respect for linguistic and cultural diversity is mentioned in Article 3, paragraph 3, of the EU Treaty and Article 165 of the Treaty on the Functioning of the European Union (FEU). Among numerous publications on the European Union's language regime, several contributions in Arzoz (2008) and Hanf et al. (2018) provide useful reference points.

10 "Multilingualism" and (linguistic) "diversity" are often mentioned together in the literature, and the relationship between them is not always clear, even if most authors make a point of distinguishing (societal) multilingualism from individual "plurilingualism," a convenient borrowing from the French "plurilinguisme." For the purposes of this chapter, I propose to treat "diversity" (D) as a macro-level element of context; individual "plurilingualism" (P) is a set of language skills embodied in individual actors, and societal multilingualism (M) denotes the distribution of skills through society *and* patterns of use of the languages concerned. P and M are both *responses* to diversity and *determinants* of it. We may think of it as a causal chain of the form: $\{D \rightarrow (P \leftrightarrow M) \rightarrow D' \rightarrow (P' \leftrightarrow M') \rightarrow D' \rightarrow \text{etc.}\}$, where primes denote successive stages. For a formal treatment, using dynamic modelling, of the passage of time and linguistic equilibria in successive periods, see e.g. Grin (1992) or Wickström (2013).

11 Note that the criticism does not bear upon the effectiveness (or lack thereof) of measures adopted to protect and promote small languages as elements of diversity; rather, it targets the way in which the policy object is conceptualized (or "recast" as a commodity), which is dismissed as a matter of principle. Thus, it is hard to see what is actually being bemoaned – perhaps the loss of a pure, spotless relationship to language in which the latter was unsullied by base materialistic associations.

12 The "new economy" may describe: (1) an economy from which traditional business cycles and inflation have largely disappeared (obviously no longer a credible notion, if it ever was); (2) an economic sector centred on high-tech activities; (3) an economy with fast-paced productivity growth; or (4) the "full effects on social, economic, and political systems of the [information and

communications technologies] revolution" centred on the computer; see Lipsey and Nakamura (1991).

13 For an early application of these tools to language dynamics, see Grin and Rossiaud (1997); for a discussion focused on identity, see Kraus (2018).

14 Let us for example recall that in 2011, out of the 500m residents of the European Union, 6.6% were foreigners in their country of residence (including from other EU member states). Even if we assume that interactions are purely randomly distributed (which is probably not the case), "exolingual" communication between people who do *not* share a language represents a small proportion of total interaction.

15 D is not defined over negative values, since nothing can be less diverse than zero diversity (or absolute uniformity).

16 See http://www.mime-project.org (accessed 6 July 2019).

17 For example, is it adequate, in the case of the official and working languages of the EU, to think in terms of communication only, or should "esteem" and "creativity potential" be taken into account as well? And if a focus on communication is considered acceptable, what types of communication are relevant?

18 An interesting case is Switzerland, where centuries of common political destiny may have resulted in a measure of cultural convergence between the French-, German-, and Italian-speaking communities despite language barriers. Consequently, there is abundant circumstantial evidence that a stronger sense of community exists, within the country, across internal language boundaries, than with neighbouring countries speaking the same language. Relatedly, the notion of "kin-state" is irrelevant to the Swiss context (Dardanelli 2012).

REFERENCES

Arzoz, Xabier, ed. 2008. *Respecting Linguistic Diversity in the European Union.* Amsterdam: John Benjamins.

Barry, Brian. 2001. *Culture and Equality.* Cambridge, MA: Harvard University Press.

Blommaert, Jan, Ben Rampton, and Massimiliano Spotti, eds. 2011. "Language and Superdiversities." *Diversities* 13, no. 2 (thematic issue).

Comte-Sponville, André. 2004. *Le capitalisme est-il moral?* Paris: Albin Michel.

Conti, Virginie, and François Grin, eds. 2008. *S'entendre entre langues voisines. Vers l'intercompréhension*. Geneva: Georg.

Cooper, Robert. 1989. *Language Planning and Social Change*. Cambridge: Cambridge University Press.

Dardanelli, Paolo. 2012. "Multi-lingual but Mono-national: Exploring and Explaining Switzerland's Exceptionalism." In *Federalism, Plurinationality and Democratic Constitutionalism*, edited by Ferran Requejo and Miquel Caminal, 295–323. Abingdon, UK: Routledge.

De Swaan, Abram. 2001. *Words of the World. The Global Language System*. Cambridge: Polity Press.

Duchêne, Alexandre. 2007. *Discourses of Endangerment: Ideologies and Interests in the Defense of Languages*. London: Continuum.

Duchêne, Alexandre, and Monica Heller, eds. 2011. *Language in Late Capitalism. Pride and Profit*. London: Routledge.

Edwards, John. 2012. *Multilingualism. Understanding Linguistic Diversity*. London: Continuum.

European Commission. 2008. EVALSED: *The Resource for the Evaluation of Socio-Economic Development*. Luxembourg: Office for the Official Publications of the European Communities.

Fishman, Joshua. 1989. *Language and Ethnicity in Minority Sociolinguistic Perspective*. Clevedon, UK: Multilingual Matters.

Fishman, Joshua, Charles Ferguson, and Jyotirindra Dasgupta, eds. 1968. *Language Problems of Developing Nations*. New York: Wiley.

Gazzola, Michele. 2014. *The Evaluation of Language Regimes. Theory and Application to Multilingual Patent Organisations*. Amsterdam: John Benjamins.

Gazzola, Michele, and François Grin. 2017. "Comparative Language Policy and Evaluation: Criteria, Indicators and Implications for Translation Policy." In *Translation and Public Policy. Interdisciplinary Perspectives and Case Studies*, edited by Gabriel González Núñez and Reine Meylaerts, 83–116. New York: Routledge.

Ginsburgh, Victor, and Shlomo Weber. 2011. *How Many Languages Do We Need? The Economics of Linguistic Diversity*. Princeton, NJ: Princeton University Press.

Grin, François. 1996. "Conflit ethnique et politique linguistique." *Relations internationales* 88: 381–96.

– 2002. "Towards a Threshold Theory of Minority Language Survival." *Kyklos* 45, no. 1: 69–97.

– 2003a. "Diversity as Paradigm, Analytical Device, and Policy Goal." In *Language Rights and Political Theory*, edited by Will Kymlicka and Allan Patten, 169–88. Oxford, UK: Oxford University Press.

– 2003b. *Language Policy Evaluation and the European Charter for Regional or Minority Languages*. Basingstoke, UK: Palgrave Macmillan.

– 2003c. "The Economics of Language Planning." *Current Issues in Language Planning* 4, no. 1: 1–66.

– 2005. "Linguistic Human Rights as a Source of Policy Guidelines: A Critical Assessment." *Journal of Sociolinguistics* 9, no. 3: 448–60.

– 2016. "Combining Immigrant and Autochthonous Language Rights: A Territorial Approach to Multilingualism." In *Language Rights, vol. 1: Principles, Enactment, Application*, edited by Tove Skutnabb-Kangas and Robert Phillipson, 349–66. New York: Routledge.

– 2018. "On Some Fashionable Terms in Multilingualism Research: Critical Assessment and Implications for Language Policy." In *The Politics of Multilingualism. Europeanisation, Globalisation and Linguistic Governance*, edited by Peter A. Kraus and François Grin, 247–74. Amsterdam: John Benjamins.

Grin, François, Jacques Amos, Klea Faniko, Guillaume Fürst, Jacqueline Lurin, and Irene Schwob. 2015. *Suisse—Société multiculturelle. Ce qu'en font les jeunes aujourd'hui*. Glarus/Chur, Switzerland: Rüegger Verlag.

Grin, François, and Jean Rossiaud. 1997. "Mondialisation, processus marchands et dynamique des langues." In *Universalisation et différenciation des modèles culturels*, edited by Sélim Abou and Katia Haddad, 113–42. Beirut: Presses de l'Université Saint-Joseph.

Gustafson, Per. 2008. "Transnationalism and Retirement Migration: The Case of North European retirees in Spain." *Ethnic and Racial Studies* 31, no. 3: 451–75.

Hanf, Dominik, Klaus Malacek, and Elise Muir. 2010. *Langues et construction européenne*. Brussels: Peter Lang.

Heller, Monica. 2007. "Bilingualism as Ideology and Practice." In *Bilingualism: A Social Approach*, edited by Monica Heller, 1–22. Houndmills, UK: Palgrave Macmillan.

Henrard, Kristin, and Robert Dunbar, eds. 2008. *Synergies in Minority Protection: European and International Law Perspectives*. Cambridge: Cambridge University Press.

Hollinger, David A. 1995. *Postethnic America: Beyond Multiculturalism*. New York: Basic Books.

Kraus, Peter A. 2012. "The Politics of Complex Diversity: A European Perspective." *Ethnicities* 12, no. 1: 3–25.

– 2018. "From Glossophagic Hegemony to Multilingual Pluralism? Re-assessing the Politics of Linguistic Identity in Europe." In *The Politics of Multilingualism. Europeanisation, Globalisation and Linguistic Governance*, edited by Peter A. Kraus and François Grin, 89–109. Amsterdam: John Benjamins.

Kymlicka, Will. 1995. *Multicultural Citizenship*. Oxford, UK: Oxford University Press.

Kymlicka, Will, and Alan Patten, eds. 2003. *Language Rights and Political Theory*. Oxford, UK: Oxford University Press.

Jørgensen, J. Normann, Martha S. Karrebæk, Lian M. Madsen, and Janus S. Møller. 2011. "Polylanguaging in Superdiversity." *Diversities* 13, no. 2: 23–37.

Lipsey, Richard G., and Alice Nakamura, eds. 1991. *Services Industries and the Knowledge-Based Economy*. Calgary, AB: University of Calgary Press.

May, Stephen. 2001. *Language and Minority Rights*. Harlow, UK: Pearson.

McElhinny, Bonnie. 2012. "Silicon Valley Sociolinguistics? Analyzing Language, Gender and Communities of Practice in the New Knowledge Economy." In *Language in Late Capitalism*, edited by Monica Heller and Alexandre Duchêne, 230–60. London: Routledge.

Muysken, Pieter. 2010. "The Demise and Attempted Revival of Uchumataqu (Uru)." In *New Perspectives on Endangered Languages*, edited by José Antonio A. Flores Farfán and Fernando Ramallo, 93–118. Amsterdam: John Benjamins.

Patten, Alan. 2009. "Survey Article: The Justification of Minority Language Rights." *Journal of Political Philosophy* 17, no. 1: 102–28.

Paulré, Bernard. 1993. "L'organisation entre information et communication." In *Dictionnaire critique de la communication*, edited by Lucien Sfez, 519–68. Paris: Presses universitaires de France.

Pavlenko, Aneta. 2019. "Superdiversity and Why It Isn't: Reflections on Terminological Innovation and Academic Branding." In *Sloganization in Language*

Education Discourse, edited by Barbara Schmenck, Stephan Breidbach, and Lutz Küster, 142–68. Clevedon, UK: Multilingual Matters.

Phillipson, Robert. 2010. *Linguistic Imperialism Continued*. London: Routledge.

Phillipson, Robert, and Tove Skutnabb-Kangas. 2013. "Review of Martin-Jones, Marilyn, Adrian Blackledge and Angela Creese (eds.), The Routledge Handbook of Multilingualism." *TESOL Quarterly* 47, no. 3: 657–9.

Robichaud, David, and Helder de Schutter. 2012. "Language Is Just a Tool! On the Instrumentalist Approach to Language." In *The Cambridge Handbook of Language Policy*, edited by Bernard Spolsky, 124–45. Cambridge: Cambridge University Press.

Rossiaud, Jean. 1997. '*MoNdernisation' et subjectivation. Éléments pour la sociologie des mouvements sociaux*. Florianópolis, Brazil: Universidade Federal de Santa Catarina.

Sanguin, André-Louis, ed. 1993. *Les minorités ethniques en Europe*. Paris: L'Harmattan.

Taylor, Charles. 1994. *Multiculturalism and the Politics of Recognition*. Princeton, NJ: Princeton University Press.

Ten Thije, Jan, and Ludger Zeevaert, eds. 2007. *Receptive Multilingualism: Linguistic Analyses, Language Policies and Didactic Concepts*. Amsterdam: John Benjamins.

Tollefson, James. 1991. *Planning Language, Planning Inequality*. New York: Longman.

Urry, John. 2007. *Mobilities*. Cambridge: Polity.

Vaillancourt, François. 1987. "The Costs and Benefits of Language Policies in Québec, 1974–1984: Some Partial Estimates." In *The Economics of Language Use*, edited by Humphrey Tonkin and Karen Johnson-Weiner, 71–91. Hartford: Center for Research and Documentation on World Language Problems.

Van Parijs, Philippe, ed. 2004. *Cultural Diversity versus Economic Solidarity*. Brussels: de Boeck-Université.

– 2011. *Linguistic Justice for Europe and for the World*. Oxford, UK: Oxford University Press.

– ed. 2011. *The Linguistic Territoriality Principle: Right Violation or Parity of Esteem?* Re-Bel e-book no. 11, http://www.rethinkingbelgium.eu/rebel-initiative-ebooks/ebook-11-linguistic-territoriality-principle-right-violation-or-parity-of-esteem (accessed 6 July 2019).

Vertovec, Steven. 2007. "Super-Diversity and Its Implications." *Ethnic and Racial Studies* 30, no. 6: 1024–54.

Wickström, Bengt-Arne. 2013. "The Optimal Babel: An Economic Framework for the Analysis of Dynamic Language Rights." In *Constitutional Economics and Public Institutions*, edited by Francisco Cabrillo and Miguel Puchades Navarro, 322–44. Cheltenham, UK: Edward Elgar.

5

Intralinguistic Justice

HELDER DE SCHUTTER

During the past decade, several normative analyses of language policy have emerged within political theory.[1] These theories of "linguistic justice" provide an answer to the question: what is a just language policy? In this literature, language policy is typically taken to refer to the political management of the presence of different language groups within a political community: the paradigmatic cases in these analyses of linguistic diversity are political communities with two or more distinct language groups, such as Canada, India, Belgium, Switzerland, South Africa, or the European Union.

But there is another dimension of language policy, to which barely any normative attention has been paid so far: the political management of linguistic diversity occurring within one and the same language group.[2] Most languages are internally marked by significant regional, class-based, and/or ethnic diversity. Yet, when we talk about or learn a language, we refer to and learn the "standard" version of the language. The standard version of the language is granted higher status than all other versions. It forms the basis for the (often official) grammar, dictionary, and spelling, and it is the version used for the codification of law, in public debate, and in the educational system.

So we can distinguish between two dimensions of linguistic justice: *interlinguistic* and *intralinguistic* justice. Interlinguistic justice pertains to the just political treatment of different language communities. Intralinguistic justice concerns the just political treatment of internal linguistic differences within a language community, consisting of regional, class-based, or ethnic dialects existing alongside a standard language.[3]

The goal of this chapter is twofold: to chart the domain of intralinguistic justice (part I), and to provide a normative exploration of its content (part

II). The first part clarifies what intralinguistic justice is, and articulates two components of it: *jus ad linguam* and *jus in lingua*. The second part explores the reasons for and against the higher status granted to the standard version of the language. I argue that, while similar arguments and interests are involved in the intralinguistic and the interlinguistic dimensions of justice, (i) identity arguments for politically accommodating non-standard versions are generally less weighty than identity arguments for protecting minority (standard) languages, and (ii) instrumental arguments point intralinguistically and interlinguistically in the same direction: towards prioritizing the standard language in the first case, and towards prioritizing one of the standard languages in the second case. I argue that these two types of arguments combined justify an overall priority of recognition of the standard language.

1. THE DOMAIN OF INTRALINGUISTIC JUSTICE

1.1 A Prior Dimension

When people refer to a language, what they very often mean is the standard language. For instance, when people talk about Spanish or Russian, what they mean by Spanish and Russian is one version of the Spanish and Russian varieties, the standard version, which is formalized in dictionaries and grammars, used in the education system, and taught as a reference point in foreign language teaching. It is also the standard language that is referred to when countries declare their official languages. When Canada says that French and English are its official languages, it refers to standard French and standard English. When Thailand declares Thai as its official language, it refers to standard Thai. When the EU translates documents into its twenty-four official languages, it translates them into the standard versions of these languages.

This focus on the standard version of the language is, very understandably, also present in the normative theories of language policy that have appeared in the last decade. These theories are really theories of interlinguistic justice, which work with standard languages as the units of analysis. When Thomas Pogge (2003) argues for an "English-first approach" in the teaching of Hispanic children in the US, he refers to the standard version of English. When Van

Parijs (2011) argues for parity of esteem between languages, he argues for parity between the standard languages, not the non-standard versions.

The result of identifying the language with the standard version of that language, however, is that we tend to forget that, under the hood, there are other, non-standard versions of the language to be found, commonly referred to as dialects. These non-standard versions are granted lower status than the standard version. The non-standard versions are usually not taught at school and government services such as documents or voting ballots are not made available in them.

Taking only standard languages as the entities of a theory of linguistic justice, then, ignores the prior question of the justice of the standard language's existence and of its superiority over non-standard versions. When some form of equality is argued for in the treatment of different standard languages in interlinguistic justice, for example, then it has to be realized that each of the equally recognized units very often is the result of an internal conflict between versions of the language with non-standard versions as victims and the standard as the victor. We would then end up with equality between internally inequality-inflicting units. Perfect interlinguistic equality is then predicated on, and leads to, vast intralinguistic inequality.

So intralinguistic justice comes prior to interlinguistic justice. Only when the higher status for the standard language is internally justified can we devise principles of justice for dealing with situations where multiple standard languages are present in a political community.[4]

1.2 Terms

I will in what follows refer to a "standard language" as the linguistic variety that has undergone standardization and is functionally superposed over other varieties of the same language.[5] I will use the term "dialects" to refer to the other linguistic varieties, which can be geographical, ethnic, or class-based. I will understand the "language" (e.g. German) then as the name for the collection consisting of the standard version of the language (standard German) and the different dialects belonging to it (including Swabian and Bavarian). By "intralinguistic justice" I then mean justice concerning the relationship between the political status accorded to the standard language and the political status accorded to dialects.

There are two features of a standard language: standardization of the linguistic form and functional superposition.[6] Standardization means that uniformity has been imposed on the linguistic form through codification: among other things by listing the vocabulary in a dictionary and by laying down spelling and grammar rules (see Milroy 2001, 531; Ammon 1986). Functional superposition over all other varieties means that the standard language is the medium of communication between speakers of different varieties of the language, and that this superposition has a functional component: the standard and the dialect serve distinct functions. The standard is used in public media, the schools and the courts, for writing, and also for communication with speakers of other varieties; the dialect is typically used for ordinary conversation with speakers of the same region, class, or ethnicity (see Haugen 1966, 927; Ferguson 1959). So for dialect speakers, the sociolinguistic situation is characterized by diglossia: they know both the dialect and the standard language and use them for different functions, even though they tend to speak the standard with a local accent. Importantly, however, some segment of the speakers doesn't speak a dialect: they speak the standard language as their native variety.[7]

In some cases, two or more geographically distinct and state-specific standard versions have emerged, each superposed over non-standard versions: the resulting linguistic pattern can be called a "pluricentric" language (Ammon 1995). This can be argued to be the case for English, French, Spanish, and German. Whether they are pluricentric or not, languages with official status in more than one state sometimes co-administer (part of) their shared linguistic code in international institutions such as the Nederlandse Taalunie, the Rat für deutsche Rechtschreibung, or the Asociación de Academias de la Lengua Española.

1.3 Some Examples

We can imagine a situation of perfect standardization where all speakers speak and identify with the standard version of the language, and non-standard versions have never existed or have effectively disappeared. An example is Icelandic, which never had dialects and today has only minor phonological variation (Auer 2005, 31). In cases of perfect standardization, the relationship between the standard and non-standard versions does not arise, and hence the domain of intralinguistic justice is empty.

But in all other cases, more than one version exists, and we need to understand the legitimacy of the hierarchy of the standard language. Intralinguistic justice is concerned with the just institutional response to this hierarchy and with the legitimacy of the way it has come about. It deals with questions such as:

- Should we standardize a group of related unstandardized language varieties by creating one shared linguistic code for all, including standards for writing including spelling, grammar, and vocabulary? Should the code include standards of speaking? Should it include accent? If we should standardize, what norms should guide the standardization process?
- Should we grant language rights to dialects? Should dialects be taught at public schools? Should we ensure that teachers only speak the standard language at schools? Should dialect speakers be corrected when using dialect forms in school essays or at university? Does refusing a job on the basis of someone's lack of command of the standard version of the language, of which the speaker speaks a non-standard variety, amount to unlawful discrimination?
- Is the disappearance of a dialect a moral loss? Should political action be undertaken to prevent it?
- Which English should be taught in countries where English is not an official or native language but where it is taught in schools: British English, American English, or some other existing standard of English? Or should (part of) the non-English world develop its own standardized version of English?
- Many standard languages have politically supported language academies that supervise the codification and maintenance of the standard form of the language. English does not have one. Jonathan Swift proposed to erect one in 1712, and John Adams proposed an academy for "federal

English" in 1780. More recently, John Honey (1997) has also argued that English should have one. Should it?

These are not merely theoretical questions. Consider some real-life examples of questions involving intralinguistic justice:

Example 1. In 1996, the school board of Oakland, California, mandated some instruction in African American Vernacular English (AAVE[8]) in public schools. This ignited intense debate. Jesse Jackson, who would later revise his position, initially reacted that "this is an unacceptable surrender, borderlining on disgrace" (*The New York Times*, 23 December 1996), and that "[y]ou don't have to go to school to learn to talk garbage" (*Los Angeles Times*, 23 December 1996). The Clinton administration declared that "Black English" does not belong in the classroom (*The Washington Post*, 25 December 1996). A month later the board's decision was amended and toned down. The discussion is still ongoing, however, and some linguists working on AAVE such as John Rickford are involved in California's attempt to give AAVE a place at school (Rickford 2010, 28).

Example 2. In several parts of the Netherlands and Belgium, people from all classes speak regional dialects that other speakers of Dutch, the official language of the Netherlands and of the Dutch-language area of Belgium, have trouble understanding. Dialect speakers understand standard Dutch and can speak it, often with a local accent, but the local dialect is the default medium of conversation in shops, between the police and a citizen on the street, or even between professors discussing their work. Questions about the status of these dialects sometimes pop up. For example, in the Dutch province of Limburg and in the Belgian province of the same name, proposals have on several occasions been formulated to teach the local dialect at school, usually as part of Dutch classes (see *Limburgs Dagblad*, 19 January 2002). Since 2009, the Flemish employment agency VDAB has organized dialect courses for unemployed immigrants living in the province of West-Vlaanderen. Insufficient cooperation in courses offered by VDAB can lead to the cancelling of unemployment benefits. The VDAB argues that immigrants don't need to learn to speak the local dialect, but they need to understand it in order to enhance their opportunities of finding a job in West-Vlaanderen (*De Standaard*, 2 October 2013).

Example 3. The Soweto-based speakers of Zulu speak a non-standard version of Zulu, sometimes referred to as Gauteng Zulu. Gauteng Zulu differs significantly from standard Zulu (especially lexically, phonetically, and morpho-grammatically), and standard Zulu is increasingly rejected by several Gauteng Zulu speakers. A discussion exists today over whether Gauteng Zulu should 1) remain a non-standard version of Zulu, or 2) become a standard variety of a bi-centric Zulu (see Lafon 2005, who argues for the latter).

In all these cases, the hierarchical relationship between the standard language and the non-standard versions of the language are put into question. This has repercussions for the varieties recognized in public education, in public media, in state institutions (laws, exams for applicants to state jobs, citizenship acquisition tests in countries where such tests are required, and state-sponsored language courses for immigrants), and in the spelling books, grammars, and dictionaries endorsed by the political community.

1.4 Two Questions

Analogous to a distinction within just-war theory between just reasons for going to war and just conduct in war, we can distinguish between two distinct issues of intralinguistic justice: *jus ad linguam* and *jus in lingua*. The first asks: should we standardize, and, if so, what are the legitimate ways of doing so? The second question asks: once there is a standard language, what form of state recognition should we give to the standard and the dialects?

1 – *Jus ad linguam*. The first issue concerns the justice of building a standard language. It concerns the standards of justice that apply in the process leading up to the formation of a standard language. We can imagine a situation without a standard language. Different linguistic varieties exist, all linguistically related, and there is no version that has been codified and is accepted by all as the superposed norm. So the question is: should we standardize this linguistic world and create one or multiple sets of hierarchy between the standard and the non-standard versions? Reasons for standardization may include: efficiency, democratic participation, and national identity. I will consider these in part II of the chapter.

If a decision is made to standardize, then a crucial question will be what norm is selected for the standardization. Some enlightened minds have suggested that we should mix the existing varieties in some way so that a veritable common standard could develop. Inspired by Dante's *De Vulgari Eloquentia*, Giangiorgio Trissino proposed to mix the Italian dialects into one common Italian language in 1525. Ponteus de Heuiter did it for Dutch in 1581. Gandhi advocated Hindustani as a mixed form between Hindi and Urdu. And, in the past few decades, Rumantsch Grischun has been developed and proposed as a pan-regional standard variety for the Romansh language varieties. However, usually one of the linguistic varieties is taken as the norm for the standard language, as was for example defended by Machiavelli for Florentine (Machiavelli 1952). Even when the standard language will be based on one variety, however, we face the issue of the justice of the selection criterion. Different candidate principles of justice for dialect norm selection can be thought of: 1) prestige: select the most prestigious variety; 2) number of speakers: select the one with the most speakers; 3) acquisition ease: select the one that is easiest to learn for the other speakers; 4) linguistic distance: select the one that is linguistically furthest away from (or the reverse: closest to) neighbouring standard languages; or 5) lottery.

Apart from reasons for standardizing and principles for norm selection, a third issue of jus ad linguam concerns the depth of the codification. Should it be limited to vocabulary, grammar, and spelling? Should style be part of it? Crucially, should the standard that all will be learning and taught in include oral speech, or should the standard only be advocated for the purpose of writing? Should accent be part of it; should Received Pronunciation (RP), for example, be taught in schools in Britain?

A final issue concerns the process of spreading the standardized variety: should the standard spread organically or should it be taught at school? Even if the standard includes oral and written codes, should only the written code be explicitly spread? Should standard language courses be free? Should immigrants be required to take a standard language course as a condition for entry or for citizenship?

2 – *Jus in lingua* concerns the dimension of linguistic justice that comes into effect once a standard language exists. How should we understand the relationship between the political recognition granted to the standard language, and the political recognition granted to the dialects? What status should state institutions grant to the standard language and to dialects?

Consider the following answers to these questions, which form intralinguistic analogues of positions we find in the interlinguistic justice literature.

One answer preaches equal treatment from the point of view of the state: the state should recognize all linguistic varieties equally, whether they are standard languages or dialects. That might mean officially recognizing many more linguistic varieties than is currently done. Unilingual states would no longer be able to retain their official recognition of just one linguistic variety. Officially multilingual countries such as trilingual Belgium or quadrilingual Switzerland might have to officially recognize ten or more additional linguistic varieties. On this view, states could, for instance, grant all standard and dialect speakers alike the right to receive state services in their own linguistic variety. Instruction might have to be offered in all the varieties in public schools. Street signs might all be rendered in the standard and the dialect(s). Since standard language speakers do not live territorially separated from dialect speakers, and since there are non-regional dialects too (such as AAVE), the case for an intralinguistic analogue of the interlinguistically popular "linguistic territoriality principle" mandating one official language variety per territory would be hard to make. A full-fledged territoriality regime, seen as one of the cornerstones of interlinguistic justice by Van Parijs (2011), is undesirable intralinguistically. If equality should become the default principle of intralinguistic justice, then it will have to be realized through a policy of personality, granting language rights to more than one variety per territory.[9]

A second position argues that "all the recognition must go to one variety." Although it might be argued that all recognition must go to the dialects (or to one dialect) and the project of the standard must be abolished, the usual argument is the reverse: "no recognition for the dialects"; all the linguistic state intervention would here work to the benefit of the standard language. An extreme version of this third position is to say not just that the state should not confer official status to the dialects but that it should seek to remove dialectal diversity. This was the position of the French Revolution: we should eradicate the patois by assimilating everyone into standard French.

A third answer argues for inequality of recognition: all the varieties may get some recognition but we should give more recognition to some. Again this could in principle mean more recognition for the dialect, but it will usually lead to the intralinguistic analogue of Thomas Pogge's interlinguistic answer:

just like we should go for an English-first approach in the education of Hispanics in the US, so should we aim for a standard-first approach in the
education of dialect speakers (Pogge 2003).

Remark, however, that what we cannot have intralinguistically is a fourth
position that is sometimes appealed to in discussions of dealing with difference: to endorse a hands-off approach by not giving any recognition to any
language variety. Schools, courts, and parliaments might take crucifixes off
their premises, and thereby achieve some form of religious disestablishment,
but they must necessarily operate in language.[10] When writing or publishing
a penal code, a constitution, or school textbooks, and when organizing a debate, state institutions use a specific version of a specific language. Of course,
they can make decisions which aim to satisfy several intralinguistic interests.
For instance, they might stipulate that the constitution be published according
to the grammar rules of AAVE alongside the rules of Standard American English, just like it can be published in French alongside English in a bilingual
state such as Canada. A real-life example is provided by the two written standard languages in Norway, Bokmål and Nynorsk, and by the right for citizens
to address the state and be addressed by it in the standard language of their
choice. But there is no way for the state to remain fully neutral in the disesta-
blished sense with regard to the political accommodation of intralinguistic
differences, in the same way that the state cannot be neutral on the question
of which language(s) will be recognized in the interlinguistic case (other than
by giving a form of equal treatment; see Patten 2003a for this claim).

One's position on jus in lingua may be incongruent with one's position on
interlinguistic justice, or the two positions may be congruent. In the first case
(incongruence), one could be a staunch defender of equal treatment of standard languages but of unequal treatment in the relationship between the
standard and the dialects to the benefit of the standard: interlinguistic equality
and intralinguistic inequality. Or one could also defend a priority in state recognition (which is a form of formal inequality of recognition) for, for
example, vulnerable or declining standard languages, and still insist on an intralinguistic priority of the standard over dialects.

In the second case of congruence, the normative principles that apply to
intra- and interlinguistic justice are identical: either (i) inequality in both cases
or (ii) equality in both cases. (i) If inequality is opted for, one might argue for

giving all the recognition to the standard version of just one language (e.g. the majority language, for example English in Canada): interlinguistic inequality is then combined with intralinguistic inequality. This is for example what the French Revolutionary theorist Bertrand Barère advocated: to eradicate not just the patois but also the foreign languages on French territory such as German. (ii) A second congruence position is to justify equal recognition of all the linguistic varieties, be they inter- or intralinguistic.

I return to this discussion in section two of the chapter, where I endorse inequality in jus in lingua in favour of the standard language.

3 – Jus ad linguam*. To this discussion a second type of jus ad linguam must be added, concerning principles of justice in transfer. Whereas the jus ad linguam discussed above concerns justice in the process starting with un-standardized linguistic varieties and ending with a standard language, in some cases an already standardized language may need to be reconsidered. This is most likely to happen when a dialect that had already been placed in a standard/dialect relationship – take Frisian – can emancipate itself from a superposed standard and become a standard language in its own right.

Principles of justice in transfer then formulate the conditions and the pro-cess under which this may happen. Should such "secession" depend purely on the will of the dialect speakers? Must a claim be made on behalf of the dialect's distinct linguistic existence? Should other speakers of the standard language to which the dialect belonged have a say in the decision? Should the transfer be subject to a certain minimal numerical threshold of speakers? Apart from upgrades, in some (exceptional) situations a standard language might need to be "downgraded" to either a dialect of the same language group or a dialect of another language group. A standard may, thirdly, also need to be "re-standardized" without being downgraded, as is advocated by Lafon (2005) in the case of Zulu, so as to make Zulu more inclusive of Gauteng Zulu.

1.5 Interdisciplinarity

Contemporary analyses of linguistic justice have focused on the differences bet-ween language groups, not on differences within these groups.[11] Almost the reverse is true of sociolinguistics, the branch of linguistics where language policy is studied. Sociolinguists from the second half of the twentieth century to this day have tended to focus on the study of intralinguistic varieties, more so than on interlinguistic diversity (see for instance Bernstein 2003; Labov 1969; Trudgill 1975; 2011; Haugen 1966; Honey 1997; Rickford 2010). This sociolinguistic debate has been characterized by an important change of perspective. Until the late 60s and early 70s, parts of sociolinguistic research were animated by a belief in the superiority of standard English, which was seen as the one legitimate language variety, and by a depreciation of geographical dialects and especially of the speech of ethnic and working-class English speakers. But, in the wake of studies such as Labov (1969), an influential literature has emerged which has applied a much more critical attitude to the very concept of a standard language (see also Tollefson 2000; Milroy 2001). Standard languages are now thought to be just one variety among many, and these theorists have gone to great pains to show that there is nothing intrinsically unworthy, cognitively inferior, or illogical about non-standard dialects, and that the "deprivation thesis" of earlier socio-linguists (such as Bernstein) is wrong. Instead the non-standard versions are rich linguistic systems with their own rules and complexity, and give children access to a form of cognitive development of equal worth to the one provided by the standard language. So this literature has rehabilitated the speech of the non-standard speakers (Bourdieu 1991, 53) and has dethroned the standard language, as is for instance clear from Milroy's critique of the influence of the "standard language ideology" on linguistics (Milroy 2001).

However, the core business of sociolinguistics is not normative theory; so-ciolinguists analyze and describe but don't generally work out normative principles. So while the recent rehabilitation of non-standard varieties may certainly have to be welcomed from the standpoint of empirical linguistics, it may still be the case that normatively, a standard language ideology of some sort, understood now as the normative position that supports the higher sta-tus of the standard language, is desirable.

The intralinguistic domain forms thus an area of research to which so-ciolinguistics and normative political theory can both meaningfully contribute. Sociolinguists emphasize linguistic or cognitive equality bet-ween linguistic varieties, but they don't normally or necessarily mean that all the linguistic varieties should receive equal recognition, or that no priority should be given to the standard. What, then, are we to make of the claims of intralinguistic justice?

2. NORMATIVE STAKES

In this second part I will provide a normative reflection on the content of intralinguistic justice. In doing so I will consider the higher political recognition granted to the standard language, focusing on the written and spoken standard. To make my task manageable, I will not consider questions of accent, and I will focus especially on jus in lingua.

Since there are no existing theories of intralinguistic justice, we are somewhat groping in the dark when it comes to answering these questions. However, we may draw some parallels from the existing research on interlinguistic justice, and we may expect that positions on interlinguistic justice will recur in the intralinguistic domain. Many approaches in interlinguistic justice revolve around two poles.

A first position holds that policies should seek to accommodate people's identity interests in language. Language policies can seek to recognize the identities associated with a specific language. For example, when language groups such as the French Canadians are able to claim language rights, or when the EU holds an official multilingual language policy rather than organizing everything in only one language, such recognition is given in order to satisfy people's identity interest in their own language. This position sees people's identity interests in language as important enough for language policy to take them into account and to accord language rights to language groups. In devising language policies, language communities should be treated as communities of identity. In the interlinguistic debate, people such as Charles Taylor (1992), Will Kymlicka (1995), Alan Patten (2001), and Philippe Van Parijs (2011) have expounded this view. When referring to such arguments, I will call them "identity" arguments in favour of recognition.

But languages are not only bearers of identity; they are also instruments of interests not related to identity. For example, sharing a standard language helps people to understand each other better. Language is then an instrument of communication. So language can be an instrument of non-identity-related interests. Although normative theories could seek to realize identity as well as non-identity interests in language (and many do), a number of scholars in the linguistic justice field have taken the view that language policies should focus on satisfying non-identity interests. People may have an identity interest in language, but, this view stipulates, we should abstain from using public policy measures to accommodate it (especially in cases where it would conflict with the non-identity interests in language). Instead we should regulate language(s) in such a way that the non-identity-related goals are realized. This is what drives the interlinguistic views of, among others, Brian Barry (2001), Thomas Pogge (2003), and Daniel Weinstock (2003). I will refer to arguments based not on the identity interest in language but on other interests as "instrumental" or "non-identity" arguments.

A relatively easy example to illustrate the distinction is the following one. All else being equal, if a language group shares a state or territory with a larger language group, then, on the non-identity view, we should try to induce the speakers of the smaller language to get to know the larger language. Doing so will benefit non-identity-related functions of language such as efficiency, communication, equality of opportunity, stability, and so on (of course, it all depends on the selected non-identity reasons). The identity view, in contrast, will generally strive to grant similar official status, rights, and recognition to both language groups. Nothing prevents, however, compromise positions between the identity- and the non-identity-related functions of language. This is what leads theorists such as Patten to call the ensuing theory "hybrid" (2003a, 386).

The same distinction between identity- and non-identity-related reasons for engaging in language policy is at work in the domain of positions in intralinguistic justice. Here non-identity reasons typically point towards recognizing the standard language. And like in interlinguistic justice, identity arguments point towards recognizing the dialects alongside the standard language.

2.1 Instrumental Interests

To show this, let's have a look at some of the instrumental functions of language which will benefit from the existence of a standard language. Consider the following instrumental interests furthered by having a shared standard language (compared to not having one) and by ensuring every speaker is proficient in it:

(i) *Communication (expressive and interpretive capacity)*. Language is an instrument of communication. The communicative benefit of a standard language over non-standard varieties lies in that fact that it enables its speakers to communicate with a much wider group of people. In particular, it allows for communication beyond the boundaries of geography, ethnicity, or class of the non-standard linguistic varieties. Having a standard language (as opposed to not having one) enhances the scope of communication drastically in a given community. A lack of proficiency in the standard language spoken in one's linguistic community (if there already is one) can lead to a lack of fulfilment of the basic interest of communication, as well as to communicative inequalities compared to those who do speak the standard language well.

(ii) *Efficiency*. More can be done more efficiently when a group of people is united in terms of language. Less money needs to be spent on translation, and money is gained from having larger linguistic markets (such as book markets) which provide for economies of scale. If we are purely interested in efficiency, then we are interested in having as few linguistic thresholds as possible. From the point of view of efficiency, then, it is useful to have a shared standardized linguistic variety, and it is important to make sure all understand and speak it well. Seen purely from this point of view, theories of intralinguistic justice favouring the standard language are welcome because they warrant drastic reduction of the number of linguistic hurdles to be considered to get things done.

(iii) *Democracy and the exercise of political rights*. People who do not understand or speak the standard language of their political community well are not able to fully exercise their political rights. They are not well informed about what is going on in the public sphere and in the political process, and they have difficulty expressing their interests publicly. They are also less effective at defending themselves in court: people's access to knowledge about legal means and practices is negatively affected by a lack of knowledge of the language variety used in the courts. More generally, a lack of knowledge of a standard language is detrimental to democracy. This argument says that citizens need to understand the linguistic variety in which the laws are written and stated publicly, and that the ideal of (deliberative) democracy is difficult to realize when citizens do not speak the same linguistic variety. This argument not only says that, if there is a standard language, all have to be made proficient in it; it also shows the need for having a standard language in the first place: in a political community that is drastically (and especially non-territorially) divided in terms of dialects without an overarching common language, deliberative democracy is an unattainable ideal.

(iv) *Equality of opportunity*. People who speak a linguistic variety different from the standard language required for certain practices that bring socio-economic benefits, or speak the standard only poorly, face socio-economic disadvantages. These disadvantages emerge when audiences are not mono-dialectal: disadvantages on the job market, in securing and interpreting contracts, in being admitted at universities, in formal situations, at convincing people when engaged in deliberation, and so on. These disadvantages are a source of socio-economic inequality. The standard language is the language needed for social mobility and the language spoken by the powerful economic groups. If we do not make sure that all children know the standard language well, then the existing socio-economic structures, which tend to be reflected in language, will tend to be passed on to the next generations. This equality of opportunity argument can also be used to argue for the existence of a standard language. Without a standard language, the members of the underprivileged social classes face significant linguistic hurdles in climbing the social ladder and finding jobs beyond their region or class.

However, although equality may gain from a standard, that very standard may also upset equality. This is the result of the fact that native speakers of the standard may have advantages compared to native speakers of the dialects. Dialect speakers may be less secure and proficient in the standard, as a result of which they will have trouble performing well in any type of interaction involving non-dialect speakers. Jobs are more easily had by native speakers of the standard, whether they require knowledge of the standard (such as for interpreters) or just communication. Dialect speakers may also be discriminated against based on ill-founded assumptions of their dialect as a marker of lesser intelligence. At the same time, many of these injustices are related to issues that don't need to form part of the standard, such as strong accent uniformity; many problems of insecurity and proficiency can be mitigated by changing the dialect attitudes of teachers and speakers (e.g.

by not talking in a depreciating way about dialects, by giving dialects some place in the classroom, and by symbolically dethroning the standard's supposed superiority by emphasizing that it is linguistically just a dialect); and potential non-native speakers could effectively be made into bilingual native speakers by early schooling in the standard, and by simple exposure of students to mass media operating in the standard. All in all, children should be made proficient in the linguistic code that gives them access to socio-economic mobility (Barry 2001, 323–4). They should not be raised in a language version too small to give them that mobility. Just like, according to Van Parijs (2011, 108), we should democratize competence in English for international mobility among non-native speakers, so should we democratize the standard code by spreading it among all non-standard speakers of the language.

(v) *Nation-building, solidarity, and political stability*. Having a shared standard language can help to create a we-feeling among the speakers of different dialects, which may lead to sufficient motivation and common identity to undertake common projects and to be prepared to share a scheme of solidarity beyond the local solidarities of one's fellow dialect speakers. While in some cases political stability and supporting dialects could be compatible if we made the circles within which we strive to attain political stability and solidarity smaller (by devolving power to more local units, by secession, or by simply limiting redistribution to small regions), in many cases the dialect will not cover a sufficiently large area, or will not be territorially concentrated enough (in the case of class-based dialects, for instance), to make this possible. And even where it is possible, it is unsatisfactory from the point of view of sharing solidarity among groups of people larger than those speaking the same dialect. Since having a shared standard language is a way of enhancing national solidarity and national stability, creating a standard and ensuring all know it well will in general benefit the nation-building project.

Remark that in both the intralinguistic and the interlinguistic cases, non-identity-related arguments tend to point upwards. They normally point upwards towards inculcating knowledge of the majority language among minority language speakers in the typical case of a minority language group sharing a state with a linguistic majority. And they point upwards towards inculcating knowledge of the standard language among the population of a linguistic community (which might also form a state) marked by intralinguistic diversity. In both cases, the non-identity functions of language are best served when there is just one language. So, as far as intralinguistic justice is concerned, the non-identity position says that in regulating language policy we should further the instrumental interests in language. If it turns out that the successful realization of central political values such as equality of opportunity or democracy benefits from sharing a standard language, then, if one is interested in non-identity reasons alone, the best language policy is the one that aims to bring about a shared standard language. In short, focusing on the non-identity functions of language leads to the position that the particular variety that is to be privileged is the one that best maximizes the favoured non-identity-related function. That variety is the standard language.

While non-identity reasons are typically upward-pointing and lead to endorsing the majority language interlinguistically and the standard language intralinguistically, there are three conditions under which they can provide arguments for supporting dialects or minority languages. First, the non-identity functions listed above are derived from a socially progressive understanding of the liberal-democratic project. The selection of other values can lead to radically different conclusions. If one is against equality of opportunity or for curtailing state power, one might explicitly seek to divide the population in terms of language rather than unite it through a shared standard language.[12]

The second condition under which non-identity arguments can support dialects rather than standard languages is based on the fact that dialects are as much instruments of communication as standards and majority languages are. Sometimes communication benefits from a smaller territorial, social, or ethnic scope. Dialects can, for example, be more effective in developing social relationships or in communicating with friends or a life partner than standard languages. In some cases, lack of knowledge of the local dialect rather than of the standard language can lead to a lack of communication or to inequality of opportunity.

A third condition occurs when the standard is not yet sufficiently known by all. In such cases, the non-identity functions are indeed best furthered by common knowledge of the standard language, but as long as it is not fully known yet, one may prefer to use the dialect, as a temporary, transitional measure. For example, if a state institution makes public announcements to its citizenry, then it is interested in being understood by the recipients of these messages. As long as dialect speakers do not understand the standard language well, there is a reason for providing these messages in the dialect.

Nonetheless, it is important to see that, even where currently the instrumental interest is only satisfied in the dialect, this non-identity position can still strive to fulfil it in the standard language by making citizens fully fluent in it, while in the meantime providing transitional services in the dialect. For example, in a situation where communication (on product labels and traffic signs; in public hospital services) would be significantly enhanced if everyone acquired the same standard variety, one can still, for instance, provide some services in the dialect of the citizens while simultaneously attempting to make them acquire the standard language. If language should be treated as an instrument of non-identity functions, then a common standard language is the more desirable solution.

A lot here will clearly depend on the strength and pervasiveness of the dialect, and on the number of communicative functions it serves. We can think of a continuum of "dialectal strength" with on the left side perfect standardization (no dialectal difference) and on the right side the perfect linguistic independence of the dialect. In general the non-identity reasons will support efforts towards getting or staying nearer to the left side of the axis.

2.2 Identity Interests

A different picture emerges when we take into account the identity reasons for engaging in language policy. It is here that dialects usually differ from minority languages.[13] In the interlinguistic justice literature, we can find two major accounts of the types of interest people have in language identity, and of why these deserve political support. One account says that languages matter because they provide us with dignity. The other account is based on the view that autonomy requires a linguistic context of choice.

Let us have a look at the first. On this view, language recognition is seen as a source of collective and personal status and dignity (see especially Van Parijs 2011). People's self-respect and dignity are often affected by the esteem their language gets from others or from the state. For example, if there are several language groups in a society, and the language of only one such group is officially endorsed as a state language, and made into the only language of the education system, the parliament, and the judicial system, then this may be felt as a direct assault on the dignity of the speakers of the un-recognized languages.

Notice that it is important for this dignity view that the absence or inequality of official support given to a language is perceived as a lack of equal status and dignity. Where recognition or support of one's native language is not seen as constitutive of one's dignity, the dignity reason for engaging in language policy doesn't get off the ground. In that case, one could as well recognize the language which brings about instrumental benefits.

Now, interestingly, people appear to be more concerned about the linguistic conditions of dignity in the case of national standard languages compared to in the case of dialects. It appears that equality of dignity is more important interlinguistically than intralinguistically. Minority speakers of (standard) languages are often seriously concerned about the lack of state recognition of their language, and couch their concerns in terms of the importance of equal dignity for their own language. This is, however, not the case with dialects, or at least significantly less so. For example, while many people in Flanders are seriously concerned about the interlinguistic inequality of recognition and respect between Dutch and French in Belgium, they are not worried about accepting standard Dutch as the official language of Flanders. For many native speakers of West-Flemish and Limburgish, there is considerable linguistic difference to be bridged when switching to or learning standard Dutch. Nonetheless, standard Dutch is the default option for public media, schools, and parliaments, and there is no public indignation regarding this fact. This intralinguistic inequality of official recognition is rarely perceived as a matter of dignity. If anything, the main intralinguistic dignity concern seems to be about ensuring proficiency in standard Dutch: it is seen as a token of respect and civility to address speakers from other regions in the standard.

Very often, people don't mention the relevance of dignity at all in the case of dialects. If there are complaints about the dominance of the standard language over dialects, then these are based on non-identity concerns rather than dignity-related identity concerns. Take the debate over whether or not to transitionally teach (in) AAVE: this possibility is usually discussed in non-identity terms. The question seen as central to these debates is whether such transitional dialect education helps or hinders the social mobility of speakers:

is the teaching of the dialect a ticket to proficiency in the standard, or is it blocking that very knowledge? Consider what Labov, of all linguists the one best known for rehabilitating non-standard speech forms, says about the AAVE debate: "if the mixed populations of our Philadelphia schools should actually be integrated, we may even reach a time when young Black children use elements of the White vernacular, and take part in the radical sound changes that sweep over the White community. At that point, AAVE as a whole might be in danger of losing its own distinct and characteristic forms of speech. I am sure that many of us would regret the decline of the eloquent syntactic and semantic options that I have presented here. But we might also reflect at that time that the loss of a dialect is a lesser evil than the current condition of endangered people" (Labov 2010, 24–5).

The idea here is that the disappearance of AAVE might be beneficial to the condition of the speakers of AAVE. The loss of dialect identity is not mentioned as a concern – what would be regretted by many is not identity loss but the loss of AAVE's rich linguistic options. The value of AAVE is essentially assessed in non-identity terms. Even when dignity is mentioned in such debates, this is often only in relation to the greater non-identity benefits to be had by conferring some linguistic dignity to speakers. Perhaps learning the standard language may be enhanced by granting some linguistic dignity to AAVE in the classroom, either by teaching it or by not speaking of it as an undignified entity. Dignity is in such cases "non-identified": we confer linguistic dignity to the dialect not because of the identity-related importance of dignity itself, but as an instrument of the non-identity-related interest of ensuring the standard is spoken.

So the debate over the relationship between standard languages and dialects is often held in non-identity terms, even by the theorists speaking on behalf of the dialect. Very few of the sociolinguists who argue against the standard's linguistic superiority deny the normative importance of ensuring that dialect speakers master the standard language. They thereby confirm the higher status granted to the standard language, even if they argue for linguistic-cognitive equality of the dialect and for tolerance towards dialects. Much of the standard language debate in Britain in the 1980s, for example, revolved around whether or not dialect speakers should be taught the standard at school in a prescriptive way, by having the teacher state clear norms and explicitly declare non-standard norms to be illegitimate. The conservative position advocated this prescriptive view, whereas a more progressive view, backed by most linguists, stressed the negative educational and confidence-related effects of prescriptivism. But even the progressive camp did not invoke dialectal identity or dignity as a reason against teaching the standard language in the first place. British linguist Peter Trudgill, clearly in the progressive camp, stresses that "I have never known a linguist who believed that Anglophone pupils should not be taught to write Standard English." He adds: "children with no ability in Standard English will be at a disadvantage ... The social and educational role of Standard English in modern society should be dealt with, and the benefits of mastery of Standard English stressed" (Trudgill 1998, 457). What these sociolinguists attack is the view that the standard language is cognitively or linguistically superior or more complex, and that dialect speakers should for that reason be belittled or discriminated against, not the view that the standard's higher status is normatively desirable or that dialectal identity is an argument against that status. The debate is about the best strategies of getting children to learn the standard – for example, by showing tolerance for dialect forms or by building on the dialect at school.[14] And dialectal identity is usually not seen as an argument in itself to be used against the higher status for the standard.

At the same time, while the higher status of the standard is not challenged by dialect speakers, it is not the case that there is no perceived dialectal dignity involved at all. This is, for example, shown by the requests for some limited identity recognition for West-Flemish and Limburgish and for Gauteng Zulu in the examples given earlier in this chapter. People do find their non-standard varieties to some extent important and they do derive some pride and dignity from speaking them and from getting recognition for them. But it is nonetheless striking that unequal recognition of dialects is less strongly perceived as a threat to dignity than unequal recognition of standard languages. Dignity can be layered, and varying degrees of dignity can be felt in different language varieties.

Of course this difference in perceived threats to dignity between dialects and languages has causes: it is very the result of the success of linguistic nation-building. The modern nation-state has over the course of its history attempted to unite the citizenry and create a common national language, for precisely some of the non-identity reasons discussed above. The more successful it has been at doing so, the less dialects have survived as sources of identification and the more national standard languages are seen as sources of dignity and pride.

It appears, however, that, on the dignity view, the historical cause of why one identifies with a particular language and derives dignity from its equal status does not matter when it comes to answering the question of what sort of language policy should be pursued now. If what matters is whether something is perceived as a matter of dignity, then whether this perception results out of involuntary assimilation of one's ancestors, a self-conscious "free" choice, or softly induced linguistic nation-building is not directly relevant to the question of political recognition. Groups may use past injustice as an extra argument for being granted linguistic dignity, but they will only do so when they already feel the need for dignity in the first place: the language of one's ancestors may fortify one's existing demands for language rights, but it will not create these demands.

What about the other, autonomy-based account of the identity reason for engaging in language policy? Does it point to dialects or to standard languages as the protection-worthy entities? The argument says that a cultural context, which is taken to include a language context, is a precondition for autonomy (Kymlicka 1995, 83; Gans 2003, 39–66). Autonomy, so the argument goes, requires the disposition of a set of options. Languages are option packages: they provide us with the options available to us, and with the means to evaluate options. Languages and cultures are therefore "contexts of choice." Without knowledge of the language spoken in the society in which one lives, or when one speaks only a single language which is too small to sustain a full context of choice, one does not have sufficient access to a set of choices.

What does the autonomy argument say in the context of intralinguistic differences? Two points must be stressed here. The first is that, in a linguistic situation marked by a standard language and different dialects, the linguistic context of choice will be partly provided for by the standard language. The standard language is used as the language of the public sphere, and it is the language of media and of schools. It is also used within a political community for certain linguistically structured civic rituals, such as the text of the anthem, the constitution, and the presidential oath (see Deumert 2003). It also has a certain shared linguistic vocabulary consisting of nationally specific catch-phrases which are common knowledge.

What this means is that we can partly satisfy the autonomy interest through the standard language in a way that is not typically possible interlinguistically. Of course, there are again historical reasons for why the autonomy interest is already realized through the standard language. It is in part successful linguistic nationalism that explains why even dialect speakers also have standard language interests in autonomy. Just like the history of nation-building and standardization has led to a layered sense of dignity, so has it led to the formation of a "diglossic" (dialect/standard) context of choice. And here again, if we are interested in providing a context of choice, we are not really interested in the historical coming-about of the currently existing contexts of choice; from the point of view of autonomy for citizens, the fact that past languages were destroyed as a result of linguistic injustice is irrelevant.

Second, in some cases dialects may be strong, big, or widespread enough to be able to in principle sustain a full context of choice in the dialect alone. In such cases, it might be argued that the context of choice argument could be compatible with lending full political support to the dialect. However, it is also perfectly compatible with the context of choice argument to embark on a "smart" and slow assimilation project, which does not aim to suddenly transplant a speaker into an entirely different language community but aims to provide for a gradual transition from one context of choice to another, while ensuring full linguistic autonomy at each stage. And the autonomy argument is also consistent with full assimilation of future (or newborn) children into either the standard language or one of the dialects. The choice for the standard or the dialect, then, cannot be based on the autonomy argument alone. That choice can be informed either by non-identity reasons or by dignity reasons.

3. CONCLUSION: THE STRONGER CASE FOR THE STANDARD LANGUAGE

The previous discussion has shown that the domain of intralinguistic justice contains two distinct linguistic entities: standard languages and dialects. Speakers tend to see their standard language as normatively equal to other standard languages. They want the language to be given equal status in transnational settings, and where a state has more than one standard language they expect their standard to be one of the official languages of the country. Equal treatment is the norm for standard languages.

This call for equality is not advocated for dialects. Instead, the norm for dialect speakers consists of full inclusion in the standard language consistent with some limited recognition for their dialects. They endorse the importance of being taught to speak and write the standard language and accept the greater status given to the standard. At the same time they may claim some special recognition of their dialectal difference. Special recognition may consist of some dialect rights such as financial support for dialect festivals, the construction of a dialect dictionary, or even the right to teach the dialect as a subject at public schools. It may also include efforts to make the standard more linguistically inclusive and thereby to reconceive jus ad linguam, as in the case of Gauteng Zulu.

Such special recognition measures are not thought to stand in the way of learning the standard. On the contrary, they are often proposed as ways to smooth inclusion in the standard by invoking adaptation measures to remove prejudices towards dialect speakers. These may include attempts to avoid the belittling of dialects (for example, by celebrating a "dialect of the week" at school) and changes to the view taught at schools about the history of the language, including some symbolic dethroning of the role of the standard language in that history by emphasizing the fact that the standard was originally just the variety spoken in one region.

So while people in general have the idea that their standard language should be equally treated, they don't endorse equal treatment of the dialect and the standard. Instead they argue for inclusion in the standard consistent with some special rights for dialects.

This difference in demands for the standard and for dialects has implications for intralinguistic justice. The normative analysis provided in this chapter did not work out a complete normative theory of intralinguistic justice. I have provided an analysis of the normative stakes, which can serve as a backdrop for developing concrete theories. Still, a relatively clear normative indication emerges from this analysis. All else being equal, there are fewer arguments for politically supporting dialects than there are for supporting minority languages in the interlinguistic domain. In particular, the identity arguments for politically supporting dialects are less compelling than those for minority languages. This is because people's autonomy is embedded also (and only so for standard-only speakers) in a standard language, but especially because people tend to experience fewer dignity interests in their dialects than they do in their (standard) language.

At the same time, the non-identity arguments point upwards in both the intralinguistic and the interlinguistic cases. In both cases, apart from some exceptions, non-identity reasons emphasize the benefits involved in sharing the same linguistic code as well as in being able to use larger-scale linguistic codes rather than smaller-scale ones. Communication, socio-economic equality, and the creation of economies of scale, efficiency, and national solidarity all benefit from linguistic unity. Judging the world from the perspective of the non-identity dimensions to language leads us to perceive extensive or equal dialectal recognition as undesirably costly. In the few cases where desirable non-identity interests do point to smaller rather than larger linguistic spheres, or where they are compatible with smaller spheres, we can nonetheless opt for a slow transition to larger spheres, while transitionally realizing people's interests in those smaller dialects.

In the end, then, it appears that the main issue involved in deciding whether or not we should accord important status to dialects depends on the dignity argument (if we accept the dignity argument). And it is especially the dignity interest that tends to be weaker in the case of dialects than it is in the case of national standard languages. Having said that, it could well be that certain regionally based dialects might transform into "national" standard languages. Some of the dialects in the Netherlands and Flanders, for instance, exhibit weak forms of national identity: they are territorially concentrated, they differ significantly from the standard, and people often talk of the Limburg or West-Flemish "character." It is conceivable that, in due time, identification with these regional identities may significantly increase, such that it becomes sensible to see them as national identities and their dialects as standard languages of the newly emerged nations.

So dignity depends on what people feel. If they identify strongly with their dialects and derive an important sense of dignity from their status, the identity arguments point towards politically supporting them rather than standard languages, or even towards upgrading these dialects to standard languages in their own rights. Realizing this makes the following argument possible. If dignity depends on what people feel, if it is felt less strongly in the intralinguistic case, and if the non-identity arguments for supporting standard languages are as strong as I claimed they are, then there are good reasons for attempting to make sure that the course of future identification of citizens will lean closer to the standard pole of the continuum between full dialectal identity and full standard language identity. There are important interests served by linguistic unification through standardization, and as long as people's dignity is not imperilled by attempting to achieve unification, we should pursue it. It appears, then, that it is desirable for the standard language to be granted higher recognition by state institutions than the non-standard versions. Equality of recognition seems less weighty intralinguistically than interlinguistically. The linguistic justice debate may after all be justified in taking the standard language as its starting point. While it then works with internally hierarchical entities entrenching recognitional inequality, doing so is not unjust.

I should end by remarking that, although the mentioned interests generally justify a higher status for the standard, we should go no further in the recognition of the standard than necessary for their fulfillment. Most arguments for supporting the standard are consistent with the existence and prosperity of dialects, as long as the dialect speakers also become proficient in the standard language: there is no need to resort to the French Revolutionaries' theory of intralinguistic justice, mandating the eradication of the dialects. Full proficiency in the standard language by all dialect speakers suffices. This brings us close to the intralinguistic analogue of the interlinguistic proposals formulated by Anna Stilz and Daniel Weinstock. Stilz defends the "least cost model," according to which states should promote citizens' fundamental non-identity interests (in political participation and economic opportunity) "by imposing rationalization policies at the least cost to individuals invested in other languages" (Stilz 2009, 272). Weinstock has interlinguistically called for a language policy "that goes no further in its imposition of the language of the majority than what is required in order for the state to be able to communicate effectively with its citizens" (Weinstock 2003, 267). Intralinguistically, too, we should promote the standard only insofar as it is important for the fulfilment of the instrumental functions discussed above. That means that there remains room for granting some political support to dialects. Political support can be given in the form of special attention to dialect-speaking children when teaching them the standard language version, whereby their language variety is not belittled or depreciated. But it could also come down to political support for dialects in their own right through special "dialect rights," if people do (partly) have dignity interests in their dialects. The ensuing position then supports a "standard first" rather than a "standard only" approach.

NOTES

Many thanks go to David Bellos, Adam Clulow, Raf Geenens, Michael Gordin, David Kiwuwa, Pritipushpa Mishra, Alan Patten, Yael Peled, Brigitte Rath, Anna Stilz, Yin-Yin Tan, and Daniel Weinstock, and the audiences of the Montreal conference on "Language Ethics as a Field of Inquiry" (November 2011) and the Princeton "Fung Seminar on Languages and Authority" (December 2013) for helpful comments on previous versions of this chapter.

1 See Kymlicka and Patten (2003), and more recently Ricento, Peled, and Ives (2015), for collections of papers on the topic, and Van Parijs 2011 for a monograph on linguistic justice.

2 For one of the very few applications of linguistic justice to such issues of intralinguistic justice as dialect and accent, see Peled and Bonotti (2016).

3 Examples are: for regional dialects, Bavarian versus standard German; for class-based (and regional), Cockney (a version of English associated with working-class Londoners) versus standard (British) English in the United Kingdom; and, for ethnic, African-American Vernacular English (AAVE) versus standard (American) English in the United States.

4 That does not mean that intralinguistic and interlinguistic justice are necessary subsets of linguistic justice, because it could be possible for a general theory of linguistic justice to treat standard and non-standard versions alike. My reasons for separately raising intralinguistic justice are fourfold: (i) because, as I explain below, people's intuitions of linguistic justice may and often do differ between these two dimensions of linguistic justice and it is important to make theoretical sense of this; (ii) because, as also explained below, the default case of intralinguistic justice is a superposed standard which

stands in a diglossic relationship with dialects, which is different from the default case of interlinguistic justice; (iii) because seeing intralinguistic justice as one dimension of linguistic justice may have the benefit of keeping the interlinguistic justice debate uncluttered by difficult intralinguistic questions; and (iv) because the standard/dialect relationship has so far not been raised in its own right since interlinguistic justice theories focus on standard languages and not on dialects.

5   I take the relationship between a standard language and the non-standard versions to be the central question of intralinguistic justice. But there are additional questions of intralinguistic justice, such as for example the status relationship between dialects, or between different standard versions of the same language in pluricentric languages.

6   The distinction between a standard language and dialects is not identical to the distinction between language and dialect. Not all languages are standard languages, and some dialects may themselves be functionally superposed varieties for communication between sub-dialectal varieties. One may see a "language" as the name for the totality of the standard version(s) of the language and the non-standard versions (the dialects) (see also Ammon 1986). For example, German is the name used to refer to Swiss standard German, Austrian standard German, German standard German, and all the dialects, including Bavarian or Rhine Franconian.

7   Ferguson (1959) reserves the term "diglossia" for cases where what he calls the higher variety is not used by any segment of the community for ordinary conversation.

8   AAVE is the term commonly used by linguists. Other ways of referring to the dialect are "Ebonics," "Black English," or "African American English."

9   A state-wide personality principle would not be necessary in the case of regional dialects; smaller territories could be imagined each with an internal personality principle that grants non-territorial rights to standard language speakers and to non-regional dialects. See Patten (2003b), Van Parijs (2011), and De Schutter (2011) for interlinguistic discussions of territoriality and personality.

10 See Kymlicka (1995), 111, for this argument in the context of the interlinguistic debate.

11 In his critique of multiculturalism, Brian Barry has at points talked explicitly

about standard languages, arguing for the teaching of the standard since "being able to speak and write only in a non-standard form of English is a one-way trip to a dead-end job" (2001, 323–4).

12 The fear of excessive state power was the central motivation behind Lord Acton's argument for multinational states, since, as he argued, the presence in a state of more than one nation makes the central state weaker. Acton saw the nations within the multinational state as bulwarks of self-government and resistance to the central state. He opposed the nation-state ideal as defended by John Stuart Mill to engender unity and common sympathies within the state (Acton 1862).

13 I shall limit myself here to *jus in lingua*. Before we have a standard language, identity concerns will place significant limits on how to build standard language identities. However, two factors mitigate those limits: the fact that the chosen standard will be a linguistic cognate variety which provides for easier identity links and fewer non-identity obstacles, and the fact that language identities will tend to still be malleable and less profoundly shaped, since otherwise the dialects would already have acquired some standard form and would usually be seen as languages rather than dialects.

14 To some extent it is also about the legitimate scope of the reach of the standard language. One might, for instance, argue against the need to make dialect speakers proficient in the spoken standard (see Trudgill 2011).

REFERENCES

Acton, Lord. 1862. "Nationality." *Home and Foreign Review* 1 (July): 1–25.

Ammon, Ulrich. 1986. "Explikation der Begriffe 'Standardvarietät' und 'Standardsprache' auf normtheoretischer Grundlage." In *Sprachlicher Substandard*, edited by Günter Holtus and Edgar Radtke, 1–63. Tübingen, Germany: Max Niemeyer Verlag

– 1995. *Die deutsche Sprache in Deutschland, Österreich und der Schweiz: das Problem der nationalen Varietäten*. Berlin: de Gruyter.

Auer, Peter. 2005. "Europe's Sociolinguistic Unity, or: A Typology of European Dialect/Standard Constellations." In *Perspectives on Variation: Sociological, Historical, Comparative*, edited by Nicole Delbecque, Johan van der Auwera, and Dirk Geeraerts, 7–42. Berlin: Mouton de Gruyter.

Barry, Brian. 2001. *Culture and Equality. An Egalitarian Critique of Multiculturalism*. Cambridge: Polity Press.

Bernstein, Basil. 2003 [1971]. *Class Codes and Control: Applied Studies towards a Sociology of Language*. London: Routledge.

Bourdieu, Pierre. 1991. *Language and Symbolic Power*. Cambridge: Polity Press.

Deumert, Ana. 2003. "Standard Languages as Civic Rituals: Theory and Examples." *Sociolinguistica* 17: 31–51.

De Schutter, Helder. 2011. "Let's Brusselize the World!" In *Arguing About Justice: Essays for Philippe Van Parijs*, edited by Axel Gossiers and Yannick Vanderborght, 199–206. Louvain, Belgium: Presses Universitaires.

Ferguson, Charles A. 1959. "Diglossia." *Word* 15: 325–40.

Gans, Chaim. 2003. *The Limits of Nationalism*. Cambridge: Cambridge University Press.

Haugen, Einar. 1966. "Dialect, Language, Nation." *American Anthropologist* 68, no. 4: 922–35.

Honey, John. 1997. *Language Is Power. The Story of Standard English and Its Enemies*. London: Faber and Faber.

Kymlicka, Will. 1995. *Multicultural Citizenship*. Oxford, UK: Oxford University Press.

Kymlicka, Will, and Alan Patten, eds. 2003. *Language Rights and Political Theory*. Oxford, UK: Oxford University Press.

Labov, William. 1998 [1969]. *Language in the Inner City: Studies in the Black English Vernacular*. Philadelphia, PA: University of Pennsylvania Press.

– 2010. "Unendangered Dialects, Endangered People." *Transforming Anthropology* 18, no. 1: 15–27.

Lafon, Michael. 2005. "The Future of Zulu Lies in Gauteng." In *The Standardisation of African Languages in South Africa. Report on the workshop held at the University of Pretoria. 30 June–1 July, 2005*, edited by Victor Webb, Ana Deumert, and Biki Lepota. Pretoria: PanSALB.

Machiavelli, Niccolo. 1952 [1514 or 1522–23]. "Discours ou plutôt dialogue dans lequel on examine si la langue dans laquelle ont écrit Dante, Boccace et Pétrarque doit s'appeler italienne, toscane ou Florentine." In *Œuvres complètes*, edited and translated by Edmond Barincou, 169–84. Paris: Gallimard.

Milroy, James. 2001. "Language Ideologies and the Consequences of Standardization." *Journal of Sociolinguistics* 5, no. 4: 530–55.

Patten, Alan. 2001. "Political Theory and Language Policy." *Political Theory* 29, no. 5: 683–707.

— 2003a. "Liberal Neutrality and Language Policy." *Philosophy and Public Affairs* 31, no. 4: 356–86.

— 2003b. "What Kind of Bilingualism?" In *Language Rights and Political Theory*, edited by Will Kymlicka and Alan Patten, 296–321. Oxford, UK: Oxford University Press.

Peled, Yael, and Matteo Bonotti. 2016. "Tongue-Tied: Rawls, Political Philosophy and Metalinguistic Awareness." *American Political Science Review* 110, no. 4: 798–811.

Pogge, Thomas. 2003. "Accommodation Rights for Hispanics in the U.S." In *Language Rights and Political Theory*, edited by Will Kymlicka and Alan Patten, 105–22. Oxford, UK: Oxford University Press.

Ricento, Tom, Yael Peled, and Peter Ives, eds. 2015. *Language Policy and Political Theory: Building Bridges, Assessing Breaches*. New York: Springer.

Rickford, John R. 2010. "Geographical Diversity, Residential Segregation, and the Vitality of African American Vernacular English and Its Speakers." *Transforming Anthropology* 18, no. 1: 28–34.

Tollefson, James W. 2000. "Language Ideology and Language Education." In *Partnership and Interaction: Proceedings of the Fourth International Conference on Language and Development, Hannoi, Vietnam*, edited by Jonathan Shaw, Diana Lubelska, and Michelle Noullet. Bangkok: Asian Institute of Technology.

Trudgill, Peter. 1975. *Accent, Dialect and the School*. London: Edward Arnold.

— 1998. "Review of 'Language Is Power' by John Honey." *Journal of Sociolinguistics* 2, no. 3: 457–61.

— 2011. "Standard English: What It Isn't," revised version. In *Standard English: The Widening Debate*, edited by Tony Bex and Richard J. Watts, 117–28. http://lagb-edu cation.org/wp-content/uploads/2016/01/SEtrudgill2011.pdf (accessed 16 March 2020).

Stilz, Anna. 2009. "Civic Nationalism and Language Policy." *Philosophy and Public Affairs* 37, no. 3: 257–92.

Van Parijs, Philippe. 2011. *Linguistic Justice for Europe and for the World*. Oxford, UK: Oxford University Press.

Weinstock, Daniel. 2003. "The Antinomy of Language Rights." In *Language Rights and Political Theory*, edited by Will Kymlicka and Alan Patten, 250–70. Oxford, UK: Oxford University Press.

6

Liberalism and Language Policy in "Mere Number Cases"

DANIEL M. WEINSTOCK

1. INTRODUCTION

Many languages find themselves under threat because their speakers have been subjected to injustices. Colonialism and nation-building are the two most prominent political forces that have led to considerable pressure being placed on speakers of languages deemed to be "backward" and "uncivilized" to abandon the languages of their forebears in order to take up those of their colonial or metropolitan masters.

I have argued elsewhere (Weinstock 2014) that where the loss of language is due to unjust political projects such as these, some form of redress is justified on grounds of corrective justice. Now, it does not follow from this that redress need take the form of language reclamation. Some groups may decide that their language is simply no longer viable, and claim compensation for past and present harms in another currency. But in cases in which such groups do decide to enact what may in other contexts seem to be illiberal measures geared toward reclaiming or stabilizing a language, such measures can be justified on grounds of justice, where they might not be justified absent the context of injustice.

My argument leaves open (at least) three questions. First, there is the question of time. How long in the past must injustices be buried before they can no longer be appealed to in order to justify measures aimed at preserving a language? This is a difficult question. Injustices can continue to have causal consequences well beyond the actual occurrence of unjust political acts. For example, as we shall see in this chapter, the size of a language group can make a difference to its being able to retain its members in the face of the attractions presented by larger, and thus more communicatively effective, languages. But the size of a language group can result from injustices that have occurred in the distant past (Waldron 1992; Perez 2012).

A second question has to do with the nature of the policies and measures that can be deemed to constitute injustices. Colonialism and the more aggressive kinds of nation-building that occurred in Europe in the nineteenth century involved forcibly removing children from their linguistic communities, prohibiting the use of local languages in education, and instilling in speakers of languages of oppressed groups a sense that their languages were somehow of lesser value than those of their masters. But what of the high levels of asymmetry in terms of power and influence that characterize the current global economic scene? For some, this asymmetry is simply a consequence of market processes that are largely beneficial to all concerned, including to those people who find themselves at the bottom of the economic hierarchy. For others, the rules and treaties that make up the contemporary financial and economic scene amount to a form of "neo-colonialism." For the former observers of contemporary international and transnational interactions, the linguistic impact of economic activity, though arguably regrettable, does not present the kinds of injustices that might justify groups in taking measures through which they constrain the linguistic choices of their members in order to preserve a threatened language. For the latter, the pressures that are brought to bear upon economically weak language groups to adopt the languages of the economically powerful are redolent of the same species of injustice that characterized the more blatantly coercive and violent periods of European colonialism.

A third question, upon which I will be focusing in the present chapter, has to do with the question of whether, within the context of a broadly liberal-democratic ethics, justification can be given to policies which constrain the linguistic choices of members with a view to preserving a language in contexts in which none of the injustices that have been mooted thus far in this chapter obtain. Let me refer to such cases as "mere number cases." The term is used to denote the idea that where linguistic groups of radically different sizes interact against otherwise fair background conditions, the effect of mere number may be to incentivize the speakers of the smaller language to move to the language of the larger group. The question I will be asking myself is whether there can be a (broadly) liberal justification for the adoption of policies aimed at arresting such processes.

I will proceed as follows. A first section will be devoted to some conceptual ground-clearing. I will describe in greater detail what I mean by a "broadly" liberal political philosophy, and I will show why such a philosophy gives rise to a *prima facie* objection to policies aimed at arresting language drift in such cases through the constraining of people's linguistic choices. I will then examine three possible justifications for such policies. A first, which might be dubbed "luck-egalitarian," holds that the failure to correct for an unchosen and undeserved disadvantage itself constitutes injustice. A second argues that liberals can and should countenance certain moderate forms of paternalism – that is, policies that run against people's preferences – in cases in which agents themselves can be made to recognize that their preferences do not track their good. The third argues that states appropriately act in order to get their citizens out of predictable collective action problems, and that the processes that lead speakers of a "small" language to move to "big" languages in "mere number cases" are an instance of precisely this kind of a collective action problem.

2. LIBERALISM AND CASES OF MERE NUMBER: THE *PRIMA FACIE* INCOMPATIBILITY

There are many ways in which to bring out the *prima facie* incompatibility between a liberal political morality on the one hand, and policies that would purport to constrain the linguistic choices of citizens in "mere number cases" on the other. A fairly plausible and intuitive route would be to note that in most of its versions, liberalism views the role of the state as being in part to protect and promote the conditions that allow its citizens to conceive of and to pursue their own conceptions of the good. Liberals are suspicious of moral and political philosophies that do not represent citizens as *agents*. They worry, for example, that utilitarians represent citizens not so much as artisans of their own lives, but as passive receptacles of pleasant or unpleasant states. They oppose perfectionists who would substitute their own conception of the good for that which citizens define for themselves on the basis of their own reflections on the good.

Now when citizens decide to express themselves in one language rather than another, when they decide to emphasize the teaching of one language rather than another to their children, when they transact business in one language rather than another, they are through their choices making precisely the kinds of choices that liberals believe agents should be able to make without the imposition of external constraint or coercion, and, *a fortiori*, without the coercion of the state. Language is, after all, an important dimension of human existence. Policies that prevent individual agents from making linguistic decisions for themselves are therefore on this view purporting to intervene in an area of life that is central to individuals being able to live according to their conceptions of the good. Proponents of policies that would prohibit individuals from acting on some of their linguistic preferences are moreover in a very weak position to deny this, since their policy preferences are themselves premised upon the importance of language.

Thus, there is at least a *prima facie* case for liberals who view the protection of a sphere of independent choice within which individuals can act on the basis of their preferences as one of the prime responsibilities of the state to oppose policies that would prevent people from acting on these preferences.

But perhaps this opposition raises only theoretical difficulties. After all, why should we expect that there will be any kind of a tension between the linguistic priorities of the state and those of its citizens in mere number cases? Won't citizens be naturally led to want to speak the language in which the state addresses them, without any coercion being required?

The mechanisms which might lead citizens to choose to abandon their language for that of another group have been well modelled by Jean Laponce (Laponce 1984). When two linguistic groups of different sizes interact peacefully – that is, in contexts where, all things equal, members of both groups want interaction to increase rather than decrease – there is greater incentive for all involved to use the "bigger" of the two languages, in order to increase communicative potential. This means that in contexts in which members of the two groups interact, the larger language will tend to eclipse the smaller. The latter will tend only to get used in "private" contexts, and thus to become folklorized and, over time, to disappear.

These are the kinds of mechanisms that led Philippe Van Parijs, in his seminal book on linguistic justice, to argue that language groups that might find their languages threatened in such an untrammelled context of (friendly) interaction should establish jurisdiction over a territory. Van Parijs argues that sovereignty over a territory will immunize speakers of smaller languages against the corrosive impact of friendly interaction among members of language groups of radically different sizes (Van Parijs 2011).

Two remarks seem apposite in the light of Van Parijs's suggestion. First, it is an empirical question whether statehood will constitute a sufficient bulwark against linguistic erosion in the case of very small language groups. For example, statehood has not prevented English from being adopted by Scandinavian states as a *de facto* second language, and from achieving dominance there in certain contexts. (Doctoral dissertations are for example standardly written in English in several countries throughout Europe.) Though for the time being this has led to bilingualism rather than to the abandonment of "smaller" languages, there is no guarantee that the "asymmetrical bilingualism" which I have just described will be stable, even within the context of a fully sovereign nation-state.

Another way of putting the point is that there are two ways in which to interpret Van Parijs's plea for language groups to "grab a territory." According to the first, weak interpretation, the mere fact of being able to control the levers of the state will represent a sufficient counterweight to the centripetal force of the global *lingua franca* to guard against the language shift that might occur absent the protection afforded by statehood. Thus, the fact that the state addresses itself to its citizens in the local language, and the fact that it accords 'official' status to that language, with all of the symbolic freight that attaches to that status, will on this weak interpretation suffice to protect smaller languages from erosion.

According to a second, stronger interpretation, the reason that small language groups should "grab a territory" is precisely in order to be able to enact legislation aimed at protecting their language. Statehood would allow a small linguistic group which would by virtue of its having grabbed a territory become a local linguistic majority to use its control of majoritarian institutions in order to enact coercive legislation aimed at preventing its members from using any other language in key contexts such as business, education, and law.

Liberals, as defined above, would have no problem with the first interpretation of Van Parijs's principle. After all, it does not follow from the liberal principle that agents should be afforded latitude within which to live according to their conception of the good that they should be able to live in a social environment free of all state-generated incentives. When the state chooses to address itself through public institutions in one language rather than another, it sets up a powerful incentive for citizens to achieve proficiency in that language, and to use it in their interactions with the state. The *prima facie* tension between liberal principles and language protection in a mere number context only emerges where a language group uses its control of the levers of the state in order to *prohibit* certain language choices outright. The empirical assumptions that need to be made in order for the weaker interpretation of the "grab a territory" principle to be sufficient to protect languages are fairly optimistic. It is therefore unlikely that Van Parijs's proposal will succeed in dissipating the tension.

A second, much briefer, remark should be made in the present context. As Van Parijs is well aware, there is not institutional space on the planet for every vulnerable language to grab a territory. The empirical feasibility of political self-determination for language groups requires, first, that we abandon the expectation that all of the roughly six thousand languages that currently exist will be able to survive, and second, that some language groups exercise self-determination not through full sovereignty, but through appropriate federal arrangements. Van Parijs's argument therefore cannot be seen as holding that *all* languages should have a secure territorial basis. The question of how many languages should be secured from erosion remains an open one, even if we accept Van Parijs's main claims (Ginsburgh and Weber 2011).

I prescind from commenting at any length on the first of these issues. Suffice it to say that many groups which are linguistically the most vulnerable, and would therefore presumably be sacrificed at the altar of feasibility by Van Parijs's principle, are those that have suffered the gravest injustices – think of the First Nations in North America, whose languages are in almost all cases teetering on the verge of viability.

As many political philosophers have noted in recent years, federalism is the solution to the problem of how to make broad and meaningful self-determination compatible with feasibility constraints (Norman 2009). It must be noted, however, that federations are typically sites of linguistic contestation. With rare exceptions (the case of Belgium comes to mind), federations are made up of units of quite different sizes. What's more, in many federations, history and size often conspire to give rise to a situation in which one of the federated entities is able to behave as a "senior partner" within the federation, with all of the attendant linguistic effects that one might expect. Even in a context in which all federal actors behaved in a perfectly just manner, it is difficult to imagine English and Spanish not exercising a powerful centripetal force on all citizens in the United Kingdom, Canada, and Spain. Self-determination within a federal context will therefore afford the speakers of smaller languages less protection than full statehood. There will therefore be even more of a felt need on the part of the smaller federated linguistic group to use whatever jurisdiction they have in order to constrain the linguistic choices of their members. The tension with liberal principles that we have noted above will thus almost certainly obtain.

Liberals are largely united in the thought that individuals should be afforded latitude within which to live their lives as they see fit, and that one of the main responsibilities of the state is to protect this area of freedom. Language policies that constrain the choices of individuals are, in a context of mere numbers, problematic. This tension is moreover not likely to remain purely theoretical, since sociolinguistic dynamics will, in contexts in which linguistic groups of different sizes coexist, exercise powerful incentives for speakers of the smaller languages to achieve proficiency in and to use the larger language. A highly unstable form of asymmetrical bilingualism will result, one that may require the use of coercive legislation to address.

I have spoken thus far of a *prima facie* incompatibility. Is it possible to moderate or to dissolve it once we dig a bit deeper, beyond the conflict of principles expressed in their most abstract form? After all, liberal states do not systematically defer to the preferences of their citizens. There are many contexts in which states override such preferences. What's more, some of the justifications of infringement are ones which liberals can under some circumstances and within certain limits accept.

Thus, for example, states engage in moderate forms of paternalism when the preferences of their citizens would, if acted upon, cause them considerable harm. They require that people wear seatbelts when in cars, and helmets when on motorcycles. They subsidize the arts and tax cigarettes and alcohol. Though each of these measures can arguably be justified on non-paternalist grounds, the most plausible way in which to interpret and to justify the broad swath of measures that even quite liberal states such as the United States engage in in order to protect citizens against the impact of their own choices is to invoke a moderate paternalism.

Second, many social interactions would, if left to themselves, give rise to collective action problems. Everyone has an interest in the community they belong to achieving herd immunity against lethal diseases, but everyone prefers to be able to benefit without having to take on the moderate sacrifice of getting vaccinated. Anyone who has ever driven a car through an intersection in which the traffic light has ceased functioning knows just how collectively self-defeating human agents can be when they are left to act on their own initiative, on the basis of what they construe to be their self-interest in strategic contexts. The government appropriately steps in to solve such collective action problems. Were it not to do so, the production of "public goods," that is goods that are both non-excludable and non-rival, and to which individual agents therefore have an incentive not to contribute, would be impossible. As Hobbes correctly saw centuries ago, collective action problems require for their solutions that some coercive agent take the defection strategy off the table.

Third, states often act to offset unchosen and undeserved disadvantage, even when it does not result from the unjust actions of some third party. For some liberal theorists, the guiding intuition behind the liberal state's approach to distributive justice ought to be that, though agents should be held responsible for the consequences of their freely undertaken actions, the advantages and disadvantages that flow from brute luck should not be allowed to lie where they fall. In other words, people should be compensated when through no fault of their own they end up disadvantaged, and the state acts unjustly when it fails to so compensate them. This insight is at the core of what has come to be known as the "luck-egalitarian" position in political philosophy.

There are thus a variety of reasons for the state to get in the way of people's choices, even within the context of a broadly liberal-democratic ethics. It can engage in mild paternalism. It can (indeed, according to some, it must) solve collective action problems. And it can (and again, according to some, must) correct for the effects of brute luck. Can any of these paths be employed to justify coercive language policies in mere number cases? It is to this question that I now turn.

3. LUCK-EGALITARIANISM AND LINGUISTIC JUSTICE

Luck-egalitarianism is grounded ethically in what from a liberal point of view seems an unobjectionable premise. That premise is that a society justly holds people responsible for the foreseeable consequences of freely undertaken choices, but it treats the effects of "brute" luck as social, at least to a significant degree. The "socialization" of the effects of brute luck affects those at both the winning and the losing ends. Those who find themselves disadvantaged through no fault of their own ought, according to the luck-egalitarian frame-work, to be compensated (or at least they have a strong, *prima facie* claim to compensation). At the other end of the spectrum, those upon whom luck smiles are not entitled to the advantages that flow from their good fortune. The bads and goods that flow from the operation of luck from this point of view constitute a common pool before which all are equally situated, from an ethical point of view, regardless of where the operation of luck happens to have distributed the positive and negative elements within this pool (Cohen 1989).

An implication of luck-egalitarianism is that injustice occurs not solely when some act unjustly toward others, or when the state fails to correct the results of such unjust actions, but also when the effects of bad luck go uncompensated.

One can see quite readily why those whose intuitions lead them to believe that liberalism (as I have characterized it above) provides the wrong answer to mere number cases would be attracted by luck-egalitarianism. After all, such cases are ones in which speakers of some languages find themselves al-most inexorably drawn toward speaking another language, not because they have been victimized by colonialism or aggressive nineteenth-century-style nation-building, but rather simply because they happen to have had the linguistic misfortune of having been born into a small language group. Luck-egalitarianism provides those who think that there may be reasons of justice (as opposed to perfectionist reasons) to compensate such unlucky speakers with a plausible rationale for their intuition. On this view, linguistic injustice arises not just through the perpetration of unjust actions, but through the failure to compensate for unchosen linguistic circumstances.

Let us in what follows assume the truth of luck-egalitarianism. I want to suggest that it fails to provide the required theoretical succour to those whose intuitions incline them to want to justify laws that coercively constrain language choice in the name of language preservation, at least in mere number cases. This is so for at least two reasons. First, luck-egalitarianism, taken on its own terms, fails to provide us with what might be called a theory of priority. That is, it fails to indicate the goods with respect to which the operations of brute luck warrant correction. And second, it fails to indicate the currency in which compensation should be paid.

Let me begin with the first of these two problems. There are innumerable dimensions along which individuals are through no fault of their own differently situated. For example: some men keep luxuriant hair throughout their lives, while others (such as the present author) succumb to male-pattern baldness early in life. Some people are tall, while others are short. Some people are born in difficult climates, while others come into the world in much more clement climates.

What's more, all of the asymmetries just mentioned, though they may in and of themselves seem trivial,[1] have measurable impacts on people's lives. For example, studies have shown that height in men correlates positively with income.[2] Those who live in difficult meteorological conditions must expend considerable time, energy, and money coping with the elements in order to achieve a level of comfort that those who live in moderate conditions can achieve, as it were, for free.

Two questions arise as a result of this observation. First, is there a way of distinguishing those unchosen asymmetries that call for correction or compensation from those that do not? And second, with respect to any of these asymmetries, is compensation or correction due in virtue of intrinsic properties of the dimensions along which people are asymmetrically situated, or because of the causal impacts of this asymmetrical distribution on the distribution of other goods?

In a recent article that carefully and insightfully attempts to outline the implications of the luck-egalitarian framework for language justice, Helder De Schutter and Lea Ypi list the plural impacts that being born into a smaller linguistic community might have. This list encompasses tangible goods such as socio-economic status (speakers of smaller languages may be at a disadvantage in finding well-paying jobs in a globalized economy in which communicative reach is an important competitive asset), and more difficult-to-quantify goods such as status and dignity (people whose native language suffers from competitive disadvantage as a result of the low number of speakers who speak it as a mother tongue may feel personally belittled by the lowly status of their language). It also includes the various political obstacles that may result from one's disadvantaged linguistic status. Thus, on their view, the problem with linguistic asymmetry is not that it places people in a disadvantaged situation on the dimension of language *per se*, but rather that it does so on the various dimensions (economics, politics, status and dignity, etc.) with which linguistic asymmetry is causally implicated. These dimensions are moreover structured around goods that are standardly considered to be central to the task of creating a just society.

In considering the kinds of corrections or compensations that are due to members of linguistic minorities, however, De Schutter and Ypi focus on fixes that are exclusively linguistic. They imagine, first, a "universal language solution," which would put in place something like a global Esperanto, only to opt for what they refer to as "language advantages for all," a solution to the problem of language inequality that would see such groups receive resources of various kinds, including monetary resources, with which to strengthen their markets and fund their (native language) educational systems.

But if what really matters about language asymmetry is its impact upon the distribution of goods such as socioeconomic success, political rights, security, dignity, and the like, then these goods can arguably just as easily be achieved by using the resources that are, on the luck-egalitarian account, due to the linguistically disadvantaged in order to put measures in place that would see "smaller"-language speakers achieve fluency in the "bigger" language. One can ensure the socio-economic flourishing of one's citizens by securing one's markets, or by overcoming the linguistic obstacles to their full inclusion in bigger markets.

Ultimately, therefore, the argument that linguistic disadvantage requires a linguistic fix is premised upon an account that would explain the priority of being able to exercise rights, compete in the marketplace, and so on in the language in which one was raised, rather than in another language.

De Schutter and Ypi argue that while a solution of linguistic shift might address the impact that one's status as a member of a linguistic minority might have upon more tangible goods, it may actually worsen one's position with respect to the goods of "status" and "dignity." Presumably, the argument would be to the effect that one is somehow made to feel inferior to others in a fairly fundamental way when circumstances are such that one can only exercise political rights effectively and take part in market activities by doing so in someone else's language.

Arguably, however, the language/dignity nexus in the case of mere number is established not by any "natural" connection between language and identity, but rather by institutional responses to linguistic asymmetry. As De Schutter and Ypi themselves point out, what is problematic from the point of view of dignity is not linguistic asymmetry *per se*, nor is it the system of (from the point of view of smaller languages) highly centripetal incentives that numerical asymmetry puts in place. Rather it is the use of majority status to turn the "bigger" language into an "official" language, one that is compulsorily imposed upon people through the education system, the courts, and so on, and provided with the symbolic freight that accompanies status as a "state" language (De Schutter and Ypi 2012, 362).

To the extent that the use of majority status as a tool to assert political domination in this way predictably affects the status and sense of dignity of members of linguistic minorities in a deleterious manner, it arguably transforms what was at the outset a mere number case into a case of injustice. One can, however, imagine a situation in which the facts of linguistic (and more generally of cultural) asymmetry are not so treated by the majority. In such a situation, various numerical asymmetries exist and generate incentives, but these are not enshrined through official language policies and coercive legislation. In such a situation, one can well imagine members of linguistic minorities not suffering from dignity deficits, because nothing is done by any actor that betokens their belief that the languages of minorities are not due equal respect. Where the state is not in the business of doling out the social bases of self-respect on the basis of such factors as language, then people will not be led to the belief that the numerical status of their language somehow connotes anything to do with their worth as persons.

Luck-egalitarians find themselves faced with a dilemma. They can either, implausibly, claim that *any* unchosen unequal distribution among individuals along any dimension constitutes an injustice. Or, they can recognize that injustice occurs when inequality that occurs along a more limited band of dimensions, to do with the goods that theories of distributive justice have traditionally been concerned with (socioeconomic resources, political rights, and the like), goes uncompensated. De Schutter and Ypi's argument consists in grabbing the second horn of this dilemma, but in claiming that there is a very strong contingent connection between language and one of these more traditional goods, namely the good of "status" or "dignity." My argument is that they are on firmer ground in claiming a strong connection between dignity and the symbolic and institutional entrenchment of a majority language. But then their argument is therefore not one from which those who think that injustice occurs in the case of mere number can take solace.

Let me briefly address the second of the questions I formulated in setting up this discussion of the putative luck-egalitarian argument for language justice. Even if we put aside the concerns that have just been raised and accept, *arguendo*, that cases of mere number warrant compensation or correction, and that that compensation is to be paid out in the currency of language, the question still arises as to the nature of the linguistic resources that are due a linguistic group that finds itself in a situation of numerical inferiority. It is one thing to say that linguistic disadvantage warrants "resources" that might allow a group to strengthen the context within which the language is used by members – for example subsidies for schools and cultural production, or financial supporting of local markets.

It is however quite another thing to justify coercive measures. Subsidies of the kinds just mooted simply change the space of incentives within which people make their linguistic choices. As Sunstein and Thaler have shown, however, the spaces within which people make choices about just about anything are never completely free of incentives that incline the situation of choice in one direction or another (Sunstein and Thaler 2008). By "incentivizing" the use of a smaller language, political actors who purport to secure a language are not doing anything that is not already being done by other forces. In mere number cases, however, in which *ex hypothesi* no one is doing anything unjust that might be coercively prohibited, additional premises are required in order to justify the kind of measure that is being envisaged in the context of this chapter: namely, measures that coerce individuals into using a smaller language where incentives to do so are insufficient.

Such an argument might be provided by a mild form of paternalism. Briefly stated, the argument might be put forward that there are reasons for even a political authority that cleaves to a broadly liberal political philosophy not to defer to the preferences of people who choose to abandon the language of their forebears. It is to such arguments that I now turn.

4. A LIBERAL PATERNALIST APPROACH TO LANGUAGE POLICY? THE CASE OF "MODERATE MORALISM"

Political paternalism is the view that the state can, or even more strongly that it ought to, enact coercive legislation forcing citizens to do what political authorities consider to be good for them, regardless of citizens' actual preferences (Raz 1986; Conly 2012). There is a strong liberal presumption against political paternalism. As noted above, the state evinces its equal concern and respect for all citizens by prescinding from imposing a particular conception of the good life upon them, one that would lead citizens who do not share this conception to acquire the justified sense that they are not equal to others. To rehearse the (admittedly vague) slogan that John Stuart Mill made famous, states should only prohibit people from acting according to their own preferences and values where they would in so doing cause "harm to others."

Despite their anti-paternalistic biases, no liberal state is perfectly anti-perfectionist. States are constantly meddling in people's lives on grounds that seem best accounted for if some form of paternalism is assumed. They enact "sin taxes" to effectively price certain forms of activity deemed to be harmful to individuals out of the range of some citizens. They prohibit certain forms of sexual activity, even among consenting adults. And perhaps most importantly, they allow us to act on preferences that are rendered ineligible from the strategic settings in which we often find ourselves with respect to our fellow citizens. These are settings in which we prefer X to Y if enough people choose X as well, but we prefer Y to X if that condition is not met. States act paternalistically, but in a way that liberals would countenance, when they (as it were) take Y off the table by prohibiting it.

Let me begin by investigating the degree to which a state or a political authority can appeal to "mild moralism" in imposing a language upon its speakers by placing serious limits on their access to the bigger languages. By mild moralism I mean to refer to justifications for paternalistic interventions which, though they override people's preferences, do so on the basis of fairly uncontroversial judgments about the good. (For the purposes of the present argument, I do not need to be more precise than this rather vague condition.) One prominent "liberal paternalist," Joseph Raz, has argued for example that the role of the state is not to promote a particular set of valuable goals, but rather, to rule out worthless ones. While care must be taken in interrogating the degree to which judgments of "worthlessness" do not end up masking contestable value judgments, we can probably agree that there are certain pursuits that are so thoroughly incompatible with any conception of human flourishing that they are appropriately placed out of bounds by political authorities. What's more, inasmuch as political action along these lines does not prevent people from making choices among a plurality of eligible conceptions of the good, it does not fall afoul of liberal ethical strictures.

Whatever one might say about the decision to adopt another language, it is quite clear that it is difficult to classify as the kind of action so incompatible with basic conditions of human flourishing as to justify state action prohibiting it. After all, those who decide to use a language with a greater number of users than the language in which they were raised do so in order to increase the range of people with whom they can interact in the pursuit of worthwhile human goods. They increase the number of people with whom they can transact business, with whom they can fall in love, with whom they can communicate through poetry, novels, plays, and the like.

Is there, despite the first appearances that I have just expressed, any way in which the decision to adopt another language can be represented that would make it seem an appropriate target of moderate paternalism? One direction that has been taken historically is to invoke notions such as authenticity. The argument would be that people's identities are deeply constituted by the language in which they are raised, so that the decision to turn one's back upon one's language does violence to them. Giving up one's language is on this view incompatible with equality in the conditions of self-esteem (Van Parijs 2011, ch. 4).

The challenge is to arrive at an account of how actions that many people seem to take in an entirely voluntary manner are, despite appearances, incompatible with the social conditions underwriting their status as equal citizens. One way in which this thought might be articulated invokes the notion of "false consciousness." This term denotes the phenomenon of changes of preferences that allow one to adapt to unjust circumstances. Paradigmatic examples include that of the traditional (usually female) homemaker who ends up forming preferences that are functional to the maintenance of the system of patriarchal domination in which she participates, or the slave who ends up loving his chains. Deference to such preferences amounts to complicity in a system of injustice rather than respect for the autonomy of agents.

This possible justification for the overriding of people's preferences is not available in the present context, however. Mere number cases are ones in which there is no system of domination for people to adapt to, no set of unjust background conditions against the backdrop of which false consciousness might develop.

Thus, a justification for the overriding of people's linguistic preferences on moderately moralistic grounds in a mere number case cannot avail itself of the claim that the adoption of another language is somehow incompatible with any conception of human flourishing, nor can it rest on the view that people can legitimately be protected against themselves by political superiors when their preferences would make them complicit in the perpetuation of a system of domination that oppresses them. It is difficult to see how such a justification would not ultimately be forced to reach beyond what I have here termed "moderate moralism," for example by invoking a notion such as "authenticity," where authenticity refers to one's "true" self. It lies well beyond the scope of this chapter to engage in any kind of a critique of this more thoroughgoing form of perfectionism.[3] My intention here is more modestly to suggest that appeals to "true" or "authentic" selves in order to justify people's linguistic preferences involves stepping outside the bounds of a "modest paternalism" the broad outlines of which I have very roughly sketched here, and which a broadly liberal ethics would conceivably countenance.

5. A LIBERAL PATERNALIST APPROACH TO LANGUAGE POLICY? LANGUAGE AS COLLECTIVE ACTION PROBLEM

I noted above that there were two possible roads toward a justification of mild paternalism which a broadly liberal political theory could accept. The first looks at the individual in isolation, and asks whether there are options that the state can remove from his repertoire while still respecting his status as an autonomous chooser. The second places the individual in a broader social context, and recognizes that the preferences people act on are often a function of the choices made by others.[4]

For example, the creation of public goods – that is, of goods that are both non-rival and non-excludable, and that thus generate considerable incentive for free riding – would be difficult, if not impossible, without the intervention of the state. Indeed, were everyone, or even a significant number of citizens, to succumb to the free rider logic, then the good in question would simply not be produced. If we accept that the state has a responsibility to ensure the production of at least certain particularly important public goods, and that language is one of them, then we may have a case for state intervention aimed at protecting languages that might in the absence of such intervention succumb to the tendency that many citizens may experience to free ride.

Security, clean air, and "herd immunity" are paradigmatic cases of public goods, in that everyone would rather be able to enjoy them without paying for them rather than enjoying them while having to pay for them. They are, however, important goods with respect to which the state cannot simply stand by idly if it turns out that their provision is vulnerable to significant free riding. Is language part of this set of vulnerable yet important public goods?

On the face of it, language does not seem to fit this description, for the defectors we are imagining in the context of this chapter are not obviously free riding. That is, they are not enjoying a good without contributing to its provision. Rather, they are doing without it altogether. When, for example, Francophone Quebeckers sent their children to English schools before the advent of coercive legislation preventing them from doing so, they were not obviously expressing the preference that French continue to be a common language while choosing not to contribute to it. Rather, they arguably failed to express a preference in favour of the French language.[5]

Another way of looking at the asymmetry between language protection on the one hand, and herd immunity or clean air on the other, is that those who choose to defect from actions that would contribute to the protection of a vulnerable language are not defecting from language altogether. They are simply defecting from *this particular* language. To the extent that the state has a responsibility to ensure that all citizens have access to *language*, it need not protect any particular language. However, arguing that the state has a responsibility to protect a particular language requires that we go beyond the analogy with such important goods as herd immunity and clean air. And that is a challenge, as opting out of a particular language, even if it is one's native language or the language of one's forebears, is not as clearly irrational and objectionable as would be, say the claim of a person who would claim to opt out of the good of security, or clean air, or immunity from infectious disease. Such a choice would be irrational because it would place an individual in a position that would make it impossible for him to flourish (such decisions are thus ones against which the state can act on the basis of the kinds of "moderately moralistic" justification adduced above). It would also be one to which others could reasonably object, since, first, their attainment of the good depends upon the putative defector doing his part to produce the good, and second, the interest that people have in the good is sufficiently weighty to justify their claim against others that they contribute to the production of the good as a matter of right.[6]

Much more can be said about the degree to which and the conditions under which the state can, or indeed must, contribute through its coercive authority to the production of public goods. The point I wanted to make in the present context is the limited one that the maintenance of a smaller language cannot be construed as a public good in the narrow sense that would within the context of a broadly liberal ethic justify state action that would prohibit people acting on their linguistic preferences.

But perhaps I have misrepresented the structure of the collective action problem that the problem of linguistic choice puts in place. The problem with language preservation is not that people might form the thought that they will be able to enjoy the use of a language regardless of whether they themselves act in ways conducive to its survival. Rather it is that they want to continue to enjoy the good in question, and are happy to "pay" for it (that is, to engage in whatever cooperative behaviour will reliably conduce to its creation or maintenance), but only on condition that a sufficient number of others engage in such behaviour as well.

Representing the situation of speakers of a small, vulnerable language as an assurance problem leads us to interpret defection from cooperative schemes in a different manner. The defector is not someone who at the end of the day does not care which language she communicates in as long as there is one which she can make use of. Nor is she someone who is seeking strategic advantage over her fellow citizens by making use of a good that they have produced. Rather, she is someone who simply wants to avoid being a patsy. That is, she wants to avoid engaging in cooperative behaviour only to find that too few of her fellow citizens have done so to allow the goods which she was hoping to realize through her cooperative behaviour to be realized.

It does not seem implausible to suppose that many people, perhaps most people, who have been brought up in a language would, all things equal, rather be able to live in that language than have to adopt another language. Continued use of the language allows them to remain in contact with a tradition that is in large measure linguistically inscribed. It also allows them in many cases to maintain communication with living forebears. What's more, it cuts down on the transition costs attendant upon adopting a new language. They will thus tend to view state action that takes the non-cooperative option off the table as a kind of self-binding mechanism, one that extends their autonomous agency rather than short-circuiting it. Such self-binding mechanisms are common, and do not pose a particular problem for liberals. Indeed, liberal constitutionalism is premised upon the idea that liberal norms, such as rights, sometimes require for their maintenance the realization that people might sometimes in the heat of political conflict be tempted to abandon them, and thus that their hands must be tied lest they succumb to this temptation (Holmes 1987). A language policy aimed at binding people to their linguistic preference for their native tongue in the face of the siren's song of the bigger language is structurally similar to such constitutional mechanisms.

The asymmetry between liberal constitutionalism and language policies aimed at preserving minority languages by constraining people's language choices is of course that the kinds of rights that liberal constitutions, and in particular their Charters or Bills of Rights, enshrine are not just preferences, they are obligations. We have an obligation to respect each other's rights, and constitutional mechanisms place such obligations beyond the reach of mere preference. Unless we invoke the kind of authenticity-based argument that we have earlier ruled out of court as being unavailable to a liberal-democratic ethics, the choice of one language rather than another cannot be seen as an obligation in anything like the same way.

Thus, when political authorities act to keep a language viable by prohibiting certain language choices, they assist people in being able to do something that they aspire to, rather than abetting them in doing something (the respect of each others' rights) that is morally required of them.

Now imagine a linguistic community made up of several different kinds of linguistic preference profiles. Some members want to preserve the viability of the language, and are willing to act in a cooperative manner to achieve that end, on condition that a number of others sufficient to achieve viability do so as well. Call them "purists." Others would rather continue using the minority language, but are disposed to free ride on the cooperative behaviour of others. Call them "free riders." The difference between "purists" and "free riders" is that coercion is not required to get the former to act cooperatively to achieve the desired good.

Others in our imagined community are indifferent as between the smaller language and the bigger one, but are responsive to the incentives that are created by numerical considerations. Their linguistic preferences will tend to vary as a function. Call them "fence-sitters." And still others positively want to adopt the bigger language so as to extend their communicative reach. Call them "defectors."

Purists can arguably coerce free riders into acting cooperatively, since the intention of free riders is to reap unjust benefit from their cooperative behaviour. Considerations of fairness between people who all share the same goal therefore militate in favour of free riders being made to do their fair share for the attainment of the good of language maintenance. To the extent that the cooperative behaviour of the purists and the coerced compliance of free riders increases the number of people who use the threatened smaller language, this may have an impact on the number of fence-sitters who choose to use that language as well.

Is there any justification for the coercion of the defectors? Imagine two scenarios. In the first, a threshold of viability is reached through the coercion of free riders and the incentivization of fence-sitters. In this case, there seems no reason to coerce the defectors. No additional good is attained for anyone else through their compliance. One could argue that fairness considerations argue in favour of coercion. But remember that, as opposed to the kind of coercion that occurs in the pursuit of an obligatory goal such as the respect of people's rights, purists as I have defined them here are pursuing an optional goal.

In the second, the viability of the language depends upon the coerced compliance of defectors. In the latter case, there is reason for the purists to coerce the defectors, though those reasons require that they reach beyond the liberal repertoire. That is, they have a perfectionist end, one that cannot be justified on the basis of the kind of "modest moralism" described above. They are in other words coercing the defectors on the basis of an end that the defectors need not share. The question of whether, all things considered, it is preferable to pursue the perfectionist end of language preservation or to cleave to liberal democratic constraints is one that, happily, lies well beyond the bounds of this chapter. Resolving this question ultimately depends upon our responses to questions to do with the value of language preservation irreducible to the preferences and interests of individuals, and with the question of the degree and conditions under which we believe that the good of linguistic *diversity* is sufficiently great to justify mild coercion.

Thus, considering language choice within a strategic context allows us to identify at least one kind of situation in which coercive language legislation can be justified on broadly liberal democratic grounds even in mere number cases. It also allows us to identify with greater precision the moral dilemmas that attend speakers of smaller languages who find themselves in situations in which they must coerce fence-sitters and defectors in order to protect those languages.

6. CONCLUSION

I have argued in this chapter that in what I have referred to as the case of mere numbers, it is difficult, if not impossible, to justify measures aimed at constraining the linguistic choices of individuals so as to achieve the goal of language preservation. I have argued that there is one situation in which such constraint may be justified – that in which those who are willing to act cooperatively in order to achieve that end coerce free riders into compliance. I make no claim as to how frequent this kind of situation is in the real world.

Nor do I make any claim about the frequency of what I have throughout referred to as the case of mere number. Remember that I have bracketed the question of whether cases of mere number that are causally related to injustice lying in the distant past should in fact be considered as cases of mere number. That question, the question of just how long the present should be seen as marked by the moral stains of the past, is one of the deepest and most difficult that we have to face in post-colonial political philosophy. I hope to be able to turn my attention to it in future work.

Acknowledgment: A French version of this paper was published, with slight modifications, in *Constitutionnalisme, droits et diversité: Mélanges en l'honneur de José Woehrling*, edited by Alain-G. Gagnon and Pierre Noreau, 193–220 (Montreal, QC: Les éditions Thémis, 2017).

NOTES

Earlier versions of this chapter were presented in the context of a conference on the topic of "language ethics" held in Montreal, at the Department of Philosophy Colloquium, McGill University, and at the Research Group on Constitutional Studies, McGill University, and at a conference in honour of José Woehrling at the Université de Montréal. I thank audiences at these venues for having provided me with much food for thought.

1   Lest I be accused of insouciance with respect to issues of climate justice, I hasten to specify that the remarks made above for the sake of argument assume the absence of anthropic causes to some people being in the dire

climate situations in which they find themselves. Where desertification is caused by rising temperatures resulting from greenhouse gas emissions, there most decidedly is injustice that must be compensated, even on more traditional, "action-based" conceptions of justice.

2 Some of this research is summarized in "Walk Tall," in *The Economist*, 25 April 2002.

3 For a trenchant critique of the idea of authenticity, see Potter (2011).

4 Alan Patten pursues a closely related line of argument in a forthcoming paper entitled "Protecting Vulnerable Languages" (Patten, forthcoming).

5 I have examined the philosophical dimensions of the policy choices faced by Quebec society in Weinstock (2016).

6 For a very thorough examination of the "market failure" argument in favour of state intervention in the area of language, see Robichaud (2011).

REFERENCES

Cohen, G.A. 1989. "On the Currency of Egalitarian Justice." *Ethics* 99, no. 4: 906–44.

Conly, Sarah. 2012. *Against Autonomy. The Case for Coercive Paternalism*. Cambridge: Cambridge University Press.

De Schutter, Helder, and Lea Ypi. 2012. "Language and Luck." *Politics, Philosophy & Economics* 11, no. 4: 361–2.

Ginsburgh, Victor, and Shlomo Weber. 2011. *How Many Languages Do We Need?* Princeton, NJ: Princeton University Press.

Holmes, Stephen. 1987. *Passions and Constraint: On the Theory of Liberal Democracy*. Chicago, IL: University of Chicago Press.

Khader, Serene. 2011. *Adaptive Preferences and Women's Empowerment*. Oxford, UK: Oxford University Press.

Laponce, Jean. 1984. *Langue et Territoire*. Ste. Foy, QC: Les Presses de l'Université Laval.

Norman, Wayne. 2009. *Negotiating Nationalism*. Oxford, UK: Oxford University Press.

Patten, Alan. Forthcoming. "Protecting Vulnerable Languages: The Public Good Argument." In *Oxford Studies in Political Philosophy*.

Perez, Nahshon. 2012. *Freedom from Past Injustice*. Edinburgh: Edinburgh University Press.

Potter, Andrew. 2011. *The Authenticity Hoax.* Toronto: Emblem Books.

Raz, Joseph. 1986. *The Morality of Freedom.* Oxford, UK: Oxford University Press.

Robichaud, David. 2011. "Justice et politiques linguistiques : pourquoi les laisser-fairistes devraient exiger des interventions de l'État." *Philosophiques* 38, no. 2: 419–38.

Sunstein, Cass, and Richard H. Thaler. 2008. *Nudge. Improving Decisions about Health, Wealth, and Happiness.* New Haven, CT: Yale University Press.

Van Parijs, Philippe. 2011. *Linguistic Justice for Europe and for the World.* Oxford, UK: Oxford University Press.

Waldron, Jeremy. 1992. "Superseding Historical Injustice." *Ethics* 103, no. 1: 4–28.

Weinstock, Daniel. 2014. "The Complex Normative Foundations of Language Policy." *Language Policy* 13, no. 4: 317–33.

– 2016. "The Politics of Language: Philosophical Reflections on the Case of Quebec." In *Quebec Questions*, 2nd ed., edited by Stephan Gervais, Christopher Kirkey, and Jarett Rudy. Oxford, UK: Oxford University Press: 57–67.

7

Language Policy, Political Theory, and English as a "Global" Language

THOMAS RICENTO

Within the language policy and planning literature, coherent and explicit theories of politics and power are rarely evident. Terms such as "dominant language" and "minority language" can mean different things in different contexts. Other terms that tend to be under-theorized include globalization, market economy, and liberalism. On the other hand, within the literature of political theory, a great deal of attention is paid to liberalism, justice, and rights, but when these frameworks and their corresponding criteria are applied to matters of languages and language policies, normative approaches tend to ignore or mischaracterize the relations between language, identity, community, and the evolution of particular societies viewed from a long-term historical perspective. In this chapter, I explore some of the ways that apparently incompatible claims from the LPP literature can be disambiguated and resolved by reference to political theory. In particular, I will focus on the competing views regarding the role of English in the world today as either a) a form of linguistic imperialism, or b) a vehicle for social and economic mobility, or (c) necessary for the promotion of a global *demos*. In analyzing the nature and effects of neoliberalism, as expressed in its globalized economic and political forms, I show that the role and utility of English worldwide is a vehicle for mobility for some people, in some economic sectors, mainly the knowledge economy, but is generally not connected to socioeconomic mobility for the vast majority of the global workforce, nor is its current status as a global "lingua franca" relevant to the promotion of global justice.

My purpose in this chapter is to interrogate a construct – English as a "global" language – that is of interest to scholars in both the political philosophy and the language policy and planning literatures. In these literatures, a variety of approaches and analytic frameworks have been adopted, and a wide range of descriptions and explanations proffered, as to the nature and effects of "global" English in the contemporary world. Scholars in these literatures often borrow ideas and theories from a broad range of disciplines in the social sciences and humanities, including cultural studies, political economy, postmodernism, critical theory, history, sociology, linguistics, and education, among others that could be mentioned. To be sure, this admixture of theories and ideas from various disciplines is inevitable; when political philosophers invoke "language" in their normative theorizing on language rights and democracy, they are dependent on expertise, implicitly or explicitly, from the various language sciences literatures. Western political theorists, generally non-experts in the language sciences, whose principal aim is often to advance normative theories on desirable states of affairs within liberal democratic states, tend to deal with language as a stable nominal category, as something that one "has" or "doesn't have," that can be labelled as one thing (e.g. English) or another thing (e.g. French), that may be learned for defined purposes, that has instrumental and symbolic value, that is used principally as a modality for interpersonal communication, with "speakers," possibly with associated geographic territories, and with cultural affiliations and traditions "attached" to named languages and varieties. The fact that situated language practices and behaviours are far more complex than this and not generally explainable by using the tools of rational choice methodology common in political theorizing, that cultural affiliations and identities cannot be predicted strictly on linguistic grounds (or vice versa), and that the desire to acquire, use, maintain, or identify with a particular language/variety may have little to do with its purported instrumental value or utility are often not taken into account by political philosophers engaged in normative theory construction that involves language(s).

At the same time, while scholarly research in the language policy and planning literature may make reference to, or incorporate theories from, political philosophy and economics, the focus generally is on aspects related to how language(s) are deployed, taught/acquired, valued, threatened, and used/perceived within various contexts, such as schools, families and communities, public and private institutions, or national or supranational contexts. Constructs such as language ideologies, communities of practice, linguistic imperialism, discourses of power, and many related concepts are often invoked in explaining the roles and status that languages/varieties play in defined contexts, synchronically or diachronically. The broader picture often provided by political philosophers, who take care to ground their theorizing in carefully stipulated theories of normative justice and the role of the state in liberal democracies, is often left out of discussions in the LPP literature that may include references to "justice" or "the state" without much, or any, detail on how these terms are understood in the relevant literature.

In order to demonstrate how the under- (or non-)specification of concepts, along with the use of selective empirical data, used in the LPP literature can be problematic, I will focus on an area of research – English as a global language – that has generated a great deal of attention in recent years. I will argue that lack of clarity on key terms and concepts leads to disputes and contrary positions on important issues where there might otherwise be greater agreement, or at least a basis for identifying common ground, which could lead to a greater possibility of consilience, a term of long historical provenance revived by biologist E.O. Wilson (1998), in which "principles from different disciplines ... form a comprehensive theory" (Merriam-Webster Dictionary). In particular, I argue that language policy scholars' lack of sophistication in political economy impacts their ability to critically address the effects of neo-liberal economic policies on the status and utility of global languages, such as English, and on the status and utility of non-global languages that could play an important role in local economic and social development in low-income countries.[1] Currently, there is not enough explicit discussion or analysis in the political theory or LPP literatures on how the interests and values of transnational corporations, and the policies of states and international organizations that support those interests and values, may influence the trajectory and fate of languages.[2] This is not to posit or defend a deterministic model of cause/effect regarding a relation between political economy and language status, but is rather to say that in the absence of clearly articulated views on political economy, with robust empirical evidence to support those views, we may have fewer tools – that is, theories and associated research methods – with which to argue in support of the maintenance of minority languages and cultures and societal multilingualism. In essence, I am arguing for political theory that is more sensitive to empiricism, and a language policy approach that incorporates political theory in analyzing the status and utility of language(s) in the world.

1. THE CASE OF ENGLISH AS A "GLOBAL" LANGUAGE

To illustrate my argument about under-specification, incompleteness, or problematic appropriation of ideas from various branches of political and economic theory in research in language policy, I consider competing views on the role of English in non-English-dominant countries in the world today as either (1) a form of linguistic imperialism, or (2) a vehicle for social and economic mobility, or (3) a global lingua franca necessary for a global *demos* essential to achieving global justice. I will discuss the work of three scholars whose published research has advanced arguments associated with these three positions, respectively: Robert Phillipson, Janina Brutt-Griffler, and Philippe Van Parijs.

The first problem with these views, or ways of thinking about English in these stark terms, is that they are not falsifiable positions except on mostly ad hoc grounds, often based on case studies that are then generalized (in the case of positions 1 and 2), or based on abstract normative political theories (as is the case for position 3). Additionally, a number of constructs are used, such as social class, that are not defined, or are ideologically problematic (a well-attested problem within variationist sociolinguists' research[3]), and are usually not historically contextualized, leading to generalizations that are untenable. Finally, there is frequently a tendency to accept *doxa* uncritically, often reflexively. This combination of factors often results in arguments and claims that are easy to criticize as merely opinion or as unprovable generalizations. We need to provide more consistent and well-articulated arguments, bolstered with empirical evidence, if, for example, we are to have any hope of influencing public discourse and debates on social justice that rely on the argument that cultural and linguistic diversity are integral to the meaningful democratic participation of all citizens in a polity.

Position 1: English as an Agent of Linguistic Imperialism

Robert Phillipson (1992) is most closely associated with this position, and his work has been influential in the language policy literature. Phillipson (2001, 187) argues that "English is integral to the globalization processes that characterize the contemporary post-cold-war phase of aggressive casino capitalism, economic restructuring, McDonaldisation and militarization on all continents ... The dominance of English is also being consolidated in other dimensions of globalization such as military links (NATO, UN peace-keeping operations, the arms trade), and culture (Hollywood products, BBC World, CNN, MTV)." Phillipson acknowledges that "[w]hile there is no simple correlation between the use of English and either British culture or US corporate interests, these developments embody and entail hegemonising processes that tend to render the use of English 'natural' and 'normal', and to marginalise other languages" (191). There is undoubtedly a relation between the global economic, cultural, and political influence of the United States and the growth in the popularity of English in many countries today. Phillipson's response, an alternative to this "Diffusion of English Paradigm," is what he labels the "Ecology of Languages Paradigm" (193), which "builds on our linguistic and cultural diversity, attempts to ensure equality for speakers of all languages, and uses the human rights system as a counterweight to the 'free' market ... To advance the cause of the Ecology of Languages requires efforts at all levels from the local to the global" (193).

Whereas the conceptual apparatus for linguistic imperialism depends on an analysis of the negative effects of Western economic and political imperialism on mostly low-income countries, with putative bad effects on their thousands of languages under pressure from (neo)colonial languages, the construct "ecology of languages" is undefined and abstract; how can "equality for speakers of all languages" be understood, let alone attained? What would such "equality" look like? Phillipson says that efforts are required "at all levels from the local to the global"; but if English has gained its great global power because of a complex set of developments in global expansion, especially in the last sixty years, what actions could be implemented to halt this expansion that are relevant for the protection of languages and for achieving "equality for speakers of all languages"? This seems to be conceptually, and programmatically, an untenable project. Part of the problem is the weight Phillipson gives to English in his argument. It isn't really – or only – English, per se, that is the problem; Phillipson reveals as much in his own recitation of the components of the "Ecology of languages paradigm" which calls, among other things, for "economic democratization ... protection of local production and national sovereignties ... [and] redistribution of the world's material resources" (193). This is a call for a fundamental reformation of the current world economic order, and not for finding an alternative to the role played by English in global economic activity, which, I believe, is highly relevant to the status of local languages; however, it appears in a long list of items that are not ordered or prioritized in any coherent way. Does this paradigm presuppose economic democratization as a *condition* for "equality for speakers of all languages," or will regimes of language rights (a component of the "Ecology of Languages Paradigm") somehow be conducive to changes in political and, eventually, economic relations? We can't know, or even guess, how this paradigm might unfold, or be operationalized, as the nature of the relations between the various components described by Phillipson is not discussed. As with normative political philosophers, Phillipson is presenting particular values that he believes are consonant with a "better world"; but his alternative paradigm to the "Diffusion of English Paradigm" is not particularly coherent with regard to a discernable philosophical position or framework.

Position 2: English as a Vehicle for Social and Economic Mobility

Janina Brutt-Griffler has been a strong critic of Phillipson, particularly with regard to his supposed downplaying of the positive role that English can play in promoting social mobility in low-income countries in Africa and elsewhere. She argues (2005, 29), for example, ventriloquizing for two South African women – Mrs. L and Pamela – that "exclusion from high proficiency [in] English [is] a prime determinant of lack of access to wealth in the world they [Mrs. L and Pamela, indicative of poor black South Africans generally] inhabit." She criticizes those who support the teaching of mother tongues over English as being insensitive to the economic aspirations of oppressed and impoverished people as they seek to escape poverty with the aid of English. This argument has also been associated with supporters of the "English only" movement in the United States and by proponents of "English First" in American public education (Pogge 2003). Brutt-Griffler (2002) argues that the denial of English-language-medium education helped maintain social and economic segregation in the former British colony Basutoland (Lesotho) during the late nineteenth and early twentieth centuries, and that this pattern persists in South Africa today. However, in a critique of Brutt-Griffler (2002), Pennycook (2004, 148) points out, "Part of the argument here about access hinges on whether we are looking at individual rights to English or whether we are looking at how access to English can alleviate poverty across a broader domain. It is perhaps disingenuous to argue for a need to deal with class, and then to argue in terms of individual access." Further to the point that individual access to English does not correlate with the reduction of class-related poverty in low-income countries, Bruthiaux (2002) argues that for many of the world's poor, English language education is "an outlandish irrelevance" and "talk of a role for English language education in facilitating the process of poverty reduction and a major allocation of public resources to that end is likely to prove misguided and wasteful" (292–3). Pennycook concludes that "we need to distinguish very clearly between individually-oriented access arguments about escape from poverty, and class-oriented arguments about large-scale poverty reduction" (148). In summary, Brutt-Griffler uses a case study to make a general claim about the relation between access to English and economic mobility in South Africa; yet, even as a case study, the evidence that English plays anything more than a trivial role in reducing poverty in South Africa is lacking.

Position 3: English as a Global Lingua Franca Necessary for a Global *Demos*

Of the three positions briefly described in this chapter, the third one, represented in the work of Philippe Van Parijs, is perhaps the most ambitious and most coherent, if flawed. Van Parijs is a political theorist who has written extensively about the benefits of a lingua franca, such as English, in helping to promote social and economic justice globally. He argues (2000) that promotion of the teaching and learning of English in low-income countries could help reduce the out-migration of highly trained, English-speaking citizens, who flee in great numbers to the wealthier "knowledge economy" countries. He argues that the reclamation of lost income and increased corporate taxes could be used for massive investment in English language teaching, leading to an increase in productivity and gross domestic product (GDP). Even more ambitiously, in his latest book, *Linguistic Justice for Europe and for the World* (2011), Van Parijs argues that we need a lingua franca in Europe and across the world because "[i]ts adoption and spreading creates and expands a transnational demos, by facilitating direct communication, live or online, without the cumbersome and expensive mediation of interpretation and translation. It enables not only the rich and the powerful, but also the poor and the powerless to communicate, debate, network, cooperate, lobby, demonstrate effectively across borders. This common demos … is a precondition for the effective pursuit of justice, and this fact provides the second fundamental reason why people committed to egalitarian global justice should not only welcome the spread of English as a lingua franca but see it as their duty to contribute to this spread in Europe and throughout the world" (Van Parijs 2011, 31).

Van Parijs is a native Francophone from Belgium, fluent in English and a number of other languages, a world traveller who has certainly benefited from his multilingual abilities. However, part of his plan for dramatically increasing the numbers of English-speakers globally includes massive subsidies from the "free-riding" Anglophone countries who benefit unfairly in a number of ways by the arbitrary "luck" of having been born in English-dominant (and wealthy) countries, such as the US, the UK, Australia, Canada, and New Zealand. His argument for a global lingua franca necessary for the strengthening of global networks and institutions that could serve to advance global interests of economic justice, environmental sustainability, and the reduction of conflict is certainly appealing (if not original), as it could (at least hypothetically) help move the world towards communication networks less tethered to ethnic and nationalistic identities and the myriad languages that reflect and constitute those identities; but that is wishful thinking, at best. The vast majority of people in the world are not motivated by abstract goals of "justice" to acquire an additional language. Clearly, Van Parijs is talking about elites who have access to high-quality education and training in English, and not the average citizen. Van Parijs also downplays the contradictions between the values and goals of economic neoliberalism, which disproportionately benefit the interests of elites in wealthy nations, and the values and goals necessary to promote a meaningful "democratic world order" in which social and economic justice could *only* be feasible if the debilitating values and manifest negative effects of the current neoliberal global regime were reversed, or at least severely modified. A lingua franca cannot overcome such intractable contradictions. Another major weakness in Van Parijs's argument is his somewhat idealized conception of language, a view that sees named languages as discrete vehicles for communication in which the symbolic/affiliational aspects can be abstracted out for particular and defined instrumental purposes (see Ives 2015 for discussion), and which has little to say about the matter of language varieties, code mixing, pragmatics – in short, the complexity and limitations of language in interpersonal/intercultural communication. Beyond the fact that the language called "English" exists in myriad forms and varieties, many of which are not mutually intelligible, there is no reason to believe that a global lingua franca – and Van Parijs argues that "English" (presumably an idealized "international" variety that no one speaks) is, currently and for the foreseeable future, the only candidate for this role – would be neutral with regard to the dominant political, economic, cultural, and symbolic values that gave rise to a particular variety in the first place ("British" English and more recently "American" English[4]), at least for the foreseeable future, or that the interests of groups represented by spokespersons using a variety of English as a second or third language would be fairly heard, let alone acted upon, as if interests were unrelated to social positions in unequal power hierarchies. Furthermore, what would motivate the states, corporations, and institutions that have benefited from English-based information technology and communication systems, with their built-in ties with Western values and economic advantages, to "democratize" the world system by changing the "rules" that have benefited them for so long, especially given the inability of institutional "referees" in global trade (such as the World Trade Organization) to level the playing field among historically unequal nations? The European Union has not been successful in developing policies to make the Eurozone function. If Europe cannot get its own economic house in order, it is even more unlikely that the roughly two hundred countries in the world would work toward a common purpose, aided by greater access to a lingua franca, given the massive social and economic inequality that currently exists. The elaborate (and often impressive) argumentation and economic analyses Van Parijs provides to justify his pro-English as a lingua franca argument cannot overcome these fundamental, seemingly intractable, obstacles to finding common ground and common purpose in a world in which everything has been, or will soon be, commodified, owned, "priced," with the owners increasingly controlling decisions about economic inputs and outputs on a global scale in the service of their own economic interests. Yet, Van Parijs does provide a coherent and well-reasoned analysis that takes into account economic, political, social, and (to a limited degree) linguistic factors in an integrated way, and in this regard his work can be viewed as exemplary, and as a useful starting point for further discussions and research on the role of language(s) in the promotion of social justice on a global scale.

2. LIBERALISM AND THE ROLE OF STATES IN PROTECTING LANGUAGE MINORITY GROUPS' RIGHTS

While my focus in this chapter has been (mostly) to provide a critique on how political economy has been used (or not) by LPP scholars (Phillipson and Brutt-Griffler), and to some degree by the political theorist Philippe Van Parijs, I would also like to briefly consider some potentially inherent problems with orthodox political liberalism as it is understood and used by political theorists whose work deals with language rights and language policy regimes. If we look to orthodox political liberalism[5] for guidance about whether language minority groups have legitimate rights claims to maintain their language(s) in the face of pressures from dominant, national/international (e.g. global English), and/or official languages to assimilate linguistically, we do not find much encouragement, whether in the writings of Locke or Bentham, or of modern (re)interpreters of eighteenth- and nineteenth-century theorists, such as Rawls (1971).[6] This is because language is a *social* phenomenon, spoken and written by communities of people, and the core of liberal political philosophy is the essentialness of *individual* liberty and rights to satisfy the supposedly unquenchable acquisitive desires of individual human beings;[7]

however, as not all languages are equal in their social status, both within and across societies, with this inequality extending to individuals as members of language communities, individuals who speak primarily lower-status languages or language varieties (usually non-national/non-dominant ones) may well be disadvantaged unless and until they acquire the higher-status language(s) spoken by other social/cultural groups, if they want to pursue their "acquisitive desires," be these material or non-material in nature. The fact that language is mutable – that is, humans are able to learn other languages, given access and opportunity to do so – leads many supporters of modern orthodox liberalism to argue that minority languages (and their speakers) need no special protections, while non-mutable characteristics, such as ethnicity, race, and gender, may lead to overt discrimination against individuals as members of defined groups, and therefore may require extra protection in the form of civil and even constitutional enactments. Yet, learning a second or third "additional" language is not always a realistic option, and it certainly is not easy nor without costs (as Van Parijs correctly notes). Further, since within liberal political theory, the state should *not* favour one language over another, as that (according to Patten and Kymlicka [2003]) would constitute an impermissible abuse of government's proper role as impartial protector of fundamental *individual* human rights for all citizens, the de facto, and usually de jure, privileged status of official/dominant/(inter)national languages unfairly provides an advantage to those who acquire them natively and who are able to be educated in them. Although supporters of modern liberalism, such as Patten and Kymlicka (2003, 13), argue that "a common national language helps to promote a common civic identity without denying the 'fact of reasonable pluralism' or the liberal commitment to neutrality regarding conceptions of the good life," this is more of a theoretical position than an empirical statement (as we will see in the following paragraph). In this regard, the role of a lingua franca in Van Parijs's conception of a global *demos* is analogous to the role of a national language in modern liberal democracies; yet, the unwarranted belief in the neutrality of the state with regard to languages within its jurisdiction (including colonial languages) applies equally to unwarranted claims about the neutrality of a global lingua franca(s) within international bodies, with their particular and interested values and institutionalized systems of governance and decision-making.

Critics of orthodox liberalism, many of whom identify with the label of communitarianism, do not view national/official languages as neutral instrumentalities that do not lessen the status or viability of multilingualism, in which "other" languages are recognized and afforded space in public domains, for example, to access public services and other public goods. These critics have a problem with the strict separation of citizenship and identity and the view that "personal *autonomy* – based on the political rights attributable to citizenship – always takes precedence over personal (and collective) *identity* and the widely differing ways of life which constitute the latter" (May 2001, 103). Philosopher Charles Taylor (1994, 33–4) argues that identity "is who we are, 'where we're coming from'. As such, it is the background against which our tastes and desires and opinions and aspirations make sense." Sociolinguist Stephen May (2001, 104) points out that the problem with orthodox liberal normative philosophy is that proponents believe in the ethnic neutrality of the state: "In other words, for orthodox liberals, the civic realm of the nation-state is a forum in which ethnicity does not (and *should* not) feature. However … ethnicity is *never* absent from the civic realm. Rather, the civic realm represents the particular (although not necessarily exclusive) *communal* interests and values of the dominant ethnie *as if* these values were held by all." Or, in Charles Taylor's (1994, 43–4) words, the "supposedly neutral set of difference-blind principles [that constitute the liberal] politics of equal dignity is in fact a reflection of one hegemonic culture … [it is] a particularism masquerading as the universal." May (2001) argues that at least some minority languages and their community of speakers merit the same sorts of language rights and prerogatives afforded to speakers of the majority/dominant/(inter)national language, since many, but not all, of those who speak a minority language would find it difficult – if not impossible – to have the means to "lead a good life, in having those things that a good life contains" (Kymlicka 1989, 10) if they were detached from the cultural moorings that provide an important – but not exclusive – means (through *their* language and the cultural meanings made available through it) for making sense of the world and their place in it. Such connections, critics of orthodox liberalism argue, are *requirements* for meaningful participation in the polity for many, though not all, members of minority communities. Even Philippe Van Parijs (2011, 119) argues that "parity of esteem," or equal respect for people's collective identities, "constitut[es] an important aspect of what matters for a society to be just," even though he extols the many benefits of a global lingua franca (see my comments above on this point).

To summarize, critics of orthodox political liberalism argue that the state is not neutral with regard to language policy, and that this has some negative consequences; it demonstrably favours usually one language as the national language through a variety of institutional, political, and legal policies and practices. In general, the national language, which may or may not be officially recognized as such, and which is not always the language of the numerical majority in the country, is the predominant medium of instruction in schooling, in the courts and legislatures, the media, public services, entertainment, and so on. The process by which a language becomes the national language very often involves the marginalization, suppression, and restriction of other languages (see Ricento 1998 on the situation in the US), along with the construction of a national identity (Ricento 2003). In other words, illiberal means have often been used to impose a particular language as the national language,[8] and attempts to expand domains for other languages in public life, for example through provision of bilingual ballots, bilingual education, and access to services in "other" languages, have frequently, and ironically, been viewed as being "illiberal" (i.e., they favour one group's interests over those of other groups), and contrary to the "natural" order of things, linguistically speaking, when in fact there is or was nothing at all natural about how most national languages came to enjoy their current privileged societal status in the first place.[9] These empirical facts and findings should not be removed from debates on normative political philosophy; indeed, history and politics should be taken fully into account and inform normative theory-making if these theories are to have usefulness in understanding the world as it is, as well as providing feasible means for achieving justice (Honig 1993; Honig and Stears 2011).

3. GLOBALIZATION AND ENGLISH

When we look at English in its global role, the economic dimension – and not the identity aspect – is what determines its value and status in countries with aspirations to participate in the knowledge economy. While proficiency in

English, whether as a first, second, or third language, *may* provide an advantage for careers and employment in certain sectors of the global economy, the number of available jobs and the number of jobs being created that require significant knowledge of English is very, very small compared to the number of workers seeking jobs worldwide. While there are many factors that impact labour markets, it is possible to look at sectors of the economy and investment patterns, and from the data make informed judgments about the relative values of languages within identified employment sectors. We can also discern correlations between capital investments and the relative presence of particular educational and linguistic resources, globally. Even a cursory examination of one (albeit highly diverse) economic sector – the knowledge economy – reveals the ways in which knowledge of certain "world" languages, and especially English, provides a competitive advantage, but only if coupled with appropriate educational credentials (Grin et al. 2010).

However, before examining data on jobs, investment, and the role of lingua francas in knowledge economy employment, we should note that it would be wrong to conclude that what is being described here is simply the efficient operation of a "self-equilibrating" global market, in which (in classic market economic terms) price determines everything. No such market exists, and has probably never existed in a global context, despite claims made by (neo)liberal economists to the contrary. There are many ways in which decisions about the production, distribution, and, crucially, prices of goods and services are influenced, and often controlled, by the political class in those countries with the most to gain – and lose – in global commerce of all types. Institutions with the ability to lend money, determine interest rates on loans, and set terms of lending (often referred to as conditionality in the economics literature) are generally controlled by the nations with the most wealth, and the means to protect it (Harvey 2005; Stiglitz 2007). The agendas and policies of the International Monetary Fund, the World Bank, and the World Trade Organization, for example, are determined largely by self-interested governments of the original G-7[10] countries, which in turn are greatly influenced by the largest banks and corporations, all of whom seek to maximize their self-interest when it comes to investment and trade policies.

The jobs in low-income countries are disproportionately very low-wage jobs for which only minimal competence – if any – in English is required. In those cases in which a high degree of English is required, as with call centres in India (Sonntag 2009) and elsewhere, educated workers who also happen to speak, or can master, a variety of English acceptable to American consumers (Blommaert 2009) will have an advantage over those who don't speak this variety of English. As we will see below, a person with a high level of English literacy and tertiary educational attainment has an advantage in competing for knowledge economy jobs *in the formal economy* compared to a person with neither English literacy nor a tertiary level of education; however, given the relatively small number of these jobs available globally, and the relatively low number of persons who meet these minimal requirements, the bald claim that English is a means to social mobility, let alone necessary to promote global justice – even in the long run – while not acknowledging and addressing the underlying dynamics of transnational capitalism, the role of high-income states in maintaining and benefiting by the current system, and the effects on employment and migration patterns that often work against the sustainable development of local economies, especially in low-income countries, cannot be justified.

4. NEOLIBERALISM AND WORK

In order to back up these claims, it is necessary to consider relevant empirical data. I have endeavoured to provide data that has been gathered by official, non-partisan bodies, and that has been reported in the work of scholars from the economics, global studies, and language policy and planning literatures. The data I reference here are accurate, to the best of my knowledge, and they are used to support my argument that the views of Philippson, Brutt-Griffler, and Van Parijs discussed earlier can be reconciled if we consider the macro picture through the lens of political economic analysis.

Castells (2006, 58) estimates that only about 200 million of the world's (formal) workforce of 3 billion workers (about 7 percent) find work through the 53,000 or so multinational corporations and their related networks; yet this workforce is responsible for 40 percent of global GDP, and two-thirds of world trade (Williams 2010, 50). Lingua francas are frequently used in these companies, regardless of their location, and English is by far the most common.

Ammon (1995) reports that the German Chambers of Commerce recommend the use of English as the sole language of communication for transactions with 64 countries; German is recommended as a co-language for 25 countries and Spanish for 17. These data suggest that English is a global lingua franca for players in the knowledge economy, and English, French, German, and Spanish are European lingua francas. Given that trade involving Japan, the US, and Europe accounted for 50 percent of world GDP in 2000, the special status of these languages appears to be justified.

Again, we can turn to the processes of neoliberalism and their globalized effects to account for the movement of skilled labour to countries whose state or national language is English or to companies who use English as the primary language of their activities. European mergers and acquisitions exceeded $1 trillion USD during 2005 (Williams 2010, 28). The US alone accounted for another $1.16 trillion in the value of mergers and acquisitions in 2005, followed by the UK ($305 billion) (Williams 2010, 28). Many of these mergers involved technology companies. These new mega-companies have no obligation to retain their headquarters in the "home" country and they increasingly tend to move to countries with the most favourable corporate taxation regimes. For example, according to a story in *The Guardian*, in 2015, 700 American companies were in Ireland employing 130,000 people; the list of major firms operating in the Republic of Ireland includes Intel, Boston Scientific, Dell, Pfizer, Google, Hewlett Packard, Facebook, and Johnson and Johnson. According to *The Guardian*, "a major draw for US firms is Ireland's low 12.5% corporation tax rate and numerous controversial tax breaks."[11] In 2010, the OECD (Organization for Economic Co-operation and Development, consisting of thirty members) countries with combined corporate income tax rates significantly lower than the US included Ireland (12.5%), Iceland (15%), Switzerland (21%), Denmark (25%), Finland (26%), Sweden (26%), Norway (28%), and the UK (28%); by comparison, the US rate was 39%, well above the OECD average rate of 25.5%. Clearly, English is the dominant language in technology and the knowledge economy, and these countries have English as either the national language or a language spoken by high percentages of the relevant workforce. The combination of favourable corporate tax policies, a highly developed infrastructure, and a highly educated English-speaking workforce helps perpetuate and increase disparities between rich and poor countries by attracting corporations, beholden to shareholders' interests, to these rich countries.

Only the countries that invest massively in education and research can appropriate the foreign technologies necessary to catch up with the rich countries. The United Nations Conference on Trade and Development claims that the poorer countries are the origin of only 8.4 percent of the spending on R&D in the world, with 97 percent of this being in Asia.[12] Therefore, foreign companies are not likely to locate in these countries, but rather will locate their head offices with high-paying jobs in the rich industrialized countries.

As the London *Times* (8 November 2006) noted: "This should be a major concern since what we are witnessing is a consolidation of the global division of labour. The collusion between the states of the developed countries and multinationals in the various trade negotiations works against the poorer countries. It is estimated that the Doha round of trade talks will benefit the rich countries by $80 billion, and the developing countries by $16 billion, while the poor countries will lose" (cited in Williams 2010, 34).

As David Harvey (2005, 176) puts it: "[n]eoliberal concern for the individual trumps any social democratic concern for equality, democracy, and social solidarities."[13] Commensurate with the current and growing concentration of economic power in a relatively small number of transnational corporations and banks, a relatively few "world" languages serve the economic interests of these entities, even though those in the world's formal workforce who benefit are disproportionately the most highly educated people from the richest countries. However, even in Europe, only about 4.5 million European citizens with tertiary-level qualifications are mobile across state boundaries within Europe, which is only about 1.4 percent of the total population (Williams 2010, 50). The massive inequalities in global wealth do not occur because not enough people speak English or some other language. Patterns of investment reveal the roles different countries play in those aspects of their economies that are involved in the global production and sale of goods and services. Thus, many of the poorest countries play a very particular and narrow role in the global system, which is to provide cheap labour and natural resources to richer countries, to be used in the manufacture of finished goods, with rich countries blocking the export by poorer countries of locally manufactured products, such as textiles, through the protectionist policies of the wealthy countries (see Stiglitz 2007 for an extended discussion). This has the effect of retarding local economic development, as targeted investments are made by the rich countries for the benefit of their own short-term economic gains, with no consideration of the long-term economic or social sustainability of the less powerful nation, which would likely entail the development and use of local resources, including local/regional languages, and some level of literacy in those languages, necessary for local micro-economic projects (Bruthiaux 2002; Batibo 2009).[14] The belief that expanding access to English, or providing low-paying, temporary work to poor people, will contribute to an "economic takeoff" (Rostow 1963) has been discredited many times over. From a macro-economic perspective, Macpherson (1973/2012, 7) notes that "the claim that the capitalist market economy maximizes individual utilities has already been pretty well destroyed by twentieth-century economists, although few political theorists seem to realize this." However, even in low-income countries, there are class divisions and therefore a relatively small number of socially advantaged citizens will benefit from neoliberal policies, because they have access to the "right" education (we can see this, for example, in India and South Africa, as discussed in Ricento 2010) and they have political power, or access to it. Despite efforts by many states to safeguard and promote national and regional languages (Ricento 2007) through constitutional and other legal provisions, transnational economic factors diminish the power and authority of states to compete globally using primarily national and regional language resources (see Van Parijs 2000). This tends to strengthen the attractiveness and influence of global lingua francas, such as English, but the use of a global lingua franca does not necessarily lead to broad-based social or economic development, except in those countries that already possess highly developed educational and economic infrastructures. Attempts by low-income states to develop language policies to support education in local languages, based on principles of universal language rights, or because they have been given official recognition and status, as with the nine African languages recognized in the South African Constitution, are difficult to implement as a result of the legacy of colonialism, coupled with the effects of transnational economic forces, since the relatively small number of people who already speak and read the preferred "global" language(s), and have advanced educational credentials and training, will not need any more rights, and those who speak the "wrong" language and lack appropriate education in the colonial language will not benefit by the granting of such language rights and protections.

5. CONCLUSION

Although inequalities between languages would still exist irrespective of political domination or social stratification (Hymes 1985, vii), the ways in which inequalities evolve and are maintained can be analyzed by looking at the historical record (see Ricento 2010 for elaborated case studies), and especially by considering how prevailing models of development work against the ending of poverty, in part, by under-valuing and under-utilizing local cultural and linguistic resources in low-income countries (Romaine 2009). I have suggested that the preference for English as a global lingua franca, especially over the past half century, is conditioned by and correlates with processes of economic globalization and expansion of the digitalized knowledge economy, which greatly, and disproportionately, benefit some workers in some sectors of the formal economy in certain geographical regions, but mostly benefit the corporations which employ those workers.[15] This preference has a secondary effect on the utility of local/non-dominant languages in local and regional economic development that, in the long run, will influence the status and viability of non-dominant languages in those societies. These effects are especially pronounced in the most linguistically diverse countries, a large proportion of which are in Africa (Romaine 2009, 133).

At this point in history, it is the case that knowledge of certain varieties of English, coupled with particular skill sets obtainable only through high levels of education generally not universally accessible, is likely to enhance the social mobility of some individuals. States that have English as the dominant /national language, and those relatively wealthy states that are able to provide affordable access to high-quality English language learning, and which have highly educated workers with skills in demand in knowledge economy–

related services, will be relatively advantaged compared to workers in states lacking in both. There definitely is a "brain drain," but mostly of well-trained people from relatively high-income countries moving to other higher-income countries, with the greatest percentage of movement of this select population from one European country to another, and from Europe and other parts of the world to North America.[16] Certainly, English has value for many of these mobile individuals; however, I have tried to demonstrate that "English" is not the inherent "hegemon," nor the de facto oppressor, nor the ticket to social or economic mobility, nor the crucial factor in promoting a global *demos* that it is claimed to be, to varying degrees, by the scholars whose positions I have described in this chapter (Phillipson, Brutt-Griffler, and Van Parijs, respectively). All of these scholars make valuable contributions to our understanding of how language(s) play important roles in social, political, and economic development in various contexts. What is missing, I have argued, is an overarching framework to account for English both as a means of social mobility *and* as an inhibitor of local development, especially in low-income countries, which can be accounted for through critical analysis of neoliberal economic policy and its attendant values, goals, and effects on the status, learning, and usefulness of languages, including in sectors of the knowledge economy. The purpose of this chapter is to serve as a starting point for new research directions in the field of language policy and planning, in which economic systems and processes, in interaction with national and global political systems and processes, inform analysis of the status, utility, value, and long-term viability of minority/minoritized languages and their communities of speakers; this analysis can provide evidence that economic and social development are aided by investment in local cultural and linguistic resources, especially in those low-income countries, many of which are in Africa, that have the greatest amount of linguistic diversity (Romaine 2009, 133) and some of the highest levels of poverty.

Acknowledgment: Some material used in this chapter appeared in T. Ricento, 2012, "Political Economy and English as a 'Global' Language," *Critical Multilingualism Studies* 1, no. 1: 30–52. Permission to use that material has been granted by the editors of the journal.

NOTES

1 In a similar vein, Bruthiaux (2008) notes that "the recent applied linguistics literature on globalization shows that most applied linguists have little to say regarding its economic dimension" (19). He goes on to argue that "the reluctance of many applied linguists to consider the economic dimension of globalization and the tendency for discussions of that dimension to be cursory and one-sided severely limit the contribution the field might make to a key contemporary debate" (20).

2 The fact that languages are always changing, and that most languages that have ever existed are now "extinct," even though language itself perseveres, is not in question. Rather, the question is: How can we understand the social, economic, and political factors and forces that lead to/accelerate language attrition and obsolescence apart from the "natural" internally motivated linguistic processes which lead to syntactic, morphological, and semantic changes within named languages over time? And how do these factors correlate with the socio-economic status and prospects of marginalized peoples with little or no political power or access to power, and therefore with few, if any, options or choices as to what language(s) they will be required to learn, and which one(s) they will be forced to give up?

3 Williams (1992), for example, argues that sociolinguistics is based on outmoded and ideologically questionable social theory which views society as consisting of rational subjects manipulating language, and sees language as reflecting society within a process of consensus-building.

4 Even the use of these superordinate terms for English is highly problematic from the perspective of linguistic science; as a professional linguist and experienced ESL and EFL teacher in North America and Japan, I have met and taught hundreds of students who claim they were taught and speak "British" or "American" English while revealing accents and varieties that would be completely unrecognizable as any known variety of British or American English; often, the belief and insistence that one speaks a certain variety of English has as much to do with a person's aspirations and strong identification with a named variety than with any objective validation provided by a linguistics expert or by other speakers of the so-claimed variety of English spoken by an individual.

5   This leaves aside, for the moment, the ways in which industrialized capitalism is inconsistent with many – but not all – of the stipulations of eighteenth-century versions of liberal political theory, along with nineteenth-century (re)formulations; see e.g. Macpherson (1973/2012), who argues that "the liberal-democratic society is a capitalist market society, and that … by its very nature compels a continual net transfer of part of the power of some men to others, thus diminishing rather than maximizing the equal individual freedom to use and develop one's natural capacities which is claimed" (10–11).

6   However, see Kymlicka (1989), who argues that Rawls's framework has been misconstrued and is not incompatible with Communitarian or even Leftist conceptions of justice.

7   But see Taylor (2006, 53), who demonstrates the vacuousness of Rational Choice Theory, in which "everything is to be explained in terms of fundamental, unstructured, competing desires."

8   Williams (2005, 25) notes, and not in a critical way, that "the circumstances in which liberal thought is possible have been created in part by actions that violate liberal ideals." Although this may pose a problem for many liberals, it is openly acknowledged by political theorists who make the case for "realism" in political theorizing.

9   There is a tendency in the normative political philosophy literature to accept "national" languages as necessary, inevitable, even natural. My point here is that the processes by which a language becomes the "national" language have generally co-occurred with processes of "othering" particular ethnic/racial/national/religious groups along with their languages, so that inequalities become "normalized," and eventually institutionalized, with long-term social problems and tensions that are not resolved (see Ricento 2013 on the Canadian situation).

10 Canada, France, Germany, Italy, Japan, the United Kingdom, and the United States.

11 *The Guardian*, 5 March 2015; https://www.theguardian.com/world/2015/mar/05/ireland-attracts-soaring-level-of-us-investment.

12 These data were reported by the United Nations Conference on Trade and Development (UNCTAD), and are cited in Williams (2010), 33.

13 Harvey argues that the human rights movements over the past thirty years fit

well within the trajectory of neoliberalization: "Undoubtedly, the neoliberal insistence upon the individual as the foundational element in political-economic life opens the door to individual rights activism. But by focusing on those rights rather than on the creation or recreation of substantive and open democratic governance structures, the opposition cultivates methods that cannot escape the neoliberal frame" (2005, 176).

14 As Neville Alexander (2009, 62), commenting on the South African context, observes: "Unless African languages are given market value, i.e., unless their instrumentality for the processes of production, exchange and distribution is enhanced, no amount of policy change at school level can guarantee their use in high-status functions and, thus, eventual escape from the dominance and the hegemony of English (or French or Portuguese where these are the relevant postcolonial European languages)."

15 This more recent history, of course, is not unconnected to the much longer history of colonialism and its attendant economic policies and practices.

16 According to Williams (2010, 43), "there are nearly 2 million immigrants from the EU in each of Canada, Australia, France and Germany, and over 4.5 million in the USA," and of those European-born living in the US, almost 50% have tertiary-level qualifications. More than 440,000 foreign-born persons in the US hold a Ph.D., which is about 25% of the total number of PhDs in the country, while in Australia and Canada, the percentage of foreign-born PhDs is 45% and 54%, respectively (46).

REFERENCES

Alexander, Neville. 2009. "The Impact of the Hegemony of English on Access to and Quality of Education with Special Reference to South Africa." In *Language and Poverty*, edited by Wayne Harbert with help from Sally McConnell-Ginet, Amanda Miller, and John Whitman, 53–66. Bristol, UK: Multilingual Matters.

Ammon, Ulrich. 1995. "To What Extent Is German an International Language?" In *The German Language and the Real World*, edited by Patrick Stevenson. Oxford, UK: Clarendon.

Batibo, Herman. 2009. "Poverty as a Crucial Factor in Language Maintenance and Language Death: Case Studies from Africa." In *Language and Poverty*, edited by

Wayne Harbert with help from Sally McConnell-Ginet, Amanda Miller, and John Whitman, 23–36. Bristol, UK: Multilingual Matters.

Blommaert, Jan. 2009. "A Market of Accents." *Language Policy* 8: 243–59.

Bruthiaux, Paul. 2002. "Hold Your Courses: Language Education, Language Choice, and Economic Development." TESOL Quarterly 36, no. 3: 275–96.

– 2008. "Dimensions of Globalization and Applied Linguistics." In *Language as Commodity: Global Structures, Local Marketplaces*, edited by Peter K.W. Tan and Rani Rubdy, 16–30. London: Continuum.

Brutt-Griffler, Janina. 2002. "Class, Ethnicity, and Language Rights: An Analysis of British Colonial Policy in Lesotho and Sri Lanka and Some Implications for Language Policy." *Journal of Language, Identity, and Education* 1: 207–34.

– 2005. "'Who Do You Think You Are, Where Do You Think You Are?': Language Policy and the Political Economy of English in South Africa." In *The Globalization of English and the English Language Classroom*, edited by Claus Gnutzmann and Frauke Intemann, 27–39. Tübingen, Germany: Gunter Narr Verlag.

Castells, Manuel. 2006. "Globalisation and Identity: A Comparative Perspective." *Journal of Contemporary Culture* 1: 56–66.

Grin, François, Claudio Sfreddo, and François Vaillancourt. 2010. *The Economics of the Multilingual Workplace.* New York: Routledge.

Harvey, David. 2005. *A Brief History of Neoliberalism.* Oxford, UK: Oxford University Press.

Hymes, Dell. 1985. "Preface." In *Language of Inequality*, edited by Nessa Wolfson and Joan Manes, v–viii. Berlin: Mouton.

Honig, Bonnie. 1993. *Political Theory and the Displacement of Politics.* Ithaca, NY: Cornell University Press.

Honig, Bonnie, and Marc Stears. 2011. "The New Realism: From Modus Vivendi to Justice." In *Political Philosophy versus History? Contextualism and RealPolitics in Contemporary Political Thought*, edited by Jonathan Floyd and Marc Stears, 177–205. New York: Cambridge University Press.

Ives, Peter. 2015. "Language and Collective Identity: Theorising Complexity." In *Language and Identity Politics*, edited by Christina Späti, 17–37. New York: Berghahn Books.

Kymlicka, Will. 1989. *Liberalism, Community, and Culture.* Oxford, UK: Oxford University Press.

Macpherson, C.B. 1973 [2012]. *Democratic Theory: Essays in Retrieval*. Oxford, UK: Oxford University Press. Reissued with an Introduction by Frank Cunningham. Toronto: Oxford University Press.

May, Stephen. 2001. *Language and Minority Rights: Ethnicity, Nationalism and the Politics of Language*. Edinburgh Gate Harlow, UK: Pearson Education Limited.

Patten, Alan, and Will Kymlicka. 2003. "Introduction: Language Rights and Political Theory: Context, Issues, and Approaches." In *Language Rights and Political Theory*, edited by Will Kymlicka and Alan Patten, 1–51. New York: Oxford University Press.

Pennycook, Alastair. 2004. "Beyond Mother Tongues and Access to English." *Journal of Language, Identity and Education* 3: 145–50.

Phillipson, Robert. 1992. *Linguistic Imperialism*. New York: Oxford University Press.

– 2001. "English for Globalization or for the World's People?" *International Review of Education* 47: 185–201.

Pogge, Thomas. 2003. "Accommodation Rights for Hispanics in the United States." In *Language Rights and Political Theory*, edited by Will Kymlicka and Alan Patten, 105–22. New York: Oxford University Press.

Rawls, John. 1971. *A Theory of Justice*. Cambridge, MA: Harvard University Press.

Ricento, Thomas. 1998. "National Language Policy in the United States." In *Language and Politics in the United States and Canada: Myths and Realities*, edited by Thomas Ricento and Barbara Burnaby, 85–112. Mahwah, NJ: Lawrence Erlbaum.

– 2003. "The Discursive Construction of Americanism." *Discourse & Society* 14: 611–37.

– 2007. "Models and Approaches in Language Policy and Planning. In *Handbook of Language and Communication: Diversity and Change*, edited by Marliss Hellinger and Anne Pauwels, 211–40. Berlin: Mouton de Gruyter.

– 2010. "Language Policy and Globalization." In *The Handbook of Language and Globalization*, edited by Nikolas Coupland, 123–41. Malden, MA: Wiley-Blackwell.

– 2013. "The Consequences of Official Bilingualism on the Status and Perception of Non-official Languages in Canada." *Journal of Multilingual and Multicultural Development* 34, no. 5: 475–89.

Romaine, Suzanne. 2009. "Biodiversity, Linguistic Diversity and Poverty: Some Global Patterns and Missing Links." In *Language and Poverty*, edited by Wayne Harbert, with help from Sally McConnell-Ginet, Amanda Miller, and John Whitman, 127–46. Bristol, UK: Multilingual Matters.

Rostow, Walter. 1963. *The Economics of Take-off into Sustained Growth.* London: MacMillan.

Sonntag, Selma. 2009. "Linguistic Globalization and the Call Center Industry: Imperialism, Hegemony or Cosmopolitanism?" *Language Policy* 8: 5–25.

Stiglitz, Joseph. 2007. *Making Globalization Work.* New York: W.W. Norton & Company.

Taylor, Charles. 1994. "The Politics of Recognition." In *Multiculturalism: Examining the Politics of Recognition*, edited by Amy Gutmann, 25–73. Princeton, NJ: Princeton University Press.

Taylor, Michael. 2006. *Rationality and the Ideology of Disconnection.* New York: Cambridge University Press.

Van Parijs, Philippe. 2000. "The Ground Floor of the World: On the Socio-economic Consequences of Linguistic Globalization." *International Political Science Review* 21: 217–33.

– 2011. *Linguistic Justice for Europe and for the World.* New York: Oxford University Press.

Williams, Bernard. 2005. *In the Beginning Was the Deed.* Princeton, NJ: Princeton University Press.

Williams, Glyn. 2002. *Sociolinguistics: A Sociological Critique.* London: Routledge.

– 2010. *The Knowledge Economy, Language, and Culture.* Clevedon, UK: Multilingual Matters.

Wilson, Edward O. 1998. *Consilience: The Unity of Knowledge.* New York: Knopf.

CONTRIBUTORS

DAN AVNON holds the Leon Blum Chair in Political Science at the Hebrew University of Jerusalem, where he is chair of the Department of Political Science (2017–20). From 2001 to 2007 he established and headed the Hebrew University's Gilo Center for Citizenship, Democracy and Civic Education, after which he headed the Hebrew University's Federmann School of Governance and Public Policy (2009–11). Previously, he taught at Stanford University's Program on Cultures, Ideas and Values. He has published on a broad range of issues in Jewish and classical political philosophy, on Israel's political constitution, on pluralistic civic education, and on democratic challenges to pluralism, liberalism, and human rights advocacy.

HELDER DE SCHUTTER is a professor of Social and Political Philosophy at KU Leuven, Belgium. He works on the moral foundations of language recognition, federalism, nationalism, and differential treatment of citizens and immigrants. His papers have appeared in books and journals including *The Journal of Political Philosophy*, *Inquiry*, the *Journal of Applied Philosophy*, *Metaphilosophy*, the *British Journal of Political Science*, *Politics, Philosophy & Economics*, and *The Cambridge Handbook of Language Policy*.

JOHN EDWARDS was born in England, educated there and in Canada, and received his PhD from McGill University (Montreal). He is a senior research professor at St Francis Xavier University (Antigonish), an adjunct professor, Graduate Studies, at Dalhousie University (Halifax), and a visiting professor at Minzu University (Beijing). His main research interest is with the establishment, maintenance, and continuity of group identity, with particular reference to language. Recent books include *Challenges in the Social Life of Language* (Palgrave-Macmillan, 2011), *Multilingualism: Understanding Linguistic Diversity* (Continuum / Bloomsbury, 2012), and *Sociolinguistics: A Very Short Introduction* (Oxford University Press, 2013). Edwards is a fellow of the British Psychological Society, the Canadian Psychological Association, and the Royal Society of Canada.

FRANÇOIS GRIN is a full professor of economics at the Faculty of Translation and Interpreting (FTI) of the University of Geneva, where, in addition to economics, he teaches courses on multilingualism and language policy. He has steered large-scale international research projects and published widely on these topics, in journals such as the *International Political Science Review*, *Kyklos*, the *Journal of Multilingual and Multicultural Development*, the *International Journal of the Sociology of Language*, *Language Policy*, the *Journal of Sociolinguistics*, etc. His latest book is *The Politics of Multilingualism*, co-edited with Peter A. Kraus (John Benjamins, 2018). François Grin is Editor-in-Chief of *Language Problems and Language Planning*.

YAEL PELED is a research associate at the Institute for Health and Social Policy, McGill University (Montreal). She is a political theorist specializing in the moral and political philosophy of language, and in the interdisciplinary substance of this area of inquiry. Her work has been published in political science, philosophy, and linguistics journals including the *American Political Science Review*, the *Journal of Politics*, the *Journal of Applied Philosophy*, *Bioethics*, *Language Policy*, the *Journal of Multilingual and Multicultural Development* and the *Journal of Language and Politics*. She is the co-author (with Leigh Oakes) of *Normative Language Policy: Ethics, Politics, Principles*, and a contributor to the *Oxford Handbook of Language Policy and Planning*. She also served as a book reviewer for *Science* on the question of a scientific lingua franca, and on the history and philosophy of interdisciplinary inquiry.

THOMAS RICENTO is a professor and Research Chair Emeritus at the University of Calgary. His book *Language Policy and Political Economy* (2015) won the 2018 Book Award from the American Association for Applied Linguistics. Other publications include *Language Policy and Planning: Critical Concepts in*

Linguistics (2016) and *Language Policy and Political Theory: Building Bridges, Assessing Breaches* (2016). He has published research on language policy, politics, and ideologies in *Language Policy*, TESOL *Quarterly*, the *Journal of Sociolinguistics*, *Discourse & Society*, and the *International Journal of the Sociology of Language*, among other journals. He is a founding co-editor of the *Journal of Language and Identity* (Routledge).

DAVID ROBICHAUD is a professor of ethics and political philosophy at the University of Ottawa. His research focuses on justice in diverse societies. He has published papers on linguistic justice, social justice, and trust in diverse societies. He also brings philosophy to a broader audience as a weekly radio commentator for Radio-Canada.

DANIEL M. WEINSTOCK holds the James McGill Chair in the Faculty of Law, McGill University (Montreal). From 2013 to 2018, he was the director of McGill's Institute for Health and Social Policy. Previously, he taught Philosophy at the Université de Montréal, where he was the founding director of the Centre de recherche en éthique de l'Université de Montréal. He has published widely on a broad range of issues in moral and political philosophy. Many of his writings have to do with the implications of liberal conceptions of justice for societies marked by significant linguistic, ethno-cultural, and religious diversity.

INDEX